Critical Essays on

ERNEST HEMINGWAY'S
THE SUN ALSO RISES

CRITICAL ESSAYS
ON
AMERICAN LITERATURE

James Nagel, General Editor
University of Georgia, Athens

Critical Essays on

ERNEST HEMINGWAY'S
THE SUN ALSO RISES

edited by

JAMES NAGEL

G. K. Hall & Co.
An Imprint of Simon & Schuster Macmillan
New York

Prentice Hall International
London Mexico City New Delhi Singapore Sydney Toronto

G. K. Hall & Co.
An Imprint of Simon & Schuster Macmillan
866 Third Avenue
New York, New York 10022

Library of Congress Cataloging-in-Publication Data

Critical essays on Ernest Hemingway's The sun also rises / edited by
    James Nagel.
        p.   cm.—(Critical essays on American literature)
    Includes bibliographical references (p.) and index.
    ISBN 0-8161-7312-5
    1. Hemingway, Ernest, 1899–1961.   Sun also rises.   I. Nagel,
James.   II. Series
PS3515.E37S9223   1995
813'.52—dc20   94-34994
                                                                    CIP

The paper used in this publication meets the minimum requirements of
American National Standard for Information Sciences—Permanence of
Paper for Printed Library Materials. ANSI Z3948-1984.∞™

10   9   8   7   6   5   4   3   2   1

Printed in the United States of America

for
James J. Martine

Contents

◆

General Editor's Note

◆

This series seeks to anthologize the most important criticism on a wide variety of topics and writers in American literature. Our readers will find in various volumes not only a generous selection of reprinted articles and reviews but original essays, bibliographies, manuscript sections, and other materials brought to public attention for the first time. This volume, *Critical Essays on Ernest Hemingway's The Sun Also Rises*, is the most comprehensive collection of essays ever published on one of the most important novels in American Literature. It contains both a sizable gathering of early reviews and a broad selection of more modern scholarship as well. Among the authors of reprinted articles and reviews are Edmund Wilson, Linda W. Wagner, Allen Josephs, and Michael S. Reynolds. In addition to a substantial introduction by James Nagel that provides an overview of critical reaction to the novel since 1926, there are three original essays commissioned specifically for publication in this volume, new studies by Robert E. Fleming on the discovery of a manuscript fragment in which Ernest Hemingway began a sequel to *The Sun Also Rises*, Linda Patterson Miller on the thematic role of Brett Ashley, and Jane E. Wilson on the importance of Wilson-Harris in the value scheme of the narrative. We are confident that this book will make a permanent and significant contribution to the study of American literature.

Publisher's Note

◆

Producing a volume that contains both newly commissioned and reprinted material presents the publisher with the challenge of balancing the desire to achieve stylistic consistency with the need to preserve the integrity of works first published elsewhere. In the Critical Essays series, essays commissioned especially for a particular volume are edited to be consistent with G. K. Hall's house style; reprinted essays appear in the style in which they were first published, with only typographical errors corrected. Consequently, shifts in style from one essay to another are the result of our efforts to be faithful to each text as it was originally published.

Preface

◆

There have been many pleasures in the compilation of *Critical Essays on Ernest Hemingway's The Sun Also Rises*. One of them has been the opportunity to contemplate again the artistry and power of Ernest Hemingway's first novel, in attempting to come to terms with its position in American literary history. Another labor of love was the occasion to review the critical reaction to the book from the earliest reviews to the present, an endeavor represented in the introduction to the volume. Here I have attempted to cover the most important commentary in scholarly articles and books; I have left out the thousands of passing references in historical accounts of the period. This work led naturally to the selection of the reviews and articles to be reprinted, chosen here to represent the chronological development of insight and information, a variety of approaches, and the best commentary on key artistic and biographical issues. The original essays provide their own valuable insights and add to the critical discussion on the novel, from the discovery of a manuscript fragment by Robert E. Fleming to the exploration of the roles of central characters by Linda Patterson Miller and Jane E. Wilson, and I am deeply grateful for the contributions made by all three.

I appreciate as well the thoughtful assistance of numerous colleagues and friends during the development of this volume. In particular, the librarians at the Widener Library at Harvard University were gracious in providing access to their vast holdings. The staff of the University of Georgia Library offered not only generous help in locating obscure items but essential office space as well, and I acknowledge with gratitude their many courtesies. For research assistance, I wish to express my thankfulness for the cheerful contributions of Carol Acree and Mary Armato in Boston and Jane E. Wilson, Tony Murphy, and Andrew Burke at the University of Georgia, all of whom made detailed work a continual pleasure. At G. K. Hall in New York, Melissa Solomon gave the editorial process a benevolent professionalism that I deeply appreciate, and this book would not have been completed without her cordial guidance. My wife, Gwen L. Nagel, provided not only humane good will but the benefit of her wiser counsel, which enriches my labors. In the dedication of this volume, to James J. Martine of St. Bonaventure University, I pay tribute to a friendship that has spanned four decades, and I offer this token with admiration, affection, and the most profound respect.

J. N.

Introduction

◆

James Nagel

When *The Sun Also Rises* appeared on 22 October 1926, it changed everything. Until then Ernest Hemingway had been an aspiring young writer in Paris whose work was thought to be "promising," largely on the basis of a brief list of short stories. But with the publication of his first novel he became an international celebrity, a spokesman for American expatriates, an authority on the bullfight, the most brilliant stylist of his generation, and one of the most powerful forces in literature the United States had ever produced.

There was little in Hemingway's early life that would have predicted his eventual literary prominence. He was born in Oak Park, Illinois, on 21 July 1899, into a conservative Protestant family. His father was a physician who taught his son to hunt and fish and appreciate the tranquility of nature. His mother was a celebrated soprano and a painter who lived for culture and the arts and insisted that her young son practice the cello. In high school, young Ernest did not stand out in any way, although he wrote for the student newspaper and literary magazine, largely in imitation of Ring Lardner. After graduation in 1917, he disappointed his parents by foregoing college to take a junior position on the *Kansas City Star*, one of the leading newspapers of the day, and this experience helped shape his style. In 1918, he joined one of his colleagues at the paper and enlisted in the Red Cross Ambulance service, and, shortly after his arrival in Italy he was wounded in the leg and foot at Fossalta.[1] Recovering in a hospital in Milan, he fell in love with a nurse who later rejected him. These events, and this romance, Hemingway would later use as background for two of his novels, *The Sun Also Rises* and *A Farewell to Arms*.

When he returned to the United States after the war, Hemingway worked for a time on a magazine before marrying Hadley Richardson in 1921, and later that year they moved to Paris, where he wrote articles for the *Toronto Star*. It was here that he received his literary education, writing fiction influenced by the work of Sherwood Anderson and Gertrude Stein and later benefiting from the tutelage of Ezra Pound, the foremost proponent of imagism. Dividing his time between journalism and fiction, Hemingway began producing remarkable short stories (and unremarkable verse) for the little magazines. A small volume, *Three Stories & Ten Poems*, appeared in 1923, followed by a series of very brief sketches, *in our time*, in 1924, a volume expanded and published again that year as *In Our Time*. During this period, Hemingway became interested in the bullfight and enjoyed long holidays in Spain, fishing on the Irati River and attending the Festival of San Fermin in Pamplona. It was this event in 1925 that he would use as the background for *The Sun Also Rises*.

In July of 1925, Hemingway and Hadley went to Pamplona for the fiesta with Bill Smith (a fishing friend from Michigan) and the witty and urbane Donald Ogden Stewart. Bright and beautiful, with a boy's haircut, Lady Duff Twysden joined them with Harold Loeb (the first Jewish student at Princeton) after their interlude at the coastal resort of St. Jean-de-Luz. Her intended, an inebriated Scotsman named Pat Guthrie, was also part of the group, and they marveled at the dramatic exploits of Cayetano Ordóñez in the bull ring. Fighting under the name Niño de la Palma, he later presented Hadley with the ear of a bull, which she left in a drawer in the hotel. Unlike the previous year, this time it all went badly: When Ernest and Hadley went north with Bill Smith to fish the Irati the week before the fiesta, they found the waters fouled by the logging operations. Later, in Pamplona, Hemingway quarreled with Loeb over the attention Loeb was paying to Duff, and they nearly fought in the streets before they came to their senses. Emotions were tense, and the joy of celebration was strained. The fiesta had turned sour, and the friendships that had brought the group together were never the same, but Hemingway had found in these experiences the subject of his first extended work of fiction.

After the Pamplona festival, Hemingway remained in Spain and started his first novel, writing in French notebooks and using the bullfighter as protagonist. He gave the members of his group new names and personalities, and he altered the circumstances of the journalist, Jake Barnes, making him impotent as a result of his war wounds, but he followed the broad outlines of what had actually happened. After some reconsideration in Paris, he changed the opening to focus on Lady Ashley, giving her background in the first two chapters, and finishing the draft on 21 September 1925. The Hemingways spent that winter in Schruns, Austria, where Ernest revised the novel and sent it off to Scribners in New York. In due course F. Scott Fitzgerald read this version and recommended cutting the first two chapters, advice Hemingway followed, and the novel was published on 22 October 1926, at a price of $2.00.[2] His life would never be the same. The novel was quickly hailed as a fictional masterpiece, one widely reviewed in the major newspapers, translated over the years into scores of languages, taught at major universities throughout the world, and studied and discussed in hundreds of critical essays and books over the decades. The development of that commentary is itself a fascinating study, daunting in its size and diversity, but rewarding in portraying the incremental growth of knowledge and insight into a monumental American novel.

But the initial reviews of *The Sun Also Rises* were by no means unanimous in their praise. Hemingway's understated prose, his method of describing action but suggesting feelings and ideas only through implication, left many readers adrift and unable to make much headway. Indeed, the review in the *Cincinnati Inquirer* on 30 October 1926, was essentially negative: "Most of the author's narrative is employed in ushering his characters in and out of cafes and in recording the number, nature, and effect of their drinks." The review in *Time* was even more negative, suspecting that Hemingway's interests "appear to have grown soggy with much sitting around sloppy café tables." The response in the *Springfield Republican* was that "in a novel, absence of structure becomes a fault, and extreme moral sordidness at such length defeats artistic purpose." Allen Tate criticized Hemingway for writing a "popular" novel that does "some violence upon the integrity" of his earlier stories. The reviewer of *Fiesta* (the British title of the novel) for the *{London} Times Literary Supplement* was less than enthusiastic, objecting to "crude, meaningless conversation," finding Brett Ashley "tiresome," and calling the novel an "unsuccessful experiment." *The Dial* reviewed the novel only briefly, saying that the "characters are as shallow as the saucers in which they stack their daily emotions." Virginia Woolf pitched in, complaining that Hemingway was not a "modern" writer because his characters are "flat as cardboard" and "crude as a photograph." She concluded: "So it would seem that the thing that is faked is character; Mr. Hemingway leans against the flanks of that particular bull after the horns have passed."[3]

But most of the reviews were strongly positive. The *New York Times Book Review* praised not only the dialogue but the plot of the novel, finding it "an absorbing, beautifully and tenderly absurd, heartbreaking narrative. . . . It is a truly gripping story, told in a lean, hard, athletic narrative prose that puts more literary English to shame." Conrad Aiken's review offered praise of Hemingway as "the most exciting of contemporary American writers of fiction." He described the dialogue as "brilliant: If there is better dialogue being written today I do not know where to find it." An anonymous assessment in the *Boston Evening Transcript* was nearly ecstatic, calling *Rises* a "beautiful and searching novel." Ernest Boyd remarked that Hemingway "writes dialogue so effectively that he has merely to allow one to hear the sound of a character's voice in order to plant him vividly before the reader." Herbert S. Gorman praised Hemingway's narrative restraint and called the novel "the tale of a great spiritual debacle, of a generation that has lost its guiding purpose and has been driven by time, fate or nerves . . . into the feverish atmosphere of strained passions." Burton Rascoe did a favorable review for the *New York Sun*, praising Hemingway's style and saying that "some Americans familiar around the Dome and Rotonde in Paris appear in the novel in the thinnest of disguises, and remarkably true to character."[4] This concern was to dominate interest in the novel for several decades.

The review in the *New Yorker* described young Hemingway as "that already almost legendary figure in the Parisian group of young, American authors. . . . The author of *Torrents of Spring*, who has only to publish to be read by a certain circle of the intelligentsia, and not even to publish to be discussed, has written wittily and with a smooth deliberateness astonishingly effective in numerous passages of nervous staccato." The reviewer for the *Chicago Daily Tribune*, acknowledging that Hemingway was from Oak Park, confessed that the novel made him feel angry that such a talented writer would do something just to be "smart." Nevertheless, he suggested that "Ernest Hemingway can be a distinguished writer if he wishes to be." When Schuyler Ashley reviewed the novel on 4 December 1926 for the *Kansas City Star* he acknowledged that Hemingway had once "served an apprenticeship to letters" with the newspaper in 1917–18, and he said that Hemingway "writes with a swinging, effortless precision that puts him in the very first flight of American stylists." In the *Saturday Review*, Cleveland B. Chase presented a strongly positive evaluation, saying that "it is an interesting fact that neither in his short stories nor in this novel does Hemingway make use of a single simile. To him things are not 'like' other things. He does not write about them until he has been able to grasp their essential qualities." Henry Seidel Canby described the novel as a "story of a lost but lively generation, aimless, drunk, loyal, pathetic, cynical. The characters are the gilded waifs and broken strays expatriate in Paris, and the wandering narrative includes the first bull-fight in English which explains the grip of bull-fighting upon a whole nation." Lawrence Morris offered a more favorable opinion of the author, saying that "no other American, writing today, can match his dialogue for its apparent naturalness, its intimacy and its concealed power of revealing emotion."[5]

By 1927 it was evident that Ernest Hemingway was an established writer and a subject of almost constant public attention. Hugh Walpole included Hemingway in his discussion of the most important contemporary writers: "Ernest Hemingway seems to me the most interesting figure in American letters in the last ten years." Edmund Wilson presented a character-istically insightful response, seeing Jake Barnes as a person of "rather complex temperament and extreme sensibility." He observed that one theme is the "barbarity of the world since the War" and that the novel focuses on "the attempts of the hero and the heroine to disengage themselves from this world, or rather to arrive at some method of living in it honorably." Edwin Muir said that Hemingway's "dialogue is by turns extraordinarily natural and brilliant, and impossibly melodramatic; when he has to describe anything he has a sureness and economy which recall Maupassant." Bruce Barton called

Hemingway the "freshest voice since that of Frank Norris" and observed that "although the people of his new book have no morals, drink too much, are blown about by their passions, have no religion and no ideals, they are alive, truly real and alive, with courage and honesty." Charles W. Ferguson described Hemingway as one of the "Five Rising Stars in American Fiction" and wrote that *The Sun Also Rises* deals with the "general futility" of life."[6]

By 1928 commentary on the novel began to move beyond the initial reaction of the reviews to deal with broader issues, many of them biographical. Richmond Barrett testified to the popularity of *The Sun Also Rises* in an article covering his trip to Paris. He recounted that it was already a sensation among the college-age set, many of them having read it four times. People on board ship were reluctant to talk about anything other than Hemingway, "that brilliant black sheep from the Middle West," causing Barrett to "curse the day on which Hemingway was born." The following year André Maurois offered a brief biography of Hemingway and observed that "a story by Hemingway is stripped to the bone. The facts are nearly always intimated by means of dialogue, without any commentaries. His descriptions are condensed into the least possible volume." Ben Ray Redman, in Pamplona for the Fiesta, encountered Hemingway sitting in a square: "The vitality of the man is apparent even when he is motionless; it is an unobtrusive force which manifests itself by no overt gesture, yet it is pervasive and inescapable. Just as pervasive is his likability."[7]

After the initial round of reviews and early comment, there was enthusiasm but little critical attention in the 1930s. One of the most important books in the decade was Malcolm Cowley's *Exile's Return*, an insider's memoir of the people and places and underlying values of the expatriates in Paris. Harlan Hatcher called Hemingway "the most brilliant novelist of the War generation" for his portrayal of the loss of meaning in the 1920s. Herbert J. Muller brought the perspective of the depression era to bear on the novel, and from his viewpoint the Lost Generation writers were quaint relics who cry in their beer while there is work to be done. The new generation of Americans who must fight both the depression and fascism have plenty of causes for which to live and die, he maintained, and they have little truck with the "distress of their elders."[8]

The period of World War II established yet another context for viewing the novel and another dimension of perceptive readings. Edmund Wilson's comments in *The Wound and the Bow* in 1941 were notable for introducing the concept of the "code" to Hemingway studies, and he described Jake as the only character who "keeps up standards of conduct." Wilson formulated the theme of *Rises* as "we suffer and we make suffer, and everybody loses out in the long run; but in the meantime we can lose with honor." This idea was to have a long run in Hemingway scholarship.[9] In a well-known essay in 1943, James T. Farrell discussed Hemingway's role in the "lost generation," exploring the paradox of the popularity of the disillusionment and nihilism of the novel at a time of prosperity and international optimism. Farrell called *Rises* "one of the very best American novels of the Twenties."[10]

Writing in the aftermath of World War II, Edwin Berry Burgum devoted his attention to distinguishing between the way British and American writers portrayed the Lost Generation, the Americans developing a kind of "rebelliousness which demolished class distinctions."[11] Henry Seidel Canby addressed the same concerns, recalling how dismayed he had been at the change of values displayed in the novel: "Men of good will—successful or unsuccessful, strong or weak—had been the heroes of the nineteenth-century tradition. But in *The Sun Also Rises* the actors lacked not only good will by any definition, but will of any kind," leaving it morally irresponsible, a "defeatist literature."[12]

It was not until the 1950s that Hemingway scholarship came of age, with articles appearing regularly in scholarly journals and the publication of the first major books on his life and works. Carlos Baker took advantage of the anniversary of the novel's publication to write "25 Years of a Hemingway Classic" in 1951, arguing that it had been admired for the wrong reasons, for its use of actual people in a roman à clef. Baker suggested that Paris gossips had given *Rises* a new subtitle: "Six Characters in Search of an Author—With a Gun Apiece."[13] Baker's analysis the next year in *Hemingway: The Writer as Artist*, the first major book on Hemingway, was limited by his approach to literature as "psychological symbol-building," which lead him to see a strain of "sabidurían symbolism" throughout the fiesta, with Brett as the pagan Circe. Baker called Brett an "alcoholic nymphomaniac," Pedro the courageous man of "complete integrity and self-possession," and Jake a person of "boyish innocence of spirit."[14] Philip Young's *Ernest Hemingway* was rather more influential, and it introduced several concepts that became seminal in Hemingway scholarship, among them the idea that Jake Barnes should be read in the context of the youthful traumas of Nick Adams. Also central to Young's schema is the idea that Hemingway's protagonists have been physically and psychologically wounded. Young also developed Wilson's idea of the "code," specifying that there are "code heroes" who know the rules and antagonists, such as Robert Cohn, who do not. Young also maintained that the structure of the novel is circular; that it goes nowhere, ending where it began.[15]

In reviewing a new edition of *The Sun Also Rises* in 1953, Ben Ray Redman commented that he had come to see Hemingway's work as romantic, portraying characters who survive with "gallantry." Carlos Baker wrote that the novel was still as "fresh, as enthralling, and most of all, as undated" as when it was first published. In 1956, James B. Colvert provided an excellent assessment of the "moral system" of the novel, suggesting that the "pursuit of new values is the primary activity of all of Hemingway's heroes." Colvert offered a concise expression of the moral stance in Hemingway's works: "In completely isolating himself from a tradition in which he cannot believe, in rejecting altogether the value assumptions deriving from intellectual abstractions, he wipes clean in his profound skepticism the slate of his moral consciousness in order to record only those values which he discovers through personal experience." Frederick J. Hoffman summarized the intellectual and psychological climate of the period, concluding that *Rises* is "a perceptive portrayal of the human condition within the rigorous limits of circumstance which the postwar world had imposed."[16]

In 1957 Arthur L. Scott initiated the argument that Robert Cohn is romantic and loyal, trusting and intelligent, and ought to be admired by Jake for his artistic and athletic abilities. The following year Mark Spilka published "The Death of Love in *The Sun Also Rises*," one of the most influential essays on the novel: "Jake Barnes and Brett Ashley are two lovers desexed by the war; Robert Cohn is the false knight who challenges their despair; while Romero, the stalwart bullfighter, personifies the good life which will survive their failure." Perhaps the most important publication of 1958 was George Plimpton's interview for the *Paris Review*, in which Hemingway discussed the composition of *The Sun Also Rises* and his famous "iceberg principle," a term critics use to indicate Hemingway's tendency to keep most of his fiction beneath the surface. In "Sunrise Out of the Waste Land," Richard P. Adams explored the influence of T. S. Eliot's *The Waste Land* on Hemingway's first novel, seeing Brett in terms of fertility myths and Robert Cohn as the Grail Knight who fails to ask the right question. John Patrick Bury gave brief attention to "Hemingway in Spain," reading the novel as a "study of lostness, futility, drunkenness, purposelessness as observable in all epochs," not only the post–World War I decade.[17]

Interest in the grail legend and the role of Robert Cohn continued throughout the 1960s. Robert O. Stephens argued that Robert Cohn is the romantic Quixote figure and Jake the normative Pancho, who provides a reliable view of the events. R. W. Stallman attempted to convince readers that *The Sun Also Rises* should be read from Robert Cohn's point of view, that "Cohn is frank and simple, whereas Jake is deceptive and complex," and that "Cohn stands out as exemplar of the Christian virtues." Of greater interest was Leicester Hemingway's *My Brother, Ernest Hemingway*, in which he recalled the dismay and bewilderment of his parents, devout Christians and conservative Republicans with Victorian tastes in literature, when they first read *The Sun Also Rises*.[18]

Malcolm Cowley wrote the introduction to *Three Novels of Ernest Hemingway* in 1962, providing some excellent background on Hemingway's apprenticeship in Paris, particularly the evolution of his style and his relationship with other writers. In "Hemingway's Grail Quest" Paul B. Newman argued that Jesse Weston's portrait of the Fisher King influenced not only T. S. Eliot but Hemingway as well: "Jake is the Fisher King of a Waste Land whose inhabitants are in the same disastrous condition as himself." In his book, published in 1963, Earl Rovit gave an impressive reading of the novel with emphasis on Jake as a narrator who "must learn to become uninvolved from useless and impossible illusions if he is to remain sane." In an essay that might indicate something of the European reception of Hemingway, Geoffrey Moore said that "Hemingway does not appear to have been at home in the novel. His mind lacked the breadth and compassion for humanity which a novelist's must have; plot in the conventional sense he cared nothing for; his characters do not develop; his women are hopeless."[19]

Paul Lauter argued in 1964 that Robert Cohn is a commentary on Jay Gatsby in that both are athletic, socially formal, Romantic idealists who love a woman they cannot possess. And Sidney P. Moss concluded that the theme of the novel is the tension between "ethical traditionalism" and "ethical experimentation." A year later, in *Hemingway on Love*, Robert W. Lewis, Jr. explored the concepts of "eros, agape, and romantic love" in Hemingway's fiction, arguing that in *The Sun Also Rises* "romantic love is examined and rejected." Frances E. Skipp concluded that Jake is a more positive portrait than most readers assume; he clearly enjoys life and will be "successful within the conditions imposed by his world."[20]

In the *Yale Literary Magazine* in 1966, Donald E. Gastwirth found that "the only value system [in the novel] that has meaning is one that insists that there are no value systems" and that it is only through "honesty and style" that anything becomes meaningful. Richard B. Hovey took a bio-psychological approach and pointed out that Cohn never violates his own values and does not "separate his sexuality from his heart." Paul Ramsey argued that although *Rises* is pessimistic it presents a moral construct that requires "self-discipline, a rightness of means, a sense of honor, and consequent moral restraint." William L. Vance developed some rather confused notions about the plot of the novel as being at once naturalistic, involving a "random episodic and circular realism," and yet Aristotelian, with "dramatic unity and interest."[21]

One truly excellent essay in 1966 was John S. Rouch's "Jake Barnes as Narrator," which explored the retrospective nature of the point of view and stressed that Jake, "the most sensitive and complicated person in the book," learns through the telling that he can deal with his situation, with his injury, hopeless love for Brett, and loss of values. Of special interest, Harold Loeb published a detailed account of his version of the events in Paris and Pamplona. Acknowledging that the character of Robert Cohn was based on him, Loeb presented a sensible, and humane, view of his friendship with Hemingway and his pain and bewilderment at the way he was portrayed in the novel. Sheridan Baker devoted his attention to the background of the novel, concluding that *Rises* "is a wonderful book because it hits so deadly center the pathetic and unadmirable wish that will not die, the pleasure in wishful unfulfillment, the pleasure in pitying ourselves for not getting what we think we deserve." Arthur Mizener contributed a discussion of Hemingway's implementation of the "objective correlative" as compared to that of T. S. Eliot and Ezra Pound. Louis D. Rubin, Jr. explored the extent to which there are autobiographical elements in the novel, and concluded, uniquely, that there are none. Daniel J. Schneider maintained that Cohn is a representative of "lost men whose sterile self-absorption and vanity hurls them into a restless, desperate search for ego-validation," that Romero is a "master of control and discipline," and that Jake moves toward control and self-discipline in the novel. And Alexander Tamke explored the biblical implications of the name "Jacob," finding an ironic reference for the impotent Jake in the Jacob of *Genesis*, the epitome of fertility.[22]

In 1968, J. F. Kobler demonstrated that the chronology Jake describes, whether fiction or fact, is impossible. The historical references are incorrect (William Jennings Bryan did not die in June of 1925 but on 26 July, for example) and the fictional dates do not work out. Dewey Ganzell offered a reading of the novel in terms of *Death in the Afternoon*, attempting to establish a "symbolic context" for the novel in the bullfight. Robert W. Cochran argued that "Jake is a worldly wise acceptor of the nature of the human condition" who has developed a means of survival. Since traditional religious values are no longer viable, the codes inherent in bullfighting and fishing come to replace them. Irving A. Yevish took a biographical approach, arguing, unconvincingly, that the sexual inadequacy of Jake Barnes is a "symbol" of "Hemingway's fear of impotency as an artist."[23]

The year 1969 was notable for the appearance of the first comprehensive biography of Hemingway, Carlos Baker's *Ernest Hemingway: A Life Story*. This book was also the first approach to *The Sun Also Rises* to fill in the background and personalities that provided the framework for the novel. Working closely with letters and manuscript documents, Baker told the story of the festival of San Fermin in 1925 and the writing of the novel that followed it.[24] This excellent account, which has remained standard, was all the more remarkable because Baker did not have all of the documents available after the opening of the Hemingway manuscripts at the John F. Kennedy Library in Boston in 1980. Nonetheless, subsequent biographies have done little to improve on Baker's initial portrayal of the events. In other criticism that year, Michael J. Hoffman explored the ways in which Robert's intellectualism, sincerity, metaphysical obsessions, and need to verbalize his feelings exemplify Jewish character. Kermit Vanderbilt, apparently unaware of Kobler's work of the year before, again addressed the issue of the chronology of the novel. He pointed out errors of calendar time, plot duration, and internal inconsistency, and concluded that the structure of the novel is flawed. Josephine Z. Knopf discussed the distinction between the traditional figures of the "villainous Jew" and the "schlemiel," arguing that Robert Cohn is a failed version of the later; a schlemiel could not come from a wealthy family, go to Princeton, or become a boxing champion.[25]

Delbert E. Wylder, in *Hemingway's Heroes*, focused on Jake as "The Wounded Anti-Hero." Wylder did not regard Jake as one of the expatriates but as a dedicated working journalist whose values are at odds with those of his friends in Pamplona. Jake is antiheroic in deciding to leave Spain for the materialistic world of France. Claire Sprague provided an excellent analysis of the literal and metaphoric exchange of value in the novel, from the monetary cost of everything to the psychic price of Jake's wound. Of particular interest is her observation that during the fishing scene in Burguette, the events go by without mention of payment. Donald T. Torchiana's reconsideration of the novel resulted in a careful refutation of the "waste land" interpretation. He places the center of the novel in the ethic of the bullfight, which teaches Jake the "value of courageous rationality."[26]

Also in 1969, William White edited *The Merrill Studies in The Sun Also Rises*, a slim volume made up of eight reviews and seven reprinted essays. There was no original material, save for a brief introduction, and no bibliography. Nevertheless, this volume testified to the continuing popularity of the novel and its use in university classrooms. One of the most important articles of the year was Bertrand D. Sarason's "Lady Brett Ashley and Lady Duff Twysden," in which he presented solid biographical information about the woman upon whom Hemingway based his character, including her tragic death in 1938 and the myths that emerged about it. Jackson Benson, in *Hemingway: The Writer's Art of Self-Defense*, provided an unusual approach to the novel as Hemingway's "Book of the Grotesque," seeing Jake as wallowing (humorously) in self-pity, Cohn as a "circus clown" or a "Chaplin character," and Brett as a kind of "Lady Booby."[27]

Hemingway criticism began to change in the 1970s, partly on the basis of the *Fitzgerald/Hemingway Annual* and *Hemingway Notes*, both of which created focused venues for scholarly articles. But this was also the decade of new books on Hemingway and a more detailed interest in *The Sun Also Rises*. Matthew J. Bruccoli insisted that Bill Gorton's "irony and pity" gag "had to be Seldes' 1925 *Dial* review of *The Great Gatsby*," a point later refuted. In the same issue, J. M. Linebarger wrote about "Eggs As Huevos in *The Sun Also Rises*," pointing out that "the Spanish word 'huevos' is literally translated 'eggs' but also carries a vulgar meaning of 'cojónes' or their equivalents." He went on to make much of the eggs that are eaten for breakfast. In an excellent article the next year, Scott Donaldson observed that Jake is the only character who works for a living and that he and Bill and Pedro all offer just compensation for what they receive, whereas Brett, Mike, and Robert are all careless with money. Donaldson also drew the distinction between French morality, based upon money, and Spanish generosity and disregard of material wealth. Another valuable study was *Ernest Hemingway and the Arts*, by Emily Stipes Watts, which examined the relationship of Hemingway's craft to that of other disciplines, particularly painting. She found that Hemingway's handling of color and depiction of landscape in *The Sun Also Rises* resembles the work of Cezanne.[28]

Bruce L. Grenberg argued that because Jake's "character is intellectual and perceptual in nature rather than physical, most critics have denied or confounded his essential heroism." Harold F. Mosher, Jr., used a complex theory of style to make some rather obvious points, such as the circularity of the novel's structure. George D. Murphy, in the first issue of *Hemingway Notes*, maintained that the influence of *The Waste Land* on *The Sun Also Rises* goes beyond emotional sterility to the utilization of water symbolism for ritual purification, particularly in the Spanish fishing scenes and at San Sebastian. Brom Weber advanced the curious argument that Hemingway did not adequately deal with "the horse as tragic comedian." Weber seemed to desire the full depiction of the disemboweling of the horse. In *The Narrative Pattern in Ernest Hemingway's Fiction*, Chaman Nahal focused on alternations of diastolic and systolic action, passages of reflection and descriptions of movement and conversation.[29]

Linda W. Wagner continued her important contributions with "*The Sun Also Rises:* One Debt to Imagism," in which she traced the personal influence of Ezra Pound and of the imagist movement in general on Hemingway's early work, culminating in "methods of suggestion, compression, and speed" in *Rises*, which is a "lyric evocation of one segment of life in the 1920s." Carole Gottlieb Vopat explored the ending of the novel, arguing that Jake has undergone a "profound change" from the beginning in his "estimation of himself, his wound, his crowd, and his love for Brett Ashley," which has diminished. Arthur Waldhorn found a similar change in his excellent *A Reader's Guide to Ernest Hemingway*, a book notable throughout for its humane good sense. Waldhorn argued that in the conclusion of the novel Jake has rejected "false hope and empty illusion and salvaged integrity, discipline, and control." He also provided a normative reading of the characters, structure, and basic themes of the novel.[30]

Morton L. Ross advanced the idea that Gorton is the explicator of the Hemingway code and that he plays the role of Koheleth, the preacher of Ecclesiastes. The irony is that the code advanced by Bill carries no divine sanction, only "the fine hammered steel of woe." J. M. Linebarger assumed that hats are "symbolic" and that wearing one is a means of dominating other people; Brett takes hers off in the taxi with Jake, indicating that she does not want to subdue him. Thomas H. Pauly and Thomas Dwyer collaborated to argue that Jake does not have a just notion of compensation and that he avoids the key issues of human interaction. Richard P. Sugg published a related article showing that Jake is "just" in his dealings with others while Mike and Robert are irresponsible.[31]

The most important contribution to Hemingway scholarship in 1972 was Bertram D. Sarason's *Hemingway and The Sun Set*, a series of essays by actual persons who may have served as "models" for the characters of the novel. Harold Loeb, Kathleen Cannell (Frances Clyne), Donald Ogden Stewart (Bill Gorton), and Luis Quintana (Montoya) commented on their memories of the fiesta. In other essays, the biographies of other sources for the characters are briefly sketched, most importantly Lady Duff Twysden (Lady Brett Ashley) and Ford Madox Ford (Braddocks). Ernest Hemingway (Jake Barnes) is missing, although covered obliquely in the other essays. This volume is essential for anyone who would like to understand Hemingway's experience in 1924 and 1925.[32]

In 1973, Sheldon Grebstein, in his excellent *Hemingway's Craft*, discussed the narrative method of the novel, suggesting that Jake "lacks sufficient time to distance [himself] from the events narrated and explain them fully." Terrence Doody also addressed Jake's telling of the events, the "device of polysyndeton." Doody errs in thinking that there is no recognition by Jake that he is speaking in retrospect. Richard K. Peterson's *Hemingway: Direct and Oblique* is valuable for showing how Robert's problems derive from his being a tourist and an unskilled and uncommitted writer; his Jewishness, says Peterson, associates him with the "rich literary dilettantes" in New York.[33]

Donald A. Daiker, in "The Affirmative Conclusion of *The Sun Also Rises*" in 1975, maintained that Jake has learned how to live despite his wound and that he must confront the most vulnerable parts of himself and acknowledge that he and Brett could never have had a life together. In another essay that year, Daiker attempted to demonstrate that the children following a man playing a reed pipe during the fiesta are a subtle reference to Robert Browning's "The Pied Piper of Hamelin." Ronald Lajoie and Sally Lentz discussed "The Crystal Trench," a story by A. E. W. Mason about a wife who waits twenty-four years for her husband's body to emerge from a glacier. They point out that Jake tells only part of the story, omitting the fact that when the long-waiting wife finds her dead husband, he is wearing a locket containing a photograph of another woman. The wife has thus wasted her life, as Jake may be wasting his. Martin Light explored the role of Robert Cohn as a Quixotic character set against Jake's commonsense realism. Donald M. Murray argued that *The Sun Also Rises* is an influence on Nathanael West's *The Day of the Locust*, particularly seen in the character of Abe Kusich, who resembles Robert Cohn. Manuel Schonhorn found the traditional reading of the name "Jacob" as providing an ironic contrast between the fertile biblical patriarch and the impotent Barnes to be erroneous; Schonhorn found the allusion "heroic and affirmative." For his part, David L. Vanderwerken argued that the bridges between Paris and Pamplona have a "symbolic" function, tracing Jake's movement from the corruption of Paris to the purity of Burguette. Linda Wagner's discussion in *Hemingway and Faulkner: inventors/masters* stressed the stylistic link between Hemingway's fiction and imagist poetry, particularly the influence of Ezra Pound.[34]

In his article in 1976, Gerald T. Gordon examined the role of Harvey Stone in the novel, concluding that "Stone's only asset is his perseverance—his ability to hang on the ropes in the face of defeat." David Henry Lowenkron argued persuasively that Jake's attitude in the novel is not the stoic code of the Lost Generation but rather the pragmatism of William James, a philosophy that allows Jake to adopt ideas drawn from Catholicism, hedonism, economics, and professionalism. B. Ramachandra Rao had nothing to say about structure in "*The Sun Also Rises*: A Study in Structure," but he observed that the characters in the novel display a variety of attitudes, which Rao found "sophisticated." W. J. Stuckey attempted to read "*The Sun Also Rises* on Its Own Ground," rejecting the notion that the novel is a prose version of *The Waste Land*.[35]

In 1977 Sara Lennox explored the influence of *Rises* on Uwe Johnson's *Mutmassungen über Jakob*, stressing that romantic love no longer mitigates human isolation. David Morgan Zehr discussed the interaction between the city of Paris and the mystique of the expatriate. In *By Force of Will*, Scott Donaldson did not give an analysis of the novel but rather discussed aspects of it in more general essays on money, religion, morality, and related matters. His treatment of these issues is excellent. The next year, Sam S. Baskett addressed anew the relationships between Brett and her various admirers, arguing that Jake learns from each of them. In the end, Jake must orient himself to this spectrum of approaches and create "a world in which he can live as a moral being." In a helpful note in *Studies in American Fiction*, Fred D. Crawford and Bruce Morton provided a gloss on the reference to "Henry's bicycle" in the fishing scene in Spain, pointing out that in the manuscript the reference is clearly to "Henry James's bicycle" and suggesting that Hemingway may have been responding to the comment by Van Wyk Brooks that expatriation always exacts its cost in separation from heritage. Scott Donaldson argued, convincingly, that the "irony and pity" phrase is an allusion to Anatole France's *Le Jardin d'Epicure* and that Donald Ogden Stewart was thoroughly familiar with this book. In a challenging article, Kathleen L. Nichols maintained that Jake undergoes a linear development from romanticism to realism, going to Madrid for an unsentimental rescue of Brett. Leon F. Seltzer attempted to demonstrate that Count Mippipopolous is impotent, while Matthew J. Bruccoli, in *Scott and Ernest*, gave a valuable account of the relationship between the two writers.[36]

Wayne Kvam followed Kermit Vanderbilt in 1979, arguing that there are two separate chronologies in the novel, one for Paris and another for Spain, each consistent within itself although irreconcilable with each other. Anders Breidlid, in *Edda: Nordisk Tidsskrift for Litteraturforskning*, attempted to show that courage in Hemingway's fiction means facing death and living "authentically." Breidlid also provided a close analysis of existential issues. Cathy N. Davidson, writing in *Hemingway Notes*, pointed out the violation of chronological time in the recounting of the death of Vicente Girones, but she erred in thinking that Hemingway himself intrudes into Jake's narration to move forward in time. Stanley Wertheim compared Hemingway's treatment of expatriates in France to that of Henry James, finding that Hemingway "implicitly condemned their feverish wanderings, drunken carousels, sordid quarrels and infidelities" and yet made these things seem attractive. Raymond S. Nelson, in *Hemingway: Expressionist Artist*, developed the thesis that Hemingway's style is that of an expressionist in the manner of Cézanne, a point Hemingway suggested in *A Moveable Feast*.[37]

David Goldknopf devoted his attention to the characters as "the eternal tourists, aimlessly criss-crossing the landscape of their disenchantment." In a more insightful essay, Gerald T. Gordon discussed the role of Wilson Harris, whom he takes to be modeled on Eric Dorman-Smith: "Wilson-Harris stands for all that is good and hopeful and satisfying in a generation fraught with anxiety, with commerce, with 'making it.' " Perhaps the most important publication in 1979 was the original opening of *The Sun Also Rises*, which begins "This is a novel about a lady" and then gives the background of Brett Ashley, explains how Jake and Brett met in the war, and covers what Jake was doing in the intervening years before he and Brett met again in Paris.[38]

The 1980s brought a new era in Hemingway scholarship with the founding of the Hemingway Society, the establishment of the *Hemingway Review*, and the opening of the Hemingway manuscript collection at the John F. Kennedy Library in Boston. The documents in this archive made possible the detailed study of the composition and publication history of the novels and short stories and gave access to thousands of pages of letters, notes, and related papers. The Hemingway Society sponsored major conferences every two years, and the proceedings of those meetings appeared as books, offering what was often the most informed and sophisticated scholarship available. Given the availability of the manuscripts, composition history became the prime focus of scholarly activity, along with an emphasis on gender studies, politics, and a more detailed form of biography, often with books devoted to a year or two of Hemingway's life. If the 1950s brought Hemingway into critical focus, the 1980s represented a dramatic surge in depth and detail, one that has transformed the way Hemingway is read and taught.

In the beginning of the decade, Delbert E. Wylder argued that Brett is a " 'new woman' or 'twentieth century woman,' breaking from the strictures of Victorianism as much as most of the expatriated males in the novel." Patrick D. Morrow emphasized that Brett refuses to have sex for money and rejects materialism, but ultimately "all of the characters pay for their lack of purpose, their lack of definite goals, and their values which center around vanities." Gene D. Phillips, in *Hemingway and Film*, offered some useful background information about the 1957 film of *Rises*, chief among which is Hemingway's personal, and positive, review of the shooting script. P. G. Rama Rao's contribution in *Ernest Hemingway: A Study in Narrative Technique* is best described as "slight," but he observed that the "subject of the novel is the frustration and restlessness of a generation juxtaposed to the abiding earth. . . ."[39]

In 1981 Robert McIlvaine published an excellent brief note on the issue of Robert Cohn's fascination with W. H. Hudson's *The Purple Land*, which depicts a romantic protagonist in South America who is irresistible to women. Cohn would have been inspired to go to South America by this novel. Warren Wedin maintained that Jake's fishing with a worm and a heavy sinker on the Irati is an indication that he is about to lose everything, even his status as sport fisherman. In *Hemingway and the Movies*, Frank M. Laurence discussed the problems of filming *Rises* to meet the strict moral codes of the film industry of 1957. The screenwriter, Peter Viertel, dealt with the problem by making Jake and Brett pious. The sexual adventures were reduced in the film, and the ending was changed to conclude optimistically. Laurence's book is the best discussion of the relationship of the film and the novel. In *The Tragic Art of Ernest Hemingway*, Wirt Williams argued that the novel is a tragedy born of Jake's romanticism, which inspired him to become involved in the war in Italy and then led him to fall in love with Brett, which Williams regards as an "overreaching" on Jake's part. Two books came out in 1981 on Hemingway's reading. Michael S. Reynolds, in *Hemingway's Reading 1910–1940: An Inventory*, detailed what Hemingway covered in his high-school courses, an inventory of the books in Hemingway's library in Key West, and a list of what he is known to have read between 1910 and 1940. *Hemingway's Library: A Composite Record*, compiled by James D. Brasch and Joseph Sigman, is a list of the books in Hemingway's libraries in Paris, Key West, and Cuba.[40]

In 1982 Robert E. Meyerson presented an excellent analysis of Robert Cohn as a Jew whose presence strengthens the sentimental theme of the novel. The other characters resent Robert because he was untouched by the war and is still idealistic. Also that year James Hinkle explored "Some Unexpected Sources for *The Sun Also Rises*," but most of the "echoes" turn out to be parallels of common phrases. Much better was Elizabeth Walden Hyde's article on the fishing scene on the Irati. She covered Hemingway's journalism on trout fishing, including several articles that advocate the use of grasshoppers and worms rather than flies. Mark Spilka discussed the theme of androgyny, arguing that the novel is "designed to show the impossibility of romantic love and marriage when women assume male prerogatives, when they become the wrong kind of androgynous woman, the bitch who destroys the man she loves. . . ." Also important is a 1982 essay by Charles Stetler and Gerald Locklin in which they pointed out, to good effect, that Jake is tentative, rather than committed to a fixed code of behavior, and that the code does not work for the other characters either, particularly not for Romero, who succumbs too easily to Brett's destructive allure. H. R. Stoneback argued once again for Jake's devotion to Christianity, questioning the interpretation of his jesting about evolution during the fishing scene as a mockery of William Jennings Bryan. Stoneback regarded Jake as devout and sympathetic to Bryan, while Bill endorses the cynical humor of H. L. Mencken.[41]

The most significant contribution of 1983 was Frederic Svoboda's *Hemingway & The Sun Also Rises: The Crafting of a Style*, in which he quoted extensively from the manuscripts, including the entire excised opening and other important scenes involving Jake and Brett. Svoboda's treatment was informed, balanced, and sensitive, resulting in one of the most important books on Hemingway. Of passing interest is *The Hemingway Women* by Bernice Kert, in which she suggested that as Hemingway wrote the novel, Hadley became increasingly uncomfortable with the portrayal of Jake's intense love for Brett. In *Concealments in Hemingway's Works*, Gerry Brenner advanced the awkward formulation that in *Rises* "egoistic but selected sensuous gratification must wed selfless deference to selected social customs." This is the "thesis" Brenner thought Hemingway "conceals" throughout the narrative.[42]

In an article on Ecclesiastes, S. A. Cowan argued that this philosophical disquisition lends the novel the carpe diem abandon of Count Mippipopolous, Jake's attitude of "disillusioned wisdom," and Robert's fundamental "confusion of thought," the role of the fool. Jesse Bier maintained that Jake's impotence is moral and psychological as well as physical. In "What's Funny in *The Sun Also Rises*" James Hinkle used a curious sense of humor, and some tortured readings, to attempt to identify "sixty submerged jokes." Although there was little that was original in Andrew Hook's "Art and Life in *The Sun Also Rises*," he clarified the role of Paris as a postwar Waste Land, Burguette as a pastoral interlude, Pamplona as the locus of a collision of values, and San Sebastian as Jake's quest for ritual purification.[43]

Perhaps the most important article of 1983 was "False Dawn: A Preliminary Analysis of *The Sun Also Rises*'s Manuscript," by Michael S. Reynolds. He explored the critical implications of the holograph notebooks: the use of real names in the opening pages, the deletion of entire scenes, the selection of the title only after the manuscript was written, and the restructuring of the narrative, which originally opened in Spain. H. R. Stoneback argued that the stand that Roland made against the Moors at Roncevaux has resonance for the novel: "Roland, then, is type and paradigm for Jacob Barnes, who wrestles courageously with the angel of his fate in the country around Roncevaux."[44]

One of the notable publications of 1984 was John Raeburn's *Fame Became of Him: Hemingway as Public Writer*, in which he discussed the transforming impact of the appearance of the novel in 1926, an event that made Hemingway into "a spokesman for his generation." Robert Elbaz maintained that in Hemingway's work "repetition constitutes the basic mechanics of his fiction, that repetitive patterns cohere throughout his text at the same time producing meaning and threatening its production, because when carried to its extreme repetition breeds delirium and non-sense." Ann Brashear Moore used a stylistic approach to support the idea that the use of repetition is Gertrude Stein's greatest influence on Hemingway. In "Lovers' Discourse in *The Sun Also Rises:* A Cock and Bull Story," Nina Schwartz presented some valuable points about existentialism and, using psychoanalytic theory, concluded that Romero is a transvestite and that "according to the bull-fight, then, woman's power to destroy man is not quite the power to castrate him; it is rather the signifier's power to castrate the very mythos of castration." Carol H. Smith brought clarity to feminist issues in her "Women and the Loss of Eden in Hemingway's Mythology," in which she said that Brett's error is to allow her desire for love to intrude into the public world of the bullfight, which inspires Jake's "self-disgust and his wish for disengagement" in the concluding scene. In contrast, Wolfgang E. H. Rudat argued that the final scene in the novel represents Brett's attempt to "castrate" Jake. Adeline R. Tintner explored parallels between *The Ambassadors* and *The Sun Also Rises* in an excellent essay in which she suggested that James associated his "obscure hurt" with the wounds suffered in the Civil War.[45]

In 1985, Jeffrey Meyers added very little in his *Hemingway: A Biography* to what Carlos Baker had already contributed, although he cast the familiar events in a negative tone, making Hemingway "vindictive" and "savage" in his treatment of the characters. Meyers, however, approached his biography in terms of the people in Hemingway's life, rather than through strict chronology, and his volume is useful as a study of these relationships, particularly between Hemingway and his four wives. Nevertheless, this strategy does not allow for a systematic discussion of any of the important works, and the few comments on *Rises* are scattered. Also that year, Wolfgang Rudat again explored the parallels between Robert and Romero, arguing, perversely, that the name "Pedro" is a pun on "Peter," which is a term for the phallus. Milton A. Cohen emphasized the ways in which the fates of Jake, Mike, and Robert Cohn parallel the fate of Odysseus's crew in their encounter with the enchantress. William Adair complained that the precise nature of Jake's wound, which he saw as "funny," is not fully explained. It did not occur to Adair that Jake is sensitive about that injury and thus discloses it only obliquely. Thomas Cornellier offered an essay exploring "The Myth of Escape and Fulfillment in *The Sun Also Rises* and *The Great Gatsby*," finding these myths central to the human condition in the postwar world of the twenties. Nothing in M. A. Klug's "Horns of Manichaeus: The Conflict of Art and Experience in *The Great Gatsby* and *The Sun Also Rises*" was as impressive as the title. A compendium of problematic assumptions, Klug's article attempts to defend Fitzgerald and Hemingway against the charge of "creative failure" while speculating about their "inner conflicts." Sukrita Paul Kumar argued that Brett is the "hero" whose tragedy is that "except for Jake, she finds no man who could comprehend the multiplicity of her roles as a woman seeking the realization of her selfhood." In a valuable note, "Putting on the Riff," Michael S. Reynolds explained an allusion in the Spanish fishing scene to General Miguel Prima Rivera and the war on the Riff in 1925.[46]

Gregory S. Sojka, in his *Ernest Hemingway: The Angler As Artist*, made the point that Jake's "fishing activities dramatize the need for ordered ritualistic activity in the face of surrounding aimlessness and disorder." Wolfgang Rudat was back again to contend that the name "Brett" means "board, plank" and that "Ashley" refers to the wood "ash," and that, finally, "Brett is a plank nailed down by many men." Jim Steinke offered a much more sensitive approach, finding that by the conclusion Jake is capable of experiencing some lovely moments alone, Brett is sensitive and considerate, and they end as caring friends, no longer frustrated lovers.[47]

In 1986 John W. Aldridge wrote an assessment of *The Sun Also Rises* sixty years after its first publication in which he suggested that Hemingway had become a public embarrassment by the time of his death but that his suicide came to be regarded as the "considered and courageous act of a man who knew exactly when all the things he cared about had ended for him." John Atherton's article that year would have been much better had he realized that the novel is told in retrospect. Without this awareness, Atherton expressed amazement that Jake narrates as though he has been to all of the places before, which, of course, he has. Atherton's other observations are also problematic, as when he maintained that Pedro is the only character Jake did not know before the journey began (actually there are several others, Harris and Edna among them). There is not much to recommend in James Rother's "Close-Reading Hemingway: Risking Mispronounced Stresses in *The Sun Also Rises*," a rambling theoretical discourse to the general point that literature means nothing and that *Rises* is a "novel that is not only about pointlessness (more or less) but also without a clearly summarizable point." Readers are advised to avoid this essay (more or less). Kim Moreland did a gloss on the novel in terms of medieval romances and histories, especially the courtly love tradition, and Myler Wilkinson explored the numerous parallels between *Rises* and Turgenev's *Fathers and Sons*.[48]

Also in 1986, H. R. Stoneback presented a richly informed discussion of Jake's "Catholic sensibility, with the moral and spiritual anguish and joy of the pilgrim, a quite specifically Catholic pilgrim on a specific pilgrimage route, very much in touch with the history, the ritual, the discipline, the moral and aesthetic and salvific legacy of the great medieval pilgrimage to Santiago de Compotela." William Belassi followed with a study of the composition of the novel, and he provided a chart outlining the daily production by Hemingway between 19 July and 21 September 1925. Working through each of the six manuscript notebooks, Belassi traced the shifts in protagonists from Niño de la Palma, to "Gerald" Cohn, to Brett, and, finally, to Jake. James Hinkle presented an assessment of the status of the text in " 'Dear Mr. Scribner'—About the Published Text of *The Sun Also*

Rises," in which he picked up where Belassi left off, tracing the process of the production of the novel from the typescript through the editing stage, the revision of proof, and the publication of the novel. He reviewed 4,000 instances in which the galleys differ from the typescript, including a series of mistakes. Hinkle's basic assessment was that "Hemingway was let down by his proofreader, copyeditor, and publisher."[49]

In "Toreo: The Moral Axis of The Sun Also Rises," Allen Josephs developed the best essay on the significance of bullfighting, which, through its expression of honor and courage, becomes the measure of moral behavior. Pedro Romero is the idealized hero, "a kind of exemplar whose perfect sacrifice of the bull is the precise center and climactic moment of The Sun Also Rises." Also of interest is David Harrell's "A Final Note on Duff Twysden," in which he dispelled the rumor that at her funeral in 1938 her former lovers served as pallbearers and were so drunk they dropped the coffin. Harrell, who consulted the records at the hospital and funeral home, suggested that Duff moved to Santa Fe hoping to cure her tuberculosis, found that it could not be cured, and died on 27 June 1938. Her body was cremated the next day. There was no funeral, nor were there any pallbearers or former lovers. Robert A. Martin discussed "Hemingway's Sun as Title and Metaphor," maintaining that the frequent references to the sun emphasize the "predictable course" of the sun and the "pointless circularity of the lives of the characters." Frank Scafella recaptured six years of correspondence between Hemingway and Owen Wister in which the older writer cautioned Hemingway against foul language. George Morgan found the "socio-historical" portrait of Paris in the novel unconvincing, but he maintained that "Paris symbolizes the divergent state of mind of individual characters," their "otherness." In the Journal of Evolutionary Psychology, Wolfgang Rudat recycled his interpretation of "Brett" as a plank nailed down by many men. He played many of the same themes again in an article in Cithara, where he also advanced the unlikely thesis that Hemingway intended the dining scene at Botin's to be read in the context of Chaucer's Pardoner's Tale, which involves a eunuch. E. Miller Budick offered an unconvincing reading of the novel as a "psychological fantasy in which neurosis has overtaken literature and the story has resisted consolidation into a work of art."[50]

The most important publication in 1987 was New Essays on The Sun Also Rises, edited by Linda Wagner-Martin, a valuable collection of six original essays. Wagner-Martin explored the biographical background and composition history along with a discussion of the theme of "community." Scott Donaldson devoted himself to comedy, showing that "irreverence," satire, parody, "incongruity," and ethnic humor all play a role and that Bill Gorton is the key figure of amusement: his humor alone "directs its jibes at ideas and institutions, not human beings." Another excellent essay in the collection is Michael Reynolds' "The Sun in Its Time: Recovering the Historical Context," in which he demonstrated that the novel is not a celebration of the Lost Generation but a "moral indictment" of its lack of values and self-indulgence that reveals the "corruption of Jake Barnes." Less valuable is Wendy Martin's "Brett Ashley as New Woman in *The Sun Also Rises*" because she ignored the proliferation of New Woman figures in the 1890s and regarded Brett as a startling and original phenomenon. In "Decoding the Hemingway Hero in *The Sun Also Rises*," Arnold E. Davidson and Cathy N. Davidson offered little beyond well-established insights. They concluded that *Rises* "itself effectively refutes any standards in the novel whereby Jake might be either particularly praised or blamed." John W. Aldridge presented random ideas as his "Afterthoughts on the Twenties and *The Sun Also Rises*," but there is little of value: "Hemingway's initially most seductive attribute was and remains his powerful responsiveness to experience." Kenneth S. Lynn's *Hemingway*, published in 1987, was a bio-critical exploration of sexuality in Hemingway and his works, particularly with reference to lesbians and male homosexuals. Lynn assumed that sexual confusion, originating in Hemingway's relationship with his mother, was a dominating force in his life, and this influences his treatment of *Rises*. The result was some confused logic and bad reading, as when Lynn assumed that, because of Jake's wound, he and Brett enjoy oral sex. Lynn does not explain why, given this assumption, they cannot live happily together, sexually fulfilled. Lynn did not add anything to an understanding of Hemingway by way of research; rather, he applied his own assumptions to the data compiled by others. The result was an unconvincing, and often curious, account of Hemingway's life and the background of his first novel.[51]

In a much more important essay in 1988, Robert E. Fleming gave an excellent assessment of the significance of the count, contending that this character emerges as a code hero and a prophet "who has been tested in the fire and who has remained intact." Lee Thorn argued that the aesthetic of the novel is built on etiquette. A more helpful article is Linda Wagner-Martin's "Hemingway's Search for Heroes, Once Again," in which she stressed the endurance of the biblical Jacob in his loyalty to Rachel and the references to the *Chanson de Roland* and the events at Roncevalles.[52]

Also of interest was Sibbie O'Sullivan's energetic rejoinder to Mark Spilka on "The Death of Love." O'Sullivan argued that there are patterns of enduring love and friendship in the novel, particularly between Jake and Brett, and that the novel concludes in an affirmation of that relationship. The essay was also helpful in its survey of the changing patterns of feminine roles from the New Woman to the British Blondes, the Gibson Girl, and the flapper. In *American Literature*, Mary Ann C. Curtis explored the possible influence of *The Song of Roland* on the Spanish scenes in *Rises*, making much of Jake's reference to Roncesvalles as "Roncevaux," the name by which the monastery is called in the medieval French epic. Not one to miss a year, Wolfgang Rudat maintained that Jake is missing his penis but that "Brett brings Jake to orgasm" by employing "some kind of mental process." In an even worse article, Rudat attempted to prove that Bill Gorton is impotent and that his condition is a submerged joke. And Rudat used *Studies in the Novel* to argue again that "Pedro" is a reference to "Peter" as "phallus" and that "the bullfighter's 'peter' possesses a 'durability' which Brett's former lovers had not been endowed with." Although nothing in Denis Brian's *The True Gen* (1988) can be trusted, there are entertaining comments by Hadley Mowrer, Harold Loeb, Malcolm Cowley, and others about the events in 1925. Brian, though, made it appear that all of these people engaged in conversation with him, which was not the case.[53]

One of the most notable publications of 1989 was *Hemingway in Love and War: The Lost Diary of Agnes von Kurowsky*, by Henry S. Villard and James Nagel, a volume that presented original documents (including the diary kept by Hemingway's nurse in the hospital in Milan), reminiscences, and a scholarly account of what happened to Hemingway in World War I. Many aspects of the backgrounds of Brett Ashley and Jake Barnes seem drawn from these events, rather than the life of Duff Twysden. More important was Michael Reynolds, *Hemingway: The Paris Years*, the best biographical account of the people and events that provided the raw material for the novel. Reynolds's account was informed, detailed, and authoritative, relying on letters, manuscript drafts, and other documents to verify dates and places. Of special interest was *Hemingway and Spain: A Pursuit*, in which Edward F. Stanton explored the unique history and values of Spain. Stanton portrays Spain as the "land of the ancient truths—nature, the body, fertility, religion, ritual" set against the modern, false values of France. Frank M. Laurence, in *"The Sun Also Rises:* The NBC Version," discussed the television treatment of the novel, which ran in two parts in December of 1984. Laurence contended that the numerous changes in characterization and event from the novel are justified because television is not a serious art form but only entertainment. Wolfgang Rudat argued once again that Jake has lost his penis and that Brett makes impossible sexual demands on him. In a more valuable essay, Peter L. Hays maintained that "bullfighting in the novel should be seen as an attenuated form of religious worship culminating in live sacrifice."[54]

The momentum in Hemingway scholarship continued strong into the 1990s, with increased interest in gender issues and composition history. Perhaps the most important publication was *Ernest Hemingway, The Sun Also Rises: A Facsimile Edition*, edited by Matthew J. Bruccoli, which contained the text of the French notebooks in which Hemingway wrote the first draft. In *Hemingway's Quarrel with Androgyny*, Mark Spilka returned to the theme of sexual identity, which he had explored years earlier, this time focusing on Jake as impotent narrator, a condition Spilka saw as part of a tradition including Strether in Henry James's *The Ambassadors* and Dowell in Ford Madox Ford's *The Good Soldier*. William Belassi came back to the subject that he had tentatively addressed in 1986, the writing of the novel. In this more complete study, Balassi outlined the biographical events behind the novel's action, the day by day writing of the first draft, and the revisions that were made before publication. Balassi's astute comments about the shifts of focus as the writing progressed were of particular interest. Much less vital was Wolfgang Rudat's *A Rotten Way to Be Wounded*, a gathering of previously published essays. Rudat attempted to show that in *Rises* Hemingway is an allusive writer who "uses literary allusion in general and myth-adaptation in particular synergistically with psychological symbol-building." Eugene Kanjo concluded that Brett is "not bent on sexual gratification but on displacing the male of the species from the catbird seat." Peter Griffin had remarkably little to say about *Rises* in his *Less Than A Treason: Hemingway in Paris*, and much of what he did say is unreliable: Hemingway's having been rendered impotent and Duff Twysden's drug addiction are two important biographical examples. In his *Ernest Hemingway*, Peter L. Hays maintained that the characters in the novel are "without control over their destiny." Presumably, from his point of view, Jake's introduction of Brett to Pedro and her decision to leave the bullfighter for his own good have no moral weight, everything having been determined by outside forces. [55]

There was surprisingly little new material in Peter Messent's *New Readings of the American Novel*, except the reformulation of traditional ideas in poststructural rhetoric. He discussed matters such as "character as subordinate to action" and "action as subordinate to character." Much better was Jacqueline Tavernier-Coubin's detailed study of *A Moveable Feast*, in which she covered Hemingway's use of two scenes from the manuscript of *The Sun Also Rises* in his retrospective memoir, one dealing with Ford Madox Ford and the cutting of Hilaire Belloc, and the other an incident with Gertrude Stein when she made the comment about the Lost Generation. Kathleen Morgan did not insist on the direct influence of Homer's Helen of Troy on Brett Ashley, but she did argue that they are both strong women in a world of men, who live outside of the world of home and family; women of beauty and sexuality; women who share a concern for the young (such as Brett's for Romero). Of lesser importance, Louise R. Achuff discussed Jake's use of "nice," "fine," and "pleasant," finding the words "related to Hemingway's fear of sounding pretentious and to his predilection for understatement." For his part, Darryl Hattenhauer added to Jim Hinkle's collection of humor in the novel by citing such puns as Jake's comment that he drinks Pernod because it has "a good uplift." [56]

The most important book in 1992 was *Hemingway: The American Homecoming*, by Michael Reynolds, in which he covered the stages of revision, and the events in Hemingway's life, from March of 1926 until the publication of the novel on October 22. Characteristically, Reynolds worked from documents and manuscript drafts to present a concentrated account of this period. The biographical background provided by James R. Mellow in *Hemingway: A Life Without Consequences* was more complete; he covered the basic story informed by documents, especially letters, which were not available when Baker did his study. Mellow's comments regarding Hemingway's letters during the composition of the novel, in which he gave insights into his objectives and approach, were particularly valuable. His account of Harold Loeb's relationship with Kitty Cannell and his affair with Duff Twysden is also superior. In these respects, Mellow's biography superseded that of Baker as the most complete of the comprehensive biographies.[57]

In *Hadley*, Gioia Diliberto did not presume to offer analysis of the novel, but did comment on some of the events of 1925 involving Hemingway's first wife. Harold Bloom's *Brett Ashley* consisted almost entirely of reprinted material, but in his brief introduction he offered the opinion that the figure of Brett is "a grand period piece, rather than a fully achieved literary character." Also that year, Charles L. Ross explored the influence of Ford's *The Good Soldier* on the novel, stressing the similarities of narrative technique. George Cheatham went back to the issue of money and argued that in most ways Jake is penurious but that at the end, in his relationship with Brett, he demonstrates generosity and a "refusal to calculate debt."[58]

In 1993, Robert E. Fleming observed that the name "Zizi" is the French diminutive for penis. There is thus humor in the question Brett asks the Count, "What about your little friend, Zizi?" Peter L. Hays explored the possible influence of Catullus on the novel, speculating that Pound's interest in the poet could have touched Hemingway. As though to demonstrate that no scholarship is too bizarre to find publication somewhere, Wolfgang Rudat followed with yet another book, this one entitled *Alchemy in The Sun Also Rises: Hidden Gold in Hemingway's Narrative*, published, without a blush, by Edwin Mellen Press. Rudat here argued that Brett has gone without an orgasm since her manual stimulation by Jake in Italy, a situation rectified by Pedro Romero, who allows her to assume the superior position, copulating *recibiendo*. Rudat concluded that by the end of the novel, Jake has freed himself of his sexual obsession with Brett. Anyone who has not read enough Rudat scholarship on *Rises* should rush to purchase this book.[59]

This survey of criticism on *The Sun Also Rises* demonstrates the shifting emphasis and deepening insight of scholars as the information about Hemingway and his novel has increased over the years.[60] The initial reviews and early scholarship could only speculate about Hemingway's life, making judgments based on rumor and partial information, and the emphasis was on the Lost Generation and their spokesman. The 1950s, the first decade of sustained scholarship, brought a concern for Jake's search for values, for the influence of *The Waste Land*, and an appreciation of Hemingway's "iceberg principle" of leaving key facts unstated, working through implication. This concept inspired the first close readings of the novel and a new appreciation of the role of Jake as narrator and the chronology of the events he describes. That led, in later work, to an appreciation of Hemingway and imagism and the relationship of his fiction to painting, particularly impressionism and expressionism. With the opening of the manuscripts and letters in 1980, scholarship began to concentrate on the composition of the novel and a more detailed look at Hemingway's life. Changing interests in American culture led to a stress on gender issues and a focus on Hemingway's women characters and the lesbian and homosexual characters in his works; these concerns continued into the 1990s.

More remains to be done, partly because new documents surface virtually every year, and also because many of the key questions about the novel have never been fully explored. Attempting to deal with unresolved matters, the new essays in this volume address a series of issues. In an important new study, "Second Thoughts: Hemingway's Postscript to *The Sun Also Rises*," Robert E. Fleming explores the implications of a newly discovered manuscript fragment, a sequel to the novel that Hemingway began in 1927. In this fragment, entitled "Jimmy the Bartender," Hemingway brought Jake and Brett and Mike Campbell together again in Paris, and they discuss the effects of Jake's book on their current lives. Fleming's discovery initiates a new chapter in the discussion of the novel. Linda Patterson Miller, in "Brett Ashley: The Beauty of It All," presents a detailed examination of the novel as the story of Brett's self-discovery through her relationship with Pedro Romero. Her sensitive treatment of Lady Ashley goes well beyond previous scholarship on this subject. In the concluding essay, "Good Old Harris in *The Sun Also Rises*," Jane E. Wilson demonstrates that the role of Harris on the fishing trip to Burguete aligns him with the regenerative values of nature as opposed to the urbane destructiveness of the Lost Generation in Pamplona. But in no sense are these original essays meant to terminate serious consideration of the complex issues in the novel. Rather, they are further testimony to an enduring interest in the characters, places, and artistic richness of Hemingway's timeless fiesta, *The Sun Also Rises*.

Notes

1. The best account of Hemingway's World War I experience is *Hemingway in Love and War* by Henry S. Villard and James Nagel (Boston: Northeastern University Press, 1989).

2. Carlos Baker, *Ernest Hemingway: A Life Story* (New York: Scribner's, 1969), 147–55, 160–67, 178–79, 180–82, 186–88.

3. The major reviews of Hemingway's works have been gathered into two useful collections: *Ernest Hemingway: The Critical Reception*, ed. Robert O. Stephens (New York: Burt Franklin, 1977), and *Hemingway: The Critical Heritage*, ed. Jeffrey Meyers (Boston: Routledge & Kegan Paul, 1982). "Study in Futility," *Cincinnati Enquirer*, 30 October 1926, 5. "Sad Young Man," *Time* 8 (1 November 1926): 48. "Seeking Sensations," *Springfield Republican*, 28 November 1926, 7F. Allen Tate, "Hard-Boiled," *Nation*, 15 December 1926, 642, 644. "Fiesta," {London} *Times Literary Supplement*, 30 June 1927, 454. "*The Sun Also Rises*, by Ernest

Hemingway," *The Dial* 82 (January 1927): 73. Virginia Woolf, "An Essay in Criticism," *New York Herald Tribune Books*, 4 (9 October 1927): 1, 8.

4. "Marital Tragedy," *New York Times Book Review*, 31 October 1926, 7. Conrad Aiken, "Expatriates," *New York Herald Tribune Books*, 31 October 1926, sec. 7, p. 4. K. J. W., review of *The Sun Also Rises, Boston Evening Transcript* 6 November 1926, part 6, p. 2. Ernest Boyd, "Readers and Writers," *Independent* 117 (20 November 1926): 594. Herbert S. Gorman, "Hemingway Keeps His Promise," *New York World*, 14 November 1926, 10m. Burton Rascoe, "Diversity in the Younger Set," *New York Sun*, 16 November 1926, 10.

5. Touchstone, "The New Books," *New Yorker* 2 (20 November 1926): 88, 90. "Hemingway Seems Out of Focus in *The Sun Also Rises*," *Chicago Daily Tribune*, 27 November 1926, 13. Schuyler Ashley, "Hemingway Leads Young Ineffectuals Through Europe," *Kansas City Star*, 4 December 1926, 8. Cleveland B. Chase, "Out of Little, Much," *Saturday Review* 3 (11 December 1926): 420–21. Henry Seidel Canby, "Notes of a Rapid Reader," *Saturday Review* 111 (18 December 1926): 445. Lawrence Morris, "Warfare in Man and among Men," *New Republic*, 22 December 1926: 142–43.

6. Hugh Walpole, "Contemporary American Letters," *Nation & Athenaeum* 41 (4 June 1927): 302–03. Edmund Wilson, "The Sportsman's Tragedy," *New Republic* 53 (14 December 1927): 102–3. Edwin Muir, "Fiction," *Nation & Athenaeum* 41 (2 July 1927): 450, 452. Bruce Barton, review of *The Sun Also Rises, Atlantic Monthly* 139 (April 1927): 12, 14. Charles W. Ferguson, "Five Rising Stars in American Fiction," *Bookman* 65 (May 1927): 251–57.

7. Richmond Barrett, "Babes in the Bois," *Harper's* 156 (May 1928): 724–36. André Maurois, "Ernest Hemingway," *This Quarter* 2, no. 2 (1929): 212–15. Ben Ray Redman, "Spokesman for a Generation," *Spur* 44 (1 December 1929): 77, 186.

8. Malcolm Cowley, *Exile's Return* (New York: Norton, 1934). Harlan Hatcher, *Creating the Modern American Novel* (New York: Farrar & Rinehart, 1935), 228–33. Herbert J. Muller, *Modern Fiction: A Study of Values* (New York: Funk & Wagnalls, 1937), 383–403.

9. Edmund Wilson, *The Wound and the Bow: Seven Studies in Literature* (Boston: Houghton Mifflin, 1941).

10. James T. Farrell, "Ernest Hemingway, Apostle of a 'Lost Generation'," *New York Times Book Review*, 1 August 1943, 6, 14.

11. Edwin Berry Burghum, "Ernest Hemingway and the Psychology of the Lost Generation," in *The Novel and the World's Dilemma* (New York: Oxford University Press, 1947), 184–204.

12. Henry Seidel Canby, *American Memoir* (Boston: Houghton-Mifflin, 1947), 339–49.

13. Carlos Baker, "25 Years of a Hemingway Classic," *New York Times Book Review* 56 (29 April 1951): 5, 31.

14. Carlos Baker, *Hemingway: The Writer as Artist* (Princeton: Princeton University Press, 1952).

15. Philip Young, *Ernest Hemingway* (New York: Rinehart, 1952).

16. Ben Ray Redman, "Gallantry in the Face of Death," *Saturday Review* 36 (6 June 1953): 18. Carlos Baker, "When the Warriors Sleep," *Saturday Review* 36 (4 July 1953): 13. James B. Colvert, "Ernest Hemingway's Morality in Action," *American Literature* 27 (1955): 372–85. Frederick J. Hoffman, *The Twenties: American Writing in the Postwar Decade* (New York: Viking, 1955), 80–85.

17. Arthur L. Scott, "In Defense of Robert Cohn," *College English* 18 (March 1957): 309–14. Mark Spilka, "The Death of Love in *The Sun Also Rises*," in *Twelve Original Essays on Great American Novels*, ed. Charles Shapiro (Detroit: Wayne State University Press, 1958), 238–56. See George Plimpton, "An Interview with Ernest Hemingway," in *Ernest Hemingway: Five Decades of Criticism*, ed. Linda Welshimer Wagner (East Lansing: Michigan State University Press, 1974), 21–38. Reprinted from *Paris Review* 18 (Spring 1958): 60–89. Richard P. Adams, "Sunrise Out of the Waste Land," *Tulane Studies in English* 9 (1959): 119–31.

John Patrick Bury, "Hemingway in Spain," *Contemporary Review* 1118 (February 1959): 103–5.

18. Robert O. Stephens, "Hemingway's Don Quixote in Pamplona," *College English* 23 (December 1961): 216–18. R. W. Stallman, *The Houses That James Built and Other Literary Studies* (Athens: Ohio University Press, 1961), 173–93. Leicester Hemingway, *My Brother, Ernest Hemingway* (Cleveland: World Publishing Co., 1961), 100–2.

19. Malcolm Cowley, "Introduction" to *Three Novels of Ernest Hemingway* (New York: Scribners, 1962), ix–xxviii. Paul B. Newman, "Hemingway's Grail Quest," *University of Kansas City Review* 28 (1962): 295–303. Earl Rovit, *Ernest Hemingway* (New York: Twayne, 1963), 147–62. Geoffrey Moore, "*The Sun Also Rises*: Notes Toward an Extreme Fiction," *Review of English Literature* 4 (October 1963): 31–46.

20. Paul Lauter, "Plato's Stepchildren, Gatsby and Cohn," *Modern Fiction Studies* 9 (Winter 1963–64): 338–46. Sidney P. Moss, "Character, Vision, and Theme in *The Sun Also Rises*," *Iowa English Yearbook* 9 (Fall 1964): 64–67. Robert W. Lewis, Jr., *Hemingway on Love* (Austin: University of Texas Press, 1965), 19–35. Frances E. Skipp, "What Was the Matter with Jacob Barnes?" *The Carrell* 6 (December 1965): 17–22.

21. Donald E. Gastwirth, "Can Life Have Meaning? A Study of *The Sun Also Rises*," *Yale Literary Magazine* 134 (March 1966): 36–41. Richard B. Hovey, "*The Sun Also Rises*: Hemingway's Inner Debate," *Forum* 4 (Summer 1966): 4–10. Paul Ramsey, "Hemingway as Moral Thinker: A Look at Two Novels," in *The Twenties, Poetry and Prose: 20 Critical Essays*, ed. Richard E. Langford and William E. Taylor (Deland, FL: Everett Edwards Press, 1966), 92–94. William L. Vance, "Implications of Form in *The Sun Also Rises*," in *The Twenties, Poetry and Prose*, 87–91.

22. John S. Rouch, "Jake Barnes as Narrator," *Modern Fiction Studies* 11 (1966): 361–70. Harold Loeb, "Hemingway's Bitterness," *Connecticut Review* 1 (October 1967): 7–24. Sheridan Baker, *Ernest Hemingway: An Introduction and Interpretation* (New York: Holt, Rinehart and Winston, 1967), 40–55. Arthur Mizener, *Twelve Great American Novels* (New York: New American Library, 1967), 120–41. Louis D. Rubin, Jr., *The Teller in the Tale* (Seattle: University of Washington Press, 1967), 116–17, 129–32. Daniel J. Schneider, "The Symbolism of *The Sun Also Rises*," *Discourse* 10 (Summer 1967): 334–42. Alexander Tamke, "Jacob Barnes' 'Biblical Name': Central Irony in *The Sun Also Rises*," *The English Record* 18 (December 1967): 2–7.

23. J. F. Kobler, "Confused Chronology in *The Sun Also Rises*," *Modern Fiction Studies* 13 (Winter 1967–68): 517–20. Dewey Ganzell, "*Cabestro* and *Vaquilla:* The Symbolic Structure of *The Sun Also Rises*," *Sewanee Review* 76 (Winter 1968): 26–48. Robert W. Cochran, "Circularity in *The Sun Also Rises*," *Modern Fiction Studies* 14 (Autumn 1968): 297–305. Irving A. Yevish, "The Sun Also Exposes: Hemingway and Jake Barnes," *Midwest Quarterly* 10 (Autumn 1968): 89–97.

24. Carlos Baker, *Ernest Hemingway: A Life Story* (New York: Scribner's, 1969), 147–55, 160–67, 178–79, 180–82, 186–88.

25. Michael J. Hoffman, "From Cohn to Herzog," *Yale Review* 58 (Spring 1969): 342–58. Kermit Vanderbilt, "*The Sun Also Rises*: Time Uncertain," *Twentieth Century Literature* 15 (October 1969): 153–54. Josephine Z. Knopf, "Meyer Wolfsheim and Robert Cohn: A Study of a Jewish Type and Stereotype," *Tradition* 10 (Spring 1969): 93–104.

26. Delbert E. Wylder, *Hemingway's Heroes* (Albuquerque: University of New Mexico Press, 1969), 31–65. Claire Sprague, "*The Sun Also Rises*: Its 'Clear Financial Basis'," *American Quarterly* 21 (Summer 1960): 259–66. Donald T. Torchiana, "*The Sun Also Rises*: A Reconsideration," *Fitzgerald/Hemingway Annual* (1969): 77–103.

27. William White, ed., *The Merrill Studies in "The Sun Also Rises"* (Columbus: Charles E. Merrill Publishing Co., 1969). Bertram D. Sarason, "Lady Brett Ashley and Lady Duff Twysden," *Connecticut Review* 2 (April 1969): 5–13. Jackson J. Benson, *Hemingway: The Writer's Art of Self-Defense* (Minneapolis: University of Minnesota Press, 1969), 30–43.

28. Matthew J. Bruccoli, " 'Oh, Give Them Irony and Give Them Pity'," *Fitzgerald/ Hemingway Annual* (1970): 236. J. M. Linebarger, "Eggs As Huevos in *The Sun Also Rises*," *Fitzgerald/Hemingway Annual* (1970): 237–39. Scott Donaldson, "Hemingway's Morality of Compensation," *American Literature* 43 (1971): 399–420. Emily Stipes Watts, *Ernest Hemingway and the Arts* (Urbana: University of Illinois Press, 1971).

29. Bruce L. Grenberg, "The Design of Heroism in *The Sun Also Rises*," *Fitzgerald/ Hemingway Annual* (1971): 274–89. Harold F. Mosher, Jr., "The Two Styles of Hemingway's *The Sun Also Rises*," *Fitzgerald/Hemingway Annual* (1971): 262–73. George D. Murphy, "Hemingway's *Waste Land*: The Controlling Water Symbolism of *The Sun Also Rises*," *Hemingway Notes* 1 (Spring 1971): 20–26. Brom Weber, "Ernest Hemingway's Genteel Bullfight," in *The American Novel and the Nineteen Twenties*, ed. Malcolm Bradbury and David Palmer (London: Edward Arnold, 1971), 151–63. Chaman Nahal, *The Narrative Pattern in Ernest Hemingway's Fiction* (Rutherford: Fairleigh Dickinson University Press, 1971), 28–48.

30. Linda W. Wagner, "*The Sun Also Rises*: One Debt to Imagism," *Journal of Narrative Technique* 2, no. 2 (1972): 88–98. Carole Gottlieb Vopat, "The End of *The Sun Also Rises*: A New Beginning," *Fitzgerald/Hemingway Annual* (1972): 245–55. Arthur Waldhorn, *A Reader's Guide to Ernest Hemingway* (New York: Farrar, Straus, and Giroux, 1972), 93–112.

31. Morton L. Ross, "Bill Gorton, The Preacher in *The Sun Also Rises*," *Modern Fiction Studies* 18 (Winter 1972–73): 517–27. J. M. Linebarger, "Symbolic Hats in *The Sun Also Rises*," *Fitzgerald/Hemingway Annual* (1972): 323–24. Thomas H. Pauly and Thomas Dwyer, "Passing the Buck in *The Sun Also Rises*," *Hemingway Notes* 2, no. 2 (1972): 3–6. Richard P. Sugg, "Hemingway, Money, and *The Sun Also Rises*," *Fitzgerald/Hemingway Annual* (1972): 257–67.

32. Bertram D. Sarason, *Hemingway and The Sun Set* (Washington, D. C.: Microcard Editions, 1972).

33. Sheldon Norman Grebstein, *Hemingway's Craft* (Carbondale: Southern Illinois University Press, 1973), 67–73. Terrence Doody, "Hemingway's Style and Jake's Narration," *Journal of Narrative Technique* 4 (Sept. 1974): 212–25. Richard K. Peterson, *Hemingway: Direct and Oblique* (The Hague: Mouton, 1974), 171–207.

34. Donald A. Daiker, "The Affirmative Conclusion of *The Sun Also Rises*," *McNeese Review* 21 (1975): 3–19. Donald A. Daiker, "The Pied Piper in *The Sun Also Rises*," *Fitzgerald/ Hemingway Annual* (1975): 235–37. Ronald Lajoie and Sally Lentz, "Is Jake Barnes Waiting?" *Fitzgerald/Hemingway Annual* (1975): 229–33. Martin Light, "Sweeping Out Chivalric Silliness: The Example of *Huck Finn* and *The Sun Also Rises*," *Mark Twain Journal* 17 (Winter 1975): 18–21. Donald M. Murray, "*The Day of the Locust* and *The Sun Also Rises*: Congruence and Caricature," *Fitzgerald/Hemingway Annual* (1975): 239–45. Manuel Schonhorn, "*The Sun Also Rises*: I: The Jacob Allusion II: Parody as Meaning," *Ball State University Forum* 16 (Spring 1975): 49–55. David L. Vanderwerken, "One More River to Cross: The Bridge Motif in *The Sun Also Rises*," *CEA Critic* 37 (January 1975): 21–22. Linda Welshimer Wagner, *Hemingway and Faulkner: inventors/masters* (Metuchen: Scarecrow, 1975), 41–51.

35. Gerald T. Gordon, "Survival in *The Sun Also Rises*: (Hemingway's Harvey Stone)," *Lost Generation Journal* 4, no. 2 (1976): 10–11, 17. David Henry Lowenkron, "Jake Barnes— A Student of William James in *The Sun Also Rises*," *Texas Quarterly* 19, no. 1 (1976): 147–56. B. Ramachandra Rao, "*The Sun Also Rises*: A Study in Structure," *Banasthali Patrika* 20 (1976): 11–17. W. J. Stuckey, "*The Sun Also Rises* on Its Own Ground," *Journal of Narrative Technique* 6 (Fall 1976): 224–32.

36. Sara Lennox, " 'We Could Have Had Such a Damned Good Time Together': Individual and Society in *The Sun Also Rises* and *Mutmassungen über Jakob*," *Modern Language Studies* 7 (1977): 82–90. David Morgan Zehr, "Paris and the Expatriate Mystique: Hemingway's *The Sun Also Rises*," *Arizona Quarterly* 33 (Summer 1977): 156–64. Scott Donaldson, *By Force of Will: The Life and Art of Ernest Hemingway* (New York: Viking, 1977). Sam S. Baskett, " 'An Image to Dance Around': Brett and Her Lovers in *The Sun Also Rises*,"

The Centennial Review 22 (Winter 1978): 45–69. Fred D. Crawford and Bruce Morton, "Hemingway and Brooks: The Mystery of 'Henry's Bicycle'," *Studies in American Fiction* 6 (1978): 106–9. Scott Donaldson, " 'Irony and Pity'—Anatole France Got It Up," *Fitzgerald/ Hemingway Annual* (1978): 331–34. Kathleen L. Nichols, "The Morality of Asceticism in *The Sun Also Rises*: A Structural Reinterpretation," *Fitzgerald/Hemingway Annual* (1978): 321–30. Leon F. Seltzer, "The Opportunity of Impotence: Count Mippipopolous in *The Sun Also Rises*," *Renascence* 31 (Autumn 1978): 3–14. Matthew J. Bruccoli, *Scott and Ernest: The Authority of Failure and the Authority of Success* (New York: Random House, 1978), 40–56.

37.   Wayne Kvam, "*The Sun Also Rises*: The Chronologies," *Papers on Language and Literature* 15 (Spring 1979): 199–203. Anders Breidlid, "Courage and Self-Affirmation in Ernest Hemingway's 'Lost Generation' Fiction," *Edda: Nordisk Tidsskrift for Litteraturforskning* 5 (1979): 279–99. Cathy N. Davidson, "Death in the Morning: The Role of Vicente Girones in *The Sun Also Rises*," *Hemingway Notes* 5 (Fall 1979): 11–13. Stanley Wertheim, "Images of Exile: *The Portrait of a Lady* and *The Sun Also Rises*," *Hemingway Notes* 5 (1979): 25–27. Raymond S. Nelson, *Hemingway: Expressionist Artist* (Ames: Iowa State University Press, 1979).

38.   David Goldknopf, "Tourism in *The Sun Also Rises*," *CEA Critic* 41 (March 1979): 2–8. Gerald T. Gordon, "Hemingway's Wilson-Harris: The Search for Value in *The Sun Also Rises*," *Fitzgerald/Hemingway Annual* (1972): 237–44. Ernest Hemingway, "The Unpublished Opening of *The Sun Also Rises*," *Antaeus* 33 (Spring 1979): 7–14.

39.   Delbert E. Wylder, "The Two Faces of Brett: The Role of the New Woman in *The Sun Also Rises*," *Kentucky Philological Review* (1980): 27–33. Patrick D. Morrow, "The Bought Generation: Another Look at Money in *The Sun Also Rises*," in *Money Talks: Language and Lucre in American Fiction*, ed. Roy R. Male (Norman: University of Oklahoma Press, 1980), 51–69. Gene D. Phillips, *Hemingway and Film* (New York: Ungar, 1980), 119–33. P. G. Rama Rao, *Ernest Hemingway: A Study in Narrative Technique* (New Dehli: S. Chand, 1980), 165–75.

40.   Robert McIlvaine, "Robert Cohn and *The Purple Land*," *Notes on Modern American Literature* 5, no. 2 (1981): item 8. Warren Wedin, "Trout Fishing and Self-Betrayal in *The Sun Also Rises*," *Arizona Quarterly* 37 (Spring 1981): 63–74. Frank M. Laurence, *Hemingway and the Movies* (Jackson: University Press of Mississippi, 1981), 139–50. Wirt Williams, *The Tragic Art of Ernest Hemingway* (Baton Rouge: Louisiana State University Press, 1981), 40–64. Michael S. Reynolds, *Hemingway's Reading 1910–1940: An Inventory* (Princeton: Princeton University Press, 1981). James D. Brasch and Joseph Sigman, *Hemingway's Library: A Composite Record* (New York: Garland, 1981).

41.   Robert E. Meyerson, "Why Robert Cohn?: An Analysis of Hemingway's *The Sun Also Rises*," *Liberal and Fine Arts Review* 2, no. 1 (1982): 57–68. James Hinkle, "Some Unexpected Sources for *The Sun Also Rises*," *Hemingway Review* 2 (Fall 1982): 26–42. Elizabeth Walden Hyde, "Aficionado Fishes Worms: A Study of Hemingway and Jake," *American Fly Fisher* 9 (1982): 2–7. Mark Spilka, "Hemingway and Fauntleroy: An Androgynous Pursuit," in *American Novelists Revisited: Essays in Feminist Criticism* (Boston: G. K. Hall, 1982), 339–70. Charles Stetler and Gerald Locklin, "Does Time Heal All Wounds? A Search for the Code Hero in *The Sun Also Rises*," *McNeese Review* 28 (1982): 92–100. H. R. Stoneback, " 'For Bryan's Sake': The Tribute to the Great Commoner in Hemingway's *The Sun Also Rises*," *Christianity and Literature* 32 (Winter 1982): 29–36.

42.   Frederic Joseph Svoboda, *Hemingway & The Sun Also Rises: The Crafting of a Style* (Lawrence: University Press of Kansas, 1983). Bernice Kert, *The Hemingway Women* (New York: Norton, 1983), 165–69. Gerry Brenner, *Concealments in Hemingway's Works* (Columbus: Ohio State University Press, 1983), 42–52.

43.   S. A. Cowan, "Robert Cohn, the Fool of Ecclesiastes in *The Sun Also Rises*," *Dalhousie Review* 63 (Spring 1983): 98–106. Jesse Bier, "Jake Barnes, Cockroaches, and Trout in *The Sun Also Rises*," *Arizona Quarterly* 39 (Summer 1983): 164–71. James Hinkle, "What's

Funny in *The Sun Also Rises*," in *Up in Michigan: Proceedings of the First National Conference of the Hemingway Society*, Traverse City: 1983, 62–71. Andrew Hook, "Art and Life in *The Sun Also Rises*," in *Ernest Hemingway: New Critical Essays*, ed. Robert A. Lee (Totowa: Barnes & Noble, 1983), 49–63.

44. Michael S. Reynolds, "False Dawn: A Preliminary Analysis of *The Sun Also Rises*'s Manuscript," in *Hemingway: A Revaluation*, ed. Donald R. Noble (Troy: Whitston Publishing Co., 1983), 115–34. H. R. Stoneback, "Hemingway and Faulkner on the Road to Roncevaux," in *Hemingway: A Revaluation*, 135–63.

45. John Raeburn, *Fame Became of Him: Hemingway as Public Writer* (Bloomington: Indiana University Press, 1984), 21–23. Robert Elbaz, "The Mechanics of Repetition in the Discourse of Ernest Hemingway," *Zagadnienia Rodzajów Literackich* 27 (1984): 77–90. Ann Brashear Moore, "Hemingway's *The Sun Also Rises* and Stein: A Stylistic Approach," *Káñina: Revista de Artes y Letras de la Universidad de Costa Rica* 8 (1984): 111–17. Nina Schwartz, "Lovers' Discourse in *The Sun Also Rises*: A Cock and Bull Story," *Criticism* 26 (Winter 1984): 49–69. Carol H. Smith, "Women and the Loss of Eden in Hemingway's Mythology," in *Ernest Hemingway: The Writer in Context*, ed. James Nagel (Madison: University of Wisconsin Press, 1984), 129–44. Wolfgang E. H. Rudat, "Jake's Odyssey: Catharsis in *The Sun Also Rises*," *Hemingway Review* 4 (Fall 1984): 33–36. Adeline R. Tintner, "Ernest and Henry: Hemingway's Lover's Quarrel with James," in *Ernest Hemingway: The Writer in Context*, 165–78.

46. Jeffrey Meyers, *Hemingway: A Biography* (New York: Harper & Row, 1985). Wolfgang E. H. Rudat, "Cohn and Romero in the Ring: Sports and Religion in *The Sun Also Rises*," *Arizona Quarterly* 41 (Winter 1985): 311–18. Milton A. Cohen, "Circe and Her Swine: Domination and Debasement in *The Sun Also Rises*," *Arizona Quarterly* 41 (Winter 1985): 293–305. William Adair, "Hemingway's Iceberg Method and Jake's Wound," *Notes on Contemporary Literature* 15 (1985): 11–12. Thomas Cornellier, "The Myth of Escape and Fulfillment in *The Sun Also Rises* and *The Great Gatsby*," *Society for the Study of Midwestern Literature Newsletter* 15 (1985): 15–21. M. A. Klug, "Horns of Manichaeus: The Conflict of Art and Experience in *The Great Gatsby* and *The Sun Also Rises*," *Essays in Literature* 12 (1985): 111–24. Sukrita Paul Kumar, "Woman as Hero in Hemingway's *The Sun Also Rises*," *Literary Endeavor* 6 (1985): 102–8. Michael S. Reynolds, "Putting on the Riff," *Hemingway Review* 5 (Fall 1985): 30–31.

47. Gregory S. Sojka, *Ernest Hemingway: The Angler As Artist* (New York: Peter Lang, 1985), 66–71. Wolfgang E. H. Rudat, "Brett's Problem: Ovidian and Other Allusions in *The Sun Also Rises*," *Style* 19 (Fall 1985): 317–25. Jim Steinke, "Brett and Jake in Spain: Hemingway's Ending for *The Sun Also Rises*," *Spectrum* 27 (1985): 131–41.

48. See John W. Aldridge, "*The Sun Also Rises*—Sixty Years Later," *Sewanee Review* 94 (Spring 1986): 337–45. John Atherton, "The Itinerary and the Postcard: Minimal Strategies in *The Sun Also Rises*," *English Literary History* 53 (Spring 1986): 199–218. James Rother, "Close-Reading Hemingway: Risking Mispronounced Stresses in *The Sun Also Rises*," *Hemingway Review* 6 (Fall 1986): 79–87. Kim Moreland, "Hemingway's Medievalist Impulse: Its Effect on the Presentation of Women and War," *Hemingway Review* 6 (Fall 1986): 30–41. Myler Wilkinson, *Hemingway and Turgenev: The Nature of Literary Influence* (Ann Arbor: UMI Research Press, 1986), 47–68.

49. H. R. Stoneback, "From the rue Saint-Jacques to the Pass of Roland to the 'Unfinished Church on the Edge of the Cliff'," *Hemingway Review* 6 (Fall 1986): 2–29. William Belassi, "The Writing of the Manuscript of *The Sun Also Rises*, with a Chart of Its Session-by-Session Development," *Hemingway Review* 6 (Fall 1986): 65–78. James Hinkle, "'Dear Mr. Scribner'—About the Published Text of *The Sun Also Rises*," *Hemingway Review* 6 (Fall 1986): 43–64.

50. Allen Joseph, "*Toreo*: The Moral Axis of *The Sun Also Rises*," *Hemingway Review* 6 (Fall 1986): 88–99. David Harrell, "A Final Note on Duff Twysden," *Hemingway Review* 5

(Spring 1986): 45–46. Robert A. Martin, "Hemingway's Sun as Title and Metaphor," *Hemingway Review* 6 (Fall 1986): 100. Frank Scafella, *"The Sun Also Rises*: Owen Wister's 'Garbage Pail,' Hemingway's Passage of the 'Human Soul'," *Hemingway Review* 6 (Fall 1986): 101–11. George Morgan, "An American in Paris: Strategies of Otherness in *The Sun Also Rises*," *Cycnos* 2 (1986): 27–39. Wolfgang E. H. Rudat, "Hemingway's Brett: Linguistic Manipulation and the Male Ego in *The Sun Also Rises*," *Journal of Evolutionary Psychology* 7 (1986): 76–82. Wolfgang E. H. Rudat, "Jake Barnes, Chaucer's Pardoner, and the Restaurant Scene in Ernest Hemingway's *The Sun Also Rises*," *Cithara* 26 (May 1987): 48–55. E. Miller Budick, *"The Sun Also Rises*: Hemingway and the Art of Repetition," *University of Toronto Quarterly* 56 (Winter 1986–87): 319–37.

51. Linda Wagner-Martin, ed., *New Essays on "The Sun Also Rises"* (New York: Cambridge, 1987), 1–18. This volume cited hereafter as *New Essays*. Scott Donaldson, "Humor in *The Sun Also Rises*," *New Essays*, 19–41. Michael S. Reynolds, *"The Sun* in Its Time: Recovering the Historical Context," *New Essays*, 43–64. Wendy Martin, "Brett Ashely as New Woman in *The Sun Also Rises*," *New Essays*, 65–82. Arnold E. Davidson and Cathy N. Davidson, "Decoding the Hemingway Hero in *The Sun Also Rises*," *New Essays*, 83–107. John W. Aldridge, "Afterthoughts on the Twenties and *The Sun Also Rises*," *New Essays*, 109–29. Kenneth S. Lynn, *Hemingway* (New York: Simon and Schuster, 1987).

52. Robert E. Fleming, "The Importance of Count Mippipopolous: Creating the Code Hero," *Arizona Quarterly* 44 (Summer 1988): 69–75. Lee Thorn, *"The Sun Also Rises:* Good Manners Make Good Art," *Hemingway Review* 8 (Fall 1988): 42–49. Linda W. Wagner-Martin, "Hemingway's Search for Heroes, Once Again," *Arizona Quarterly* 44 (Summer 1988): 58–68.

53. Sibbie O'Sullivan, "Love and Friendship / Man and Woman in *The Sun Also Rises*," *Arizona Quarterly* 44 (Summer 1988): 76–97. Mary Ann C. Curtis, *"The Sun Also Rises*: Its Relation to *The Song of Roland*," *American Literature* 60 (1988): 274–80. Wolfgang E. H. Rudat, "Jacob Barnes and Onan: Sexual Response in *The Sun Also Rises* and *For Whom the Bell Tolls*," *Journal of Evolutionary Psychology* 9 (1988): 50–58. Wolfgang E. H. Rudat, "He 'Just Lay There': Bill Gorton as Wounded Preacher in *The Sun Also Rises*," *Wascana Review* 23 (1988): 22–30. Wolfgang E. H. Rudat, "Mike Campbell and 'These Literary Chaps': Palimpsestic Narrative in *The Sun Also Rises*," *Studies in the Novel* 20 (Fall 1988): 302–15. Denis Brian, *The True Gen: An Intimate Portrait of Ernest Hemingway by Those Who Knew Him* (New York: Grove Press, 1988), 55–61.

54. Henry S. Villard and James Nagel, *Hemingway in Love and War: The Lost Diary of Agnes von Kurowsky* (Boston: Northeastern University Press, 1989). Michael Reynolds, *Hemingway: The Paris Years* (Cambridge, Mass.: Basil Blackwell, 1989), 298–327. Edward F. Stanton, *Hemingway and Spain: A Pursuit* (Seattle: University of Washington Press, 1989). Frank M. Laurence, *"The Sun Also Rises*: The NBC Version," *A Moving Picture Feast: The Filmgoer's Hemingway*, ed. Charles M. Oliver (New York: Praeger, 1989), 91–113. Wolfgang E. H. Rudat, "Sexual Dilemmas in *The Sun Also Rises*," *Hemingway Review* 8, no. 2 (1989): 2–13. Peter L. Hays, "Hunting Ritual in *The Sun Also Rises*," *Hemingway Review* 8, no. 2 (1989): 46–48.

55. *Earnest Hemingway, The Sun Also Rises: A Facsimile Edition*, 2 vols., ed. Matthew J. Bruccoli (Detroit: Omnigraphics, 1990). Mark Spilka, *Hemingway's Quarrel with Androgyny* (Lincoln: University of Nebraska Press, 1990), 197–208. William Balassi, "Hemingway's Greatest Iceberg: The Composition of *The Sun Also Rises*," in *Writing the American Classics*, ed. James Barbour and Tom Quirk (Chapel Hill: University of North Carolina Press, 1990), 125–55. Wolfgang E. H. Rudat, *A Rotten Way to Be Wounded: The Tragicomedy of The Sun Also Rises* (New York: Peter Lang, 1990). Eugene Kanjo, "Signs Are Taken for Nothing in *The Sun Also Rises*," in *Hemingway in Italy and Other Essays*, ed. Robert W. Lewis (New York: Praeger, 1990), 85–97. Peter Griffin, *Less Than A Treason: Hemingway in Paris* (New York:

Oxford, 1990), 114. Peter L. Hays, *Ernest Hemingway* (New York: Continuum, 1990), 47–53.

56.   Peter Messent, *New Readings of the American Novel: Narrative Theory and Its Application* (New York: St. Martin's, 1991), 86–129. Jaqueline Tavernier-Courbin, *Ernest Hemingway's* A Moveable Feast: *The Making of Myth* (Boston: Northeastern University Press, 1991. Kathleen Morgan, "Between Two Worlds: Hemingway's Brett Ashely and Homer's Helen of Troy," *Classical and Modern Literature* 11, no. 2 (1991): 169–80. Louise R. Achuff, " 'Nice' and 'Pleasant' in *The Sun*," *Hemingway Review* 10, no. 2 (1991): 42–46. Darryl Hattenhauer, "More Humor in *The Sun Also Rises*," *Hemingway Review* 10, no. 2 (1991): 56–57.

57.   Michael Reynolds, *Hemingway: The American Homecoming* (Cambridge: Basil Blackwell, 1992), 4–73. James R. Mellow, *Hemingway: A Life Without Consequences* (Boston: Houghton Mifflin, 1992), 298–313.

58.   Gioia Diliberto, *Hadley* (New York: Ticknor & Fields, 1992). Harold Bloom, ed., *Brett Ashley* (New York: Chelsea House Publishers, 1991). Charles L. Ross, " 'The Saddest Story' Part Two: *The Good Soldier* and *The Sun Also Rises*," *Hemingway Review* 12, no. 1 (1992): 26–34. George Cheatham, " 'Sign the Wire with Love': The Morality of Surplus in *The Sun Also Rises*," *Hemingway Review* 11, no. 2 (1992): 25–30.

59.   Robert E. Fleming, "The Fun Also Rises: A Tribute to Jim Hinkle," *Hemingway Review* 13, no. 1 (1993): 90–91. Peter L. Hays, "Catulus and *The Sun Also Rises*," *Hemingway Review* 12, no. 2 (1993): 15–23. Wolfgang E. H. Rudat, *Alchemy in "The Sun Also Rises": Hidden Gold in Hemingway's Narrative* (Lewiston: Mellen, 1992).

60.   The most useful bibliographies of secondary criticism on Hemingway are Linda Welshimer Wagner, *Ernest Hemingway: A Reference Guide* (Boston: G. K. Hall, 1977), and its sequel, Kelli A. Larson, *Ernest Hemingway: A Reference Guide 1974–1989* (Boston: G. K. Hall, 1991). Although they are not comprehensive, both of these volumes are annotated and allow for a survey of changing patterns in scholarly emphasis.

REVIEWS

◆

Marital Tragedy

*THE NEW YORK TIMES BOOK REVIEW**

Ernest Hemingway's first novel, "The Sun Also Rises," treats of certain of those younger Americans concerning whom Gertrude Stein has remarked: "You are all a lost generation." This is the novel for which a keen appetite was stimulated by Mr. Hemingway's exciting volume of short stories, "In Our Time." The clear objectivity and the sustained intensity of the stories, and their concentration upon action in the present moment, seemed to point to a failure to project a novel in terms of the same method, yet a resort to any other method would have let down the reader's expectations. It is a relief to find that "The Sun Also Rises" maintains that same heightened intimate tangibility as the shorter narratives and does it in the same kind of weighted, quickening prose.

Mr. Hemingway has chosen a segment of life which might easily have become "a spectacle with unexplained horrors," and disciplined it to a design which gives full value to its Dionysian, all but uncapturable, elements. On the face of it, he has simply gathered, almost at random, a group of American and British expatriates from Paris, conducted them on a fishing expedition, and exhibited them against the background of a wild Spanish fiesta and bull-fight. The characters are concisely indicated. Much of their inherent natures are left to be betrayed by their own speech, by their apparently aimless conversation among themselves. Mr. Hemingway writes a most admirable dialogue. It has the terse vigor of Ring Lardner at his best. It suggests the double meanings of Ford Madox Ford's records of talk. Mr. Hemingway makes his characters say one thing, convey still another, and when a whole passage of talk has been given, the reader finds himself the richer by a totally unexpected mood, a mood often enough of outrageous familiarity with obscure heartbreaks.

The story is told in the first person, as if by one Jake Barnes, an American newspaper correspondent in Paris. This approach notoriously invites digression and clumsiness. The way Mr. Hemingway plays this hard-boiled Jake is comparable to Jake's own evocations of the technique of the expert matador handling his bull. In fact, the bull-fight within the story

*Reprinted from the *New York Times Book Review* (31 October 1926): 7. Copyright © 1926 by The New York Times Company. Reprinted by permission.

bears two relations to the narrative proper. It not only serves to bring the situation to a crisis, but it also suggests the design which Mr. Hemingway is following. He keeps goading Jake, leading him on, involving him in difficulties, averting serious tragedy for him, just as the matador conducts the bull through the elaborate pattern of danger.

The love affair of Jake and the lovely, impulsive Lady Ashley might easily have descended into bathos. It is an erotic attraction which is destined from the start to be frustrated. Mr. Hemingway has such a sure hold on his values that he makes an absorbing, beautifully and tenderly absurd, heartbreaking narrative of it. Jake was wounded in the war in a manner that won for him a grandiose speech from the Italian General. Certainly Jake is led to consider his life worse than death. When he and Brett (Lady Ashley) fall in love, and know, with that complete absence of reticences of the war generation, that nothing can be done about it, the thing might well have ended there. Mr. Hemingway shows uncanny skill in prolonging it and delivering it of all its implications.

No amount of analysis can convey the quality of "The Sun Also Rises." It is a truly gripping story, told in a lean, hard, athletic narrative prose that puts more literary English to shame. Mr. Hemingway knows how not only to make words be specific but how to arrange a collection of words which shall betray a great deal more than is to be found in the individual parts. It is magnificent writing, filled with that organic action which gives a compelling picture of character. This novel is unquestionably one of the events of an unusually rich year in literature.

Sad Young Man

*Time**

A lot of people expected a big novel from burly young Author Hemingway. His short work (*In Our Time*, 1925) bit deeply into life. He said things naturally, calmly, tersely, accurately. He wrote only about things he had experienced, mostly outdoors, as a doctor's son in northern Michigan and as a self-possessed young tramp in Europe. Philosophically, his implication was: "Life's great. Don't let it rattle you."

Now his first novel is published and while his writing has acquired only a few affectations, his interests appear to have grown soggy with much sitting around sloppy café tables in the so-called Latin (it should be called American) quarter of Paris. He has chosen to immortalize the semi-humorous love tragedy of an insatiable young English War widow and an unmanned U. S. soldier. His title is borrowed from *Ecclesiastes*; his motto about "a lost generation," from Gertrude Stein; his widow, Lady Brett Ashley, from Michael Arlen's *Green Hat*. She is repeatedly called "a nice piece," and "a good chap." She has a grim wit and not a shred of reticence. The hero failing, her other men are many, including a Princeton Jew and a Spanish bullfighter. The story, such as it is, comes from the eunuch, Jake, who is very generous, patient, clever and, of course, very sad.

The picture of cosmopolitan castaways going to prizefights, bars, bedrooms, bullrings in France and Spain is excessively accurate but not as trite as it might be. The ironic witticisms are amusing, for a few chapters. There is considerable emotion, consciously restrained, quite subtle. Experts may pronounce the book a masterpiece of sex-frustration psychology. But the reader is very much inclined to echo a remark that is one of Jake's favorites and, presumably, Author Hemingway's too, "Oh, what the hell!"

*Reprinted from *Time* 8 (1 November 1926): 48. © 1926 Time Warner Inc. Reprinted by permission.

The New Books

TOUCHSTONE*

"The Sun Also Rises," by Ernest Hemingway, is a new novel by that already almost legendary figure in the Parisian group of young, American authors.

This is a story of exquisite simplicity built on the sensational theme of a love affair between an American who has been sexually incapacitated during the war, and a credible and living counterpart of the jejune *Iris March*. The author of "Torrents of Spring," who has only to publish to be read by a certain circle of the intelligentsia, and not even to publish to be discussed, has written wittily and with a smooth deliberateness astonishingly effective in numerous passages of nervous staccato. An unconscious sense of security in the author carries the reader from episode to episode with mounting curiosity and no fatigue.

The story is told in a crisp procession of events in which no scene is quite without poignancy, however brutal, nor quite without wit, however poignant. Under the hard, flat glass of Mr. Hemingway's virtuosity the ever-present yet unmentionable tragedy ebbs and flows like dark water. One is shown a group of Anglo-Saxons, "the lost generation," as Gertrude Stein calls them in post-war Paris, and later at a bull-fight across the Spanish border. We see their loves, their lusts, their unutterable boredom and their amazing laughter. Related in the first person with a fierce flippancy rarely seen in the sober and surely never in the casually drunk, the book is the verbal expression of an anguish not wholly of mind nor of body, unless it is of an alcoholic mind in a tragically maimed body.

*From the *New Yorker* 2 (20 November 1926): 88, 90. Reprinted by permission; © 1926, 1954 The New Yorker Magazine, Inc.

Hemingway Leads Young Ineffectuals
Through Europe

SCHUYLER ASHLEY*

Ernest Hemingway seems here to have borrowed the Green Hat of Michael Arlen, knocked it out of shape, kicked it across the room once or twice, and then gone off to a bull fight wearing its remains pulled pugnaciously down over one eye. Personally, I prefer Green Hats worn that way: rowdiness is more palatable when it does not simultaneously affect romanticism and sentimentality. Thus described, "The Sun Also Rises" may appear a lesser novel than it really is. Mr. Hemingway, who once served an apprenticeship to letters on *The Star*, writes with a swinging, effortless precision that puts him in the very first flight of American stylists. There is almost no lost motion in his sentences; his phrases carry to their mark with a very flat trajectory.

To characterize "The Sun Also Rises" more concretely, it is a lively account of a couple of weeks spent by a small group of American and English expatriates who make highly irregular headquarters at Paris. During most of the book they are engaged upon a visit to Spain, where they fish, see bull fights and drink the wine of the country out of goat skins. All their journeying is related in great detail; it is a mannerism of Hemingway's to recount exactly his characters' physical evolutions, through doors, up and downstairs, in and out of bed, as though establishing alibis.

A VERY MIXED GROUP

The relations of the group are rather mixed. Lady Brett Ashley, a not too immaculate dove, is the decoy at its center. Jake Barnes tells the story; he represents an American newspaper syndicate at Paris and aspired to be Lady Brett's sweetheart. Robert Cohn, a well-mannered young ineffectual, had once spent a week-end with Lady Brett at San Sebastian; he had never got

*Reprinted from the *Kansas City Star* (4 December 1926): 8, with the permission of *The Kansas City Star* Co.

over it. Mike Campbell of Scotland is Lady Brett's present fancy and they consider marrying if divorces and finances can be arranged. Bill Gorton is present simply as Jake's friend, sharing his tastes for fishing and bull fighting. Lady Brett herself is really not as impossible as she sounds. She is a well portrayed example of the absolutely improvident, disorderly young woman, whose nonchalance is, possibly, a new development since the war.

To anyone who has watched in out-of-the-way parts of the world the backwash of the war generation living leisurely, reckless lives, there is more truth in Mr. Hemingway's novel than a casual reader might be ready to admit. Ever since 1918 the continent has been home for a good many young Americans who certainly do not take their Europe *à la* Henry James. Gertrude Stein told Ernest Hemingway once, "You are all a lost generation," and the remark seems to have impressed him unduly. The gentle tug of the ordinary times of life, business, marriage, getting on-in-the-world, have set most of the stranded ships afloat again. Jake Barnes's generation is not "lost," though it has suffered heavy casualties. And, as the book demonstrates quite effectively, they are not all dead yet.

A Pretty Good Time Is Had

In fact, as the novel also testifies, in sprightly fashion, some of them are having a pretty good time. It is hard not to wish one had been on that fishing trip with Jake and Bill Gorton, before trouble, with Lady Brett as its storm center, caught up with them. One could listen with pleasure to a good many of Bill's alcoholically glorified "travel stories." Or to Mike Campbell's "war stories." The one about his medals is worth quoting; it reveals to the life a certain type of Scotchman:

> "Tell him about your medals," Brett demanded.
> "I'll not," said Mike. "That story reflects great discredit on me."
> "What medals have you got, Mike?"
> "I haven't got any medals."
> "You must have some."
> "I suppose I've the usual medals. But I never sent in for them. One time there was this wopping big dinner, and the prince of Wales was to be there, and the cards and medals will be worn. So, naturally, I had no medals, and I stopped at my tailor's and he was impressed by the invitation, and I thought that's a good piece of business, and I said to him: 'You've got to fix me up with some medals.' He said: 'What medals, sir?' And I said: 'Oh, any medals. Just give me a few medals.' So he said: 'What medals have you, sir?' And I said: 'How should I know?' Did he think I spent all my time reading the bloody gazette? 'Just give me a good lot. Pick them out yourself.' So he got me some medals, you know, miniature medals, and handed me the box; and

I put it in my pocket and forgot it. Well, I went to the dinner, and it was the night they'd shot Henry Wilson; so the prince didn't come, and the king didn't come, and no one wore any medals, and all these coves were busy taking off their medals, and I had mine in my pocket."

He stopped for us to laugh.

"Is that all?"

"That's all. Perhaps I didn't tell it right."

"You didn't," said Brett. "But no matter."

We were all laughing.

"Ah, yes," said Mike. "I know now. It was a damn dull dinner, and I couldn't stick it, so I left. Later on in the evening I found the box in my pocket. What's this? I said. Medals? Bloody military medals? So I cut them all off their backing—you know, they put them on a strip—and gave them all around. Gave one to each girl. Form of souvenir. They thought I was hell's own shakes of a soldier. Give away medals in a night club. Dashing fellow."

DIALOGUE STAGGERS TOO MUCH

There is an ample dose of rather bleak *joi de vivre* in this book. At will Ernest Hemingway can recreate the good flavor of days in the open air; he knows intimately the smell of early morning at San Sebastian, or the sensation of emptiness and wind that night brings into the mountain villages of the basque country. He savors the taste and feel and smell of living with a sort of hard-boiled gusto. One must not, he seems to believe, qualify or analyze things good in themselves, like brook trout, *hors d'oeuvres*, cold spring water, coffee and buttered toast, or hard liquor.

Particularly liquor. The amount of beer, wine and brandy consumed in "The Sun Also Rises" runs, I should judge, to a higher average per page and per character than in any other fiction since Rabelais. And the conversation! Hemingway reveals what amounts to a special talent for drunken conversation, the logical illogicality of the inebriate, the earnest, disconnected stories that reveal so much of the drinker's own inner personality. Yet this subtle talent runs away with him at times. His dialogue sounds drunken almost always, even at moments when, by my careful and envious arithmetic, his characters have surely not had time to get tanked up yet.

Hard-Boiled

ALLEN TATE*

The present novel by the author of "In Our Time" supports the recent prophecy that he will be the "big man in American letters." At the time the prophecy was delivered it was meaningless because it was equivocal. Many of the possible interpretations now being eliminated, we fear it has turned out to mean something which we shall all regret. Mr. Hemingway has written a book that will be talked about, praised, perhaps imitated; it has already been received in something of that cautiously critical spirit which the followers of Henry James so notoriously maintain toward the master. Mr. Hemingway has produced a successful novel, but not without returning some violence upon the integrity achieved in his first book. He decided for reasons of his own to write a popular novel, or he wrote the only novel which he could write.

To choose the latter conjecture is to clear his intentions, obviously at the cost of impugning his art. One infers moreover that although sentimentality appears explicitly for the first time in his prose, it must have always been there. Its history can be constructed. The method used in "In Our Time" was *pointilliste*, and the sentimentality was submerged. With great skill he reversed the usual and most general formula of prose fiction: instead of selecting the details of physical background and of human behavior for the intensification of a dramatic situation, he employed the minimum of drama for the greatest possible intensification of the observed object. The reference of emphasis for the observed object was therefore not the action; rather, the reference of the action was the object, and the action could be impure or incomplete without risk of detection. It could be mixed and incoherent; it could be brought in when it was advantageous to observation, or left out. The exception, important as such, in Mr. Hemingway's work is the story Mr. and Mrs. Elliott. Here the definite dramatic conflict inherent in a sexual relation emerged as fantasy, and significantly; presumably he could not handle it otherwise without giving himself away.

In "The Sun Also Rises," a full-length novel, Mr. Hemingway could not escape such leading situations, and he had besides to approach them

*Allen Tate, "Hard-Boiled," The Nation magazine / The Nation Company, Inc., (15 December 1926): 642, 644.

with a kind of seriousness. He fails. It is not that Mr. Hemingway is, in the term which he uses in fine contempt for the big word, hard-boiled; it is that he is not hard-boiled enough, in the artistic sense. No one can dispute with a writer the significance he derives from his subject-matter; one can only point out that the significance is mixed or incomplete. Brett is a nymphomaniac; Robert Cohn, a most offensive cad; both are puppets. For the emphasis is false; Hemingway doesn't fill out his characters and let them stand for themselves; he isolates one or two chief traits which reduce them to caricature. His perception of the physical object is direct and accurate; his vision of character, singularly oblique. And he actually betrays the interior machinery of his hard-boiled attitude: "It is awfully easy to be hard-boiled about everything in the daytime, but at night it is another thing," says Jake, the sexually impotent, musing on the futile accessibility of Brett. The history of his sentimentality is thus complete.

There are certain devices exploited in the book which do not improve it; they extend its appeal. Robert Cohn is not only a bounder, he is a Jewish bounder. The other bounders, like Mike, Mr. Hemingway for some reason spares. He also spares Brett—another device—for while her pleasant folly need not be flogged, it equally need not be condoned; she becomes the attractive wayward lady of Sir Arthur Pinero and Michael Arlen. Petronius's Circe, the archetype of all the Bretts, was neither appealing nor deformed.

Mr. Hemingway has for some time been in the habit of throwing pebbles at the great—which recalls Mr. Pope's couplet about his contemporary Mr. Dennis. The habit was formed in "The Torrents of Spring," where it was amusing. It is disconcerting in the present novel; it strains the context; and one suspects that Mr. Hemingway protests too much. The point he seems to be making is that he is morally superior, for instance, to Mr. Mencken, but it is not yet clear just why.

Warfare in Man and among Men

LAWRENCE MORRIS*

The reader finds the characters of *The Sun Also Rises* gathered in Paris: an American newspaper correspondent; a Greek Count, with business experience in the Middle West; Cohn, who had graduated from Princeton and written a book; an English bankrupt; and Brett, who was the pivot of the group. Brett was a young Englishwoman, who was getting a divorce from a man she had never loved, to marry another whom she did not love, either. The development of their relations is seen through the eyes of the newspaper correspondent, who had been rendered impotent by a wound received in the War—a brutally efficient symbol of "a lost generation." It was he whom Brett loved and who loved Brett. From Paris the group migrates to the Pyrenees and shares in a week's fiesta in a Spanish town. The peak of the fiesta is the bull fights; and Hemingway gives here the only account in English of a bull fight known to this reviewer, in which the emphasis is laid not on cruelty, but on the steely beauty of skill, the perfection of workmanship in the face of danger. A bull fight becomes a hard, beautiful dance, where an awkwardness means death. Amid the rioting of the fiesta and the clear, breath-taking scenes in the bull ring, the group of characters plays its little tragedy of futility.

Although Hemingway is objectifying the bewildered anguish of an aimless generation, he does not moon about it. His mind is masculine and imaginative. He loves all the hard, stinging experiences of the senses, he loves skill, he can laugh. He knows the intonations and obliquenesses of human speech. No other American, writing today, can match his dialogue for its apparent naturalness, its intimacy and its concealed power of revealing emotion. Ring Lardner's in comparison sounds framed and self-conscious. For something against which to measure the use of over-tones in Hemingway's talk one must go to Joyce's account of a Christmas dinner in the *Portrait of the Artist* or—allowing for the greater intellectual scope and intensity of Joyce's mind—to the quarrel between Leopold Bloom and the citizen in *Ulysses*.

*Reprinted from the *New Republic*, 22 December 1926, 142–43.

Fiesta

THE [LONDON] TIMES LITERARY SUPPLEMENT*

In his first volume of short stories Mr. Ernest Hemingway got some very delicate and unusual effects by retranslating his impressions, as it were, into a primitive kind of imagery. He described his characters and their behaviour with deliberate naivety, identifying what they did and what they felt in an artful and extremely suggestive manner. Now comes a novel, FIESTA (Cape, 7s. 6d. net), which is more obviously an experiment in story-making, and in which he abandons his vivid impressionism for something much less interesting. There are moments of sudden illumination in the story, and throughout it displays a determined reticence; but it is frankly tedious after one has read the first hundred pages and ceased to hope for anything different. This is criticism we should not think of applying to the work of a less talented writer. The crude, meaningless conversation which Mr. Hemingway gives us is best taken for granted; it may be true to life, as the saying is, but there is hardly any point in putting it into a novel. Besides, so much of it consists of offers of drink and the bald confession of drunkenness that what virtue it has is staled by repetition.

Drink, indeed, is an extraordinary bugbear for these Americans in Paris, almost more troublesome than sex. However, they are all artists, and it seems to be the artistic lot to be able to consume quantities of liquid which would send most human beings to the grave. Brett, the heroine, is scarcely ever sober; Jake, who loves her, but who has been smashed up in the war (it is terrible irony that Mr. Hemingway intends—and partly achieves— here), is a reserved, rather sardonic creature, and almost the only credible person in the story. His position lends some persuasiveness to Brett's nymphomania, although it does not make her less tiresome. The other men who love her or live with her are unexciting; Cohn is a caricature, Mike never comes to life, the young matador is a mixture of perversity and convention. The Spanish scenes give us something of the quality of Mr. Hemingway's earlier book, but they hardly qualify the general impression of an unsuccessful experiment.

*Reprinted from the {London} Times Literary Supplement, 30 June 1927: 454, with the permission of The {London} Times.

The Sportsman's Tragedy

Edmund Wilson*

The reputation of Ernest Hemingway has, in a very short time, reached such proportions that it has already become fashionable to disparage him. Yet it seems to me that he has received in America very little intelligent criticism. I find Lee Wilson Dodd, for example, in the 'Saturday Review of Literature,' with his usual gentle trepidation in the presence of contemporary life, deciding with a sigh of relief that, after all, Ernest Hemingway (a young man who has published only three books) is not Shakespeare or Tolstoy; and describing Hemingway's subjects as follows: 'The people he observes with fascinated fixation and then makes live before us are . . . all very much alike: bull-fighters, bruisers, touts, gunmen, professional soldiers, prostitutes, hard drinkers, dope fiends. . . . For what they may or may not be intellectually, esthetically or morally worth, he makes his facts ours.' In the 'Nation,' Joseph Wood Krutch, whose review is more sympathetic than Mr. Dodd's, describes Hemingway as follows: 'Spiritually the distinguishing mark of Mr. Hemingway's work is a weariness too great to be aware of anything but sensations. . . . Mr. Hemingway tells us, both by his choice of subject and by the method which he employs, that life is an affair of mean tragedies. . . . In his hands the subject matter of literature becomes sordid little catastrophes in the lives of very vulgar people.' (1) I do not know whether these reviewers of 'Men Without Women' have never read Hemingway's other two books, or whether they have simply forgotten them. Do the stories in 'In Our Time' and in 'The Sun Also Rises' actually answer to these descriptions? Does 'Men Without Women' answer to them? The hero of 'In Our Time' who appears in one or two stories in the new volume, and the hero of 'The Sun Also Rises,' are both highly civilized persons of rather complex temperament and extreme sensibility. In what way can they be said to be 'very vulgar people'? And can the adventures of even the old bull-fighter in "The Undefeated" be called a 'sordid little catastrophe'?

One of the stories in 'Men without Women' also appeared in 'The American Caravan,' (2) and was thus twice exposed to the reviewers; yet in all the reviews I have read of both volumes I cannot remember one which seemed to me to give an accurate account of it. It has almost invariably been

*Reprinted from the *New Republic* 53 (14 December 1927): 102–3.

mentioned, briefly, as a simple tale of horror or a tale of brutality, or something of the sort. Let us examine this story a moment. Two young men have been skiing in the Alps: it is spring and the sun is terrifically strong; but in the shade the sweat freezes in their underclothes. They have begun to find it oppressive and are glad to get down to an inn. On their way, they have passed a burial, and at the inn they hear the story of the woman who is dead. She was the wife of a peasant and died during the winter, but the husband was snowbound and could not bring her out till spring. The peasant put the body in the wood-shed, laying it on a pile of wood; but when he had to use the wood, he stood the corpse up in a corner, and got into the habit of hanging the lantern in its mouth. Why, we ask ourselves for a moment, have we been told about the skiing expedition? Then, immediately, we realize that Hemingway, with his masterly relevance in apparent indirection, has, in the oppression felt by the tourists, supplied us with the explanation of the brutalization of the peasant. This brutalization by itself is not, however, the theme of the story. We do not see the point till the end. The peasant will not drink at the inn, where he has come immediately after the burial, but goes on to a neighboring one. "'He didn't want to drink with me,' said the sexton. 'He didn't want to drink with me, after he knew about his wife,' said the innkeeper." Similarly, "A Pursuit Race" is, as Mr. Dodd would say, a story about a dope-fiend; but what is more interesting and important, it is also about a man who has just lost a desperately prolonged moral struggle, and it derives its whole significance from the last paragraph, in which the manager of the burlesque show, understanding what has happened and pitying his recreant advance man, refrains from waking him. So in "A Simple Inquiry," in which we are shown that strange demoralization of army life which is scarcely distinguishable from stoicism, the value of the incident lies entirely in the fact that the major refrains from dismissing the boy.

It would appear, then, that Hemingway's world was not quite so devoid of interest as it has been represented by Mr. Krutch and Mr. Dodd. Even when he deals with rudimentary types—as he by no means always does—his drama usually turns on some principle of courage, of honor, of pity—in short, of sportsmanship in its largest human sense—which he discovers in them. I do not say that the world which Hemingway depicts is not a bad world; it is a bad world and a world where much is suffered. Hemingway's feelings about this world, his criticism of what goes on in it, are, for all his misleadingly simple and matter-of-fact style, rather subtle and complex; but he has, it seems to me, made it sufficiently plain what sort of emotions and ideas he intends to communicate. His first book was called "In Our Time," and it was made up of a series of brief and brutal sketches of barbarous happenings mostly connected with the War, alternated with a series of short stories about a sensitive and healthy boy in the American northwest. We were, I take it, to contrast these two series. When Hemingway gave them this title, he meant to tell us that life was barbarous, even in our civilized age; and that the man who sees the cabinet ministers shot and who finds himself potting at the Germans from the "perfectly priceless barricade" has had to come a long way from the boy who, with the fresh senses of youth, so much enjoyed the three days' fishing trip at Big Two-Hearted River. Yet has he really come so far? Is not the very principle of life essentially ruthless and cruel? What is the difference between the gusto of the soldier all on edge to hunt his fellow humans and the gusto of the young fisherman hooking grasshoppers to catch trout? Hemingway is primarily preoccupied with these problems of suffering and cruelty.

The barbarity of the world since the War is also the theme of Hemingway's next book, "The Sun Also Rises." By his title and by the quotations which he prefixes to this book, he makes it plain what moral judgment we are to pass on the events he describes: "You are all a lost generation." What gives the book its profound unity and its disquieting effectiveness is the intimate relation established between the Spanish fiesta with its processions, its revelry and its bull-fighting and the atrocious behavior of the group of Americans and English who have come down from Paris to enjoy it. In the heartlessness of these people in their treatment of one another, do we not find the same principle at work as in the pagan orgy of the festival? Is not the brutal persecution of the Jew as much a natural casualty of a barbarous world as the fate of the man who is accidentally gored by the bull on the way to the bull-ring? The whole interest of "The Sun Also Rises" lies in the attempts of the hero and the heroine to disengage themselves from this world, or rather to arrive at some method of living in it honorably. The real story is the story of their attempts to do this—attempts by which, in such a world, they are always bound to lose in everything except honor. I do not agree, as has sometimes been said, that the behavior of the people in "The Sun Also Rises" is typical of only a small and special class of American and English expatriates. I believe that it is more of less typical of certain phases of the whole western world today; and the title "In Our Time" would have applied to it with as much appropriateness as to its predecessor.

Hemingway's attitude, however, toward the cruelties and treacheries he describes is quite different from anything else which one remembers in a similar connection. He has nothing of the generous indignation of the romantics: he does not, like Byron, bid the stones of the prisoner's cell "appeal from tyranny to God"; nor, like Shelley, bid the winds to "wail for the world's wrong." Nor has he even that grim and repressed, but still generous, still passionate feeling which we find in the pessimist-realists—in Hardy's "Tess," in Maupassant's "Boule de Suif," even in those infrequent scenes of Flaubert where we are made to boil at the spectacle of an old farm servant or of a young silk-weaver's daughter at the mercy of the bourgeoisie. In his treatment of the War, for example, Hemingway is as far as possible from Barbusse or from John Dos Passos. His point of view, his state of mind, is a curious one, and one typical of the time—he seems so broken in to the agonies of humanity, and, though even against his will, so impassively resigned to them, that his only protest is, as it were, the grin and the oath of the sportsman who loses the game. Furthermore, we are not always quite sure on which side Hemingway is betting. We are sometimes afflicted by the suspicion that what we are witnessing is a set-up, with the manager backing the barbarian. Yet, to speak of Hemingway in these terms is really to misrepresent him. He is not a moralist staging a melodrama, but an artist presenting a situation of which the moral values are complex. Hemingway thoroughly enjoys bull-fighting, as he enjoys skiing, racing and prize-fights; and he is unremittingly conscious of the fact that, from the point of view of life as a sport, all that seems to him most painful is somehow closely bound up with what seems to him most enjoyable. The peculiar conflicts of feeling which arise in a temperament of this kind, are the subject of his fiction. His most remarkable effects, effects unlike anything else one remembers, are those, as in the fishing trip in 'The Sun Also Rises,' where we are made to feel, behind the appetite for the physical world, the falsity or the tragedy of a moral situation. The inescapable consciousness of this discord does not arouse Hemingway to passionate violence; but it poisons him and makes him sick, and thus invests with a singular sinister quality—a quality perhaps new in fiction—the sunlight and the green summer landscapes of 'The Sun Also Rises.' Thus, if Hemingway is oppressive, as Mr. Dodd complains, it is because he himself is oppressed. And we may find in him—in the clairvoyant's crystal of that incomparable art—an image of the common oppression.

REPRINTED CRITICISM

◆

Sunrise Out of The Waste Land

RICHARD P. ADAMS*

"You are all a lost generation," said Gertrude Stein. Perhaps they were. But if so they were lost together, and their togetherness is important. There has seldom been a literary generation the members of which were in closer communication than the American, French, and British writers of the 1920's. The liveliest center was Paris, where so many good Americans went before they died, but London, New York, and Chicago were not far away, and currents fed into the vortex from still more distant and unlikely places. Criticism has hardly begun to distinguish their relations.

Until it does, we cannot fully understand or properly assess the works of the period. They come, as all works do, from a context in which the mutual exchange of ideas was a significant element. The currents were often currents of influence in the strict sense. The New Criticism, still so-called, insofar as it tends to study individual works, out of context, is not an adequate method. We need to evolve and apply a procedure that will reassimilate the tradition of precise and careful scholarly investigation into a newer criticism, examining not only the inner structure of a work but all its outward relations too.

As a relevant instance, I offer a glance at Hemingway's *The Sun Also Rises* from a point of view determined by the hypothesis that it was directly and formatively influenced by Eliot's *The Waste Land*. This hypothesis has been suggested by others, but it has never been systematically applied.

Carlos Baker was one of the first to discuss the possibility of a close relationship between these works. His *Hemingway*, in 1952, called attention to the parallel between the "objective correlative" defined by Eliot in his essay "Hamlet and His Problems" and Hemingway's description in *Death in the Afternoon* of the way he learned to write. The resemblance is certainly close, and it is confirmed by further resemblances between the impressionistic or imagistic poems Hemingway published in various magazines beginning in 1923, together with the poetic prose sketches of *in our time*, and Eliot's "Preludes" and "Hysteria," collected in the *Prufrock* volume of 1917 and again in the *Poems* of 1920.

TSE: Tulane Studies in English, 9 (1959): 119–31. Copyright (c) 1959 by Tulane University. Reprinted by permission of the publisher.

The parallel is in fact more extended than Baker's remarks would indicate. F. O. Matthiessen has reported a talk with Eliot about "Gerontion" that sheds further light. "His design," says Matthiessen, "is to give the *exact* perceived detail, without comment, and let that picture carry its own connotations. As he said once in conversation, the images here are 'consciously concrete'; they correspond as closely as possible to something he has actually seen and remembered. But he also believes that if they are clearly rendered, they will stand for something larger than themselves; they will not depend for their apprehension upon any private reference, but will become 'unconsciously general.' " This is not the language of Hemingway, but it is very close to his substance in the various comments he has made on the submerged seven-eighths of the iceberg, on the necessity of isolating and clearly rendering the aspects of an action that cause emotion, and on the fourth and fifth dimension that may be achieved in prose "if," as he puts it, "any one is serious enough and has luck." Hemingway's implication in all such remarks seems to me to be, very clearly, that prose, like poetry, can be symbolic; that it may be made to carry overtones of feeling and meaning, partly conscious, partly unconscious, that will give it rich and permanent esthetic value. Nothing could be much closer to the effect at which Eliot aims consistently in his verse.

This is not to suggest that Eliot was the only source of such ideas and techniques, or even the most important one. Gertrude Stein was experimenting on much the same lines, and Hemingway learned more directly from her than from Eliot. The same is true of Ezra Pound, and to some extent of Sherwood Anderson. In fact, the theory and method both, as Edmund Wilson has demonstrated, are characteristic of the romantic tradition, going back to Wordsworth, Coleridge, and the Germans. The term "objective correlative" itself was used, pretty much in Eliot's sense, by Washington Allston in a lecture probably written before 1840; and Allston's thinking was largely based on that of Coleridge. But there is further evidence that part, at least, of Hemingway's early education as a writer came from Eliot.

Another of Eliot's essays with which Hemingway's published statements agree is "Tradition and the Individual Talent." What Eliot says here about the importance of the historical sense in making a writer traditional, and at the same time "most acutely conscious of his place in time, of his own contemporaneity," is the same, in substance, as what Hemingway says in *Death in the Afternoon*: "The individual, the great artist when he comes, uses everything that has been discovered or known about his art up to that point . . . and then . . . goes beyond what has been done or known and makes something of his own." Even their feelings about these ideas are closely similar. Eliot remarks that tradition "cannot be inherited, and if you want it you must obtain it by great labour," and Hemingway: "There are some things which cannot be learned quickly and time, which is all we have, must be paid heavily for their acquiring. They are the very simplest things and because it takes a man's life to know them the little new that each man gets from life is very costly and the only heritage he has to leave." Hemingway is not, as some might suppose, referring only to direct contact with life, for he goes on to say that "Every novel which is truly written contributes to the total of knowledge which is there at the disposal of the next writer who comes, but the next writer must pay, always, a certain nominal percentage in experience to be able to understand and assimilate what is available as his birthright and what he must, in turn, take his departure from." The difference in emphasis cannot obscure the fact that Hemingway, like Eliot, keenly feels the importance of a writer's relation to the literature of the past.

Parallels such as these—many more of which might easily be cited—are not the only evidence of Hemingway's debt to Eliot. There are a few direct references that deserve close study. The more or less fictitious "Author" of *Death in the Afternoon* at one point expresses his dislike of Humanists by saying to the Old Lady, "I hope to see the finish of a few, and speculate how worms will try that long preserved sterility; with their quaint pamphlets gone to bust and into foot-notes all their lust." The Old Lady likes the "line about lust," and the Author explains, "It came from Andrew Marvell. I learned how to do that by reading T. S. Eliot." This is not, in itself or in its context, an unmixed tribute. However, an earlier use of two other lines from Marvell's "To His Coy Mistress" in *A Farewell to Arms* is also connected with Eliot, less directly, and is less equivocal. Frederic Henry is about to leave his mistress, Catherine, to go back to the front. "Down below on the street a motor car honked. " 'But at my back I always hear / Time's wingéd chariot hurrying near,' " I said. 'I know that poem,' Catherine said. 'It's by Marvell.' " She does not say, but we may note, that the association between these lines and "The sound of horns and motors" was first made in *The Waste Land*.

The same sort of thing happens to another quotation used by both authors. In *The Sun Also Rises*, Jake introduces Bill Gorton, the connoisseur of stuffed animals, to Brett, and says, " 'He's a taxidermist.' " 'That was in another country,' Bill said. 'And besides all the animals were dead.' " Eliot uses a little more of Marlowe's text in his epigraph to "Portrait of a Lady": "Thou hast committed— /Fornication: but that was in another country, / And besides, the wench is dead." The reference helps, if we remember the word "fornication," to characterize Brett; but at the moment I wish only to indicate that it is a reference to Eliot as well as to Marlowe. The evidence occurs in *Across the River and into the Trees*, where the same quotation is associated not only with Eliot but specifically, though illegitimately, with *The Waste Land*. Colonel Cantwell is talking to Renata about his wife, a journalist, who is not literally dead but whose existence he prefers to ignore. " 'I told her about things once,' " he says, " 'and she wrote about them. But that was in another country and besides the wench is dead.' 'Is she really dead?' 'Deader than Phoebus the Phoenician.' " The intrusion of the sun god here suggests that the Colonel, at least, is quoting from memory and from a long time back. There are also some evident verbal echoes from *The Waste Land* in *The Sun Also Rises*, as when Jake says to Cohn, " 'I like this town and I go to Spain in the summer-time,' " and when Brett says to Jake, " 'My nerves are rotten.' "

In spite of these indications, critics have been surprisingly cautious about suggesting anything like a direct influence. Malcolm Cowley, in his Introduction to the Viking Portable *Hemingway* (1949), pointed out the fact that Hemingway's "first novel . . . deals in different terms with the same legend that T. S. Eliot was not so much presenting as concealing in *The Waste Land*." But Cowley shied away from the obvious presumption, saying, "I don't mean to imply that Hemingway owes a debt to *The Waste Land*." His explanation was that, although Hemingway had read the poem, and the notes, and obviously "dealt with the same legend that Eliot had discovered by scholarship," he somehow succeeded in "discovering it for himself, I think, by a sort of instinct for legendary situations." This formula seems to have set the tone for later comments. Baker called his chapter on *The Sun Also Rises* "The Wastelanders," but his emphasis was heavily on Hemingway's difference from and independence of Eliot. Philip Young, in his *Ernest Hemingway* (1952), cited an impressively long list of parallels, but he too insisted mainly on differences. "In the poem," he said, "a message of salvation comes out of the life-giving rain which falls on western civilization. In Hemingway's waste land there is fun, but there is no hope. No rain falls on Europe this time, and when it does fall, in *A Farewell to Arms*, it brings not life but death."

Unlike these critics, I do mean to imply that Hemingway owes a debt to *The Waste Land*. He agreed with many of Eliot's principles; he used many of the same techniques; *The Sun Also Rises* was constructed by the same method and on the same myth as *The Waste Land*; I see no reason in the evidence not to suppose that we have here a typical case of direct, formative literary influence. Incidentally, rain does fall in *The Sun Also Rises*; and Tiresias, at the end of *The Waste Land*, is no more sexually potent, fertile, or hopeful than Jake at the end of his book. My theory is that Hemingway found what he needed in *The Waste Land* and took it. This is the sovereign right of genius, now as much as when Shakespeare exercised it, and I can see no reason why Hemingway or his critics need be at all embarrassed about it.

A brief digression into the literary history of the period will help, I think, to show what happened. Hemingway established his residence in Paris early in 1922. At that time he met Ezra Pound, who had recently revised and cut *The Waste Land*. He also met James Joyce, whose *Ulysses* was published February 2. In October *The Waste Land* was published, without notes, in the same issue of *Criterion* with Valery Larbaud's essay pointing out the parallels between *Ulysses* and the *Odyssey*. On December 15 *The Waste Land* appeared in hard covers, with notes. In November, 1923, Eliot's essay "Ulysses, Order, and Myth" came out in the *Dial*. Here Eliot formulated his statement on the "mythical method," maintaining that Joyce, by "manipulating a continuous parallel between contemporaneity and antiquity," had made a discovery that others would also have to use as "a way of controlling, of ordering, of giving a shape and a significance to the immense panorama of futility and anarchy which is contemporary history."

It was not, of course, a true discovery, but rather a re-discovery of the method by which art has always made sense of the disordered futility that contemporary history always seems to present. But Eliot's insistence on its value was more than justified at a time when exaggerated reverence for a naive version of scientific method in the experiments of the naturalists had demonstrated that something other than documentation was needed to give artistic form to a literary work. Now, anyone who had read as much as the first note to *The Waste Land* must have seen that Eliot had used the method himself before recommending it to others. Hemingway knew *Ulysses*; he knew *The Waste Land*; surely he must have wondered what he in turn might do by using the same mythical method.

Obviously he did not want to do what Eliot and Joyce had done, however much it interested him. His comparison of Eliot and Conrad in the *transatlantic review* for October, 1924, is indicative. "If I knew," he wrote, "that by grinding Mr. Eliot into a fine dry powder and sprinkling that powder over Mr. Conrad's grave Mr. Conrad would shortly appear, looking very annoyed at the forced return and commence writing I would leave for London early tomorrow morning with a sausage grinder." The point, I suspect, was that Conrad had used the mythical method too, but without calling attention to it; and that is what Hemingway has done.

It appears to have been another event, however, which precipitated Hemingway's beginning of the task itself. This was the arrival in Paris of F. Scott Fitzgerald, in May, 1925. *The Great Gatsby* had appeared on April 10, and copies had been sent by the author to Gertrude Stein and to Eliot, both of whom were highly pleased with it. Eliot had a personal reason to be, for *The Great Gatsby* has the same theme, uses the same imagery, and is based on the same myth as *The Waste Land*. Fitzgerald certainly knew what he had done, for he was a great admirer of Eliot, and Hemingway was certainly a good enough reader to see the point for himself, if Fitzgerald did not explain it. The two struck up a warm friendship and spent a good deal of time together that summer; and by July Hemingway was at work on *The Sun Also Rises*.

The catalytic effect I am here attributing to *The Great Gatsby*, as it must have struck Hemingway in the spring of 1925, was probably due to its clear surface and its appearance of simplicity, directness, and realism, as well as to the fact that it was a popular success. But the more important point, in the long run, is that under its surface lay the same solid structure of traditional myth that made *The Waste Land* a great and enduring work. The Grail legend, as presented by Jessie Weston in *From Ritual to Romance*, had already had a long and honorable career. As used by Eliot, it had a sharp and cogent relevance to the state of Western civilization in the 1920's. It was itself based on a much older tradition, that of the fertility cults explored by Frazer and others and referred to by Eliot in his first note to *The Waste Land* and at many points in the poem. *The Waste Land* also invokes the tradition of pastoral elegy, which is another outgrowth of the fertility cults. In effect, Eliot had written an elegy on Western civilization, only instead of rejoicing at the end for the rebirth or metamorphosis of a demigod, he remained uncertain whether any renewal of cultural fertility or creative power was possible. The structure is a truncated version of the death-and-rebirth cycle of the fertility myths, of the successful Grail quest, and of the typical pastoral elegy. The same is true, generally, of *The Great Gatsby*, as several critics have noted.

In *The Sun Also Rises* we find the same structural principle. In the beginning, as in *The Waste Land*, there is the modern city, chaotic, sterile, inorganic, and spiritually dead. Jake's encounter with Brett and her excursion with Cohn to San Sebastian are as meaningless as the sexual relations between the men and women in "A Game of Chess" and the typist and clerk in "The Fire Sermon." In the fishing interlude at Burguete, and at Pamplona during the early part of the fiesta, there seems to be some hope of regeneration and happiness, as in the "Death by Water" of Phlebas the Phoenician and the "damp gust / Bringing rain" in "What the Thunder Said." The hope, in both works, is dissipated. After the fiasco caused by Brett's elopement and Cohn's violent reaction thereto, Jake retreats to San Sebastian, the scene of Brett's affair with Cohn, where his swimming and diving suggest the death by water theme. But when he goes to Madrid to rescue Brett, he seems to be left with nothing, not even the illusion that physical potency would have permitted him felicity with her. His ultimate recourse is the typical gesture of the early Hemingway hero, withdrawal into himself, the beaten but undefeated individual, maintaining his integrity and his dignity as a man in spite of the outrageous conditions that have isolated him. The feeling is very close to that of the speaker at the end of *The Waste Land*, shoring fragments against his ruin and lacking even the energy of Jake's final sarcasm.

The Sun Also Rises, however, is no more a simple expression of despair than is *The Waste Land*. It does embody the feeling Hemingway shared with Eliot and others that Western civilization was dying. But that feeling was not so naively entertained by these writers as it has been by some of their disciples. Both Eliot and Hemingway have remarked on this point. Matthiessen quotes Eliot as saying in 1931 that " 'when I wrote a poem called *The Waste Land* some of the more approving critics said that I had expressed the "disillusionment of a generation," which is nonsense. I may have expressed for them their own illusion of being disillusioned, but that did not form part of my intention.' " And Hemingway wrote to Maxwell Perkins on December 7, 1926, that "people aren't all as bad as some writers find them or as hollowed out and exhausted emotionally as some of the *Sun* generation." And we should always remember the second epigraph to *The Sun Also Rises*, in which the importance of a single generation, or a single cycle of any sort, is rather definitively deflated.

Accordingly, we will find, I believe, that the Waste Land imagery of *The Sun Also Rises* is a more complex and ambiguous web of sterile and creative, good and evil, cheerful and desperate implications than has generally been seen. The most conspicuous item is, of course, Jake's wound, which has made him sexually impotent and therefore physically sterile. It is the same kind of wound which, according to Miss Weston, has imposed sterility on Anfortas, the Fisher King, and on his land, and *From Ritual to Romance* appears to be the only printed source from which Hemingway could have borrowed this image. Jake serves, as an objective correlative, in the same way that Prufrock, Gerontion, and Tiresias serve Eliot, to imply an opinion about the postwar world. As Matthiessen has noted in discussing Eliot, the device is highly effective for the concrete rendering of personal emotion through a medium sufficiently detached from the author's own experience to emerge as art rather than as historical or autobiographical reporting. That is, Jake is useful precisely because he differs from his author in important ways, and because he gets caught in situations that his author would not get caught in and is therefore free to create. Jake, not Hemingway, is the Fisher King.

Brett is not qualified to be a Grail maiden, but she has some relations to the older fertility myths. One is her interest in fortune-telling, which, according to Miss Weston's account of the Tarot cards, was originally the art of predicting "the rise and fall of the waters which brought fertility to the land." Her bathing, which is frequent and obsessive, also associates her with the life-giving water. At one point she is surrounded by the celebrants at the fiesta—"They wanted her as an image to dance around"—and they rush her into a wine shop, where they seat her on a cask and decorate her with a garlic wreath. Her pagan affinities are emphasized by the fact that she has just been excluded from a church; and even as a pagan she is debauched and debased. Cohn's equation of her with Circe is not as absurd as it may seem. She does turn men into beasts, and she feels like a bitch herself when she decides to run off with Romero.

Robert Cohn's position in the pattern of characters is that of the Grail knight whose quest, if successful, will restore the Fisher King to health and the land to fertility. But, like Perceval during his first visit to the castle of Anfortas, he fails to ask the right question. His quality is described by Jake on the occasion of his meeting with Brett: "He looked a great deal as his compatriot must have looked when he saw the promised land. Cohn, of course, was much younger. But he had that look of eager, deserving expectation." He is like Gatsby in his hopeless and irredeemably innocent infatuation, but nobody says of him, as Nick says of Gatsby, "that he had committed himself to the following of a grail," much less that he is " 'worth the whole damn bunch put together.' "

The other characters are more obliquely related to the pattern of the Grail legend and of the main action. Mike Campbell is perhaps another unworthy knight; he is less innocent but not any better than Cohn. Bill Gorton is better, and appears to be intended partly as a foil, but he undertakes no quest. Montoya seems, in similar fashion, qualified to be the wise guide of the Grail stories, but he stands aside from any action. So does Count Mippipopolous, another of the insiders who "know the values" but who are too sophisticated to try to do anything more than have a good time. Bill, Montoya, and the Count help to point the direction Jake is taking and the goal he approaches at the end, a perfect detachment from this world for which nothing can be done. This is not a death or a giving-up; it is rather the conclusion that in a dying civilization the only way a man can live is by repudiating the values of society, or making what Hemingway elsewhere calls "a separate peace."

Pedro Romero is also outside the pattern and at most auxiliary to the main action, but he has a somewhat different function. He represents a primitive and, before Brett seduces him, an unspoiled virility, proved by his love for the bulls and his skill in fighting them. Since the problem is how to be fertile and civilized, his example provides no direct solution. He can only be corrupted by his involvement with the sophisticates, as Montoya, Jake, and finally Brett realize. However, he provides an impressive standard by which to measure the other characters, and he shows that power, courage, and art are real and desirable. Whether or not these goods are accessible to civilized people, Romero makes them seem worth trying for.

The largest, most complex symbol in the book is the fiesta of San Fermin. This is a vacation from work, at least for Jake, and provides recreation in that sense. But it also suggests re-creation in the more fundamental way of the pagan seasonal festivals—specifically the midsummer celebration— which it closely resembles in certain particulars. Hemingway's detailed handling of some of these, such as the wine-drinking, the dancing, the pipes and drums, and the garlic wreaths, is neither accidental nor irrelevant. The whole experience clearly suggests the cleansing and purging of emotion, particularly of guilt, which the ancient rites effected. The focus on bull-fighting, which Hemingway has elsewhere compared explicitly with tragedy, gives it added value and meaning.

Richard Ford, whose book on Spain Hemingway mentions favorably in *Death in the Afternoon*, associates modern bullfights with "*the taurobolia* of antiquity," in which "those who were sprinkled with bull blood were absolved from sin." Miss Weston mentions the *taurobolium* in connection with

Mithraism, which was spread throughout the Western Roman Empire, and with the cult of the *Magna Mater*, the Attis cult, which she says is the primitive origin of the Grail legend. Frazer, in the *Adonis Attis Osiris* volumes of *The Golden Bough*, describes the Attis festival as a ritual enactment of the demigod's rebirth. "At Rome, and probably elsewhere," he tells us, "the celebration took the form of a carnival. It was the Festival of Joy (*Hilaria*). A universal license prevailed." He adds that the *taurobolium* was one of the secret mysteries of the cult, and describes it as a ceremonial baptism in bull's blood, which was supposed to insure rebirth to eternal life. Bulls' testicles were also used. "Probably," Frazer says, "they were regarded as a powerful charm to promote fertility and hasten the new birth." He believes, further, that on the climatic "Day of Blood" the novices of the Attis priesthood castrated themselves.

It seems to me very probable that Hemingway had all or most of this material in mind when he wrote *The Sun Also Rises*, and possibly more that I have not yet found. There certainly is a mystery about bullfighting in the book, and there is a cult here and elsewhere in Hemingway's works, as critics have only too often remarked, one ticket of admission to which is a passion, or *afición*, for bullfights. Montoya, who recognizes Jake as a true *aficionado*, "always smiled as though bull-fighting were a very special secret between the two of us; a rather shocking but really very deep secret that we knew about. He always smiled as though there were something lewd about the secret to outsiders, but that it was something that we understood. It would not do to expose it to people who would not understand." If this is analogous, as it seems to be, to the attitude of the pagan worshiper in the rites of sacrifice, revival of his god, and renewal of fertility in his land, his people, and himself, then certain definite consequences follow for the criticism of *The Sun Also Rises*. Our appreciation of the bullfighting scenes, the cult, and the structural pattern of the book is greatly enhanced if we understand that members of the cult are "in" on the secrets of creative activity and power which have mostly been lost in the waste land of modern civilization. Our understanding and judgment of the characters can also be sharpened if we see why their attitudes toward bullfighting are valid measures of their worth. Brett's inadequacy, for example, is devastatingly focused by the fact that she leaves the bull's ear given her by Romero, "along with a number of Muratti cigarette-stubs, shoved far back in the drawer of the bed-table that stood beside her bed in the Hotel Montoya, in Pamplona."

"San Fermin," as Jake remarks, "is also a religious festival," and the Christian, specifically the Roman Catholic, aspect of it is kept in the foreground continually. Almost the first thing Jake does when he gets to Pamplona is to go into the cathedral and pray, at the same time regretting that he is "such a rotten Catholic . . . I only wished I felt religious and maybe I would the next time. . . ." The monastery of Roncevalles is a feature of the Burguete interlude, and perhaps has some analogy to the Chapel Perilous of the Grail legends. The Christian aspect of the fiesta is used in somewhat the same way bullfighting is to undercut the character of Brett. When she succeeds in getting into a church, she whispers to Jake that it makes her " 'damned nervous,' " and the author's innuendo is almost too obvious. On another occasion she wants to hear Jake go to confession, "but," he reports, "I told her that not only was it impossible but it was not as interesting as it sounded, and besides, it would be in a language she did not know." So she goes to a nearby gypsy camp instead and has her fortune told—from any Christian point of view, the wench is dead. Hemingway at this period seems to have shared Eliot's opinion that one prime cause of sterility in Western civilization was loss of religious faith, although, like Eliot, he apparently had more desire to believe than strong conviction. Eliot's conviction has since increased, while Hemingway has said less and less about orthodox Christianity; but in *The Sun Also Rises* Christian and pagan religious feelings work together in perfect harmony.

There is some likeness between the combination of these elements in *The Sun Also Rises* and Milton's fusing of Greco-Roman with Judaeo-Christian images and references in "Lycidas," and the result is that Hemingway's book strikes a much more positive note than it would if it were merely a chronicle of despair. This effect is not accountable to the plot, or the characters as individuals, or the intellectual content; it is mainly a matter of imagery and its connotations, the submerged seven-eighths of the iceberg. The ancient, traditional, and thoroughly religious rituals of the fiesta, reinforced by the fishing episode, keep Jake sane and healthy in spite of his wound and his arid surroundings; and they work in the same way, vicariously, for the reader whose ear is consciously or unconsciously tuned to receive their meanings. The sun does also rise, on the members of the cult, whose discipline enables them to be renewed, or figuratively reborn, with the season. They may not be many—they never have been—but they are always the hope of the future, the potentially saving remnant.

I have limited these remarks to the relation between Hemingway and Eliot, leaving out many other influences which are equally important, or more so, such as those of Pound and Gertrude Stein. These others, and Hemingway's literary backgrounds in general, need more study. One point at least is clear. Hemingway, as a literary artist, is not an isolated phenomenon. He has the usual ties with other writers and with a tradition. He is no imitator. He assimilates what he takes and turns it into something originally his own. But we can understand and value that something best if we know what its origins and external relations are.

The Sun Also Rises:
One Debt to Imagism

Linda W. Wagner*

Ernest Hemingway's appreciation for Ezra Pound is widely known—his constant praise for Pound during a life marred by broken friendships and bitter words; his 1956 check for $1000, sent to Pound seemingly in lieu of the Nobel Prize medal. Yet Hemingway's fiction is rarely read as having benefited from his intense relationship with the older writer in the early 1920's. We know the legends of the young Hemingway in Paris, apprentice to Stein, Joyce, and Pound, but we have never known what happened to Hemingway's early work. John Peale Bishop remembers, however, that the early manuscripts went to Pound and "came back to him blue penciled, most of the adjectives gone. The comments were unsparing."[1] Whereas Stein's influence was mainly general, it would seem that Pound's dicta were substantiated with practical suggestions.

By the early 1920's, Pound had enriched his earlier Imagist and Vorticist theories with precepts directed toward prose. From 1916 to 1918 he had read all of Henry James' writing, in the process of editing the James issue of *The Little Review*; and his long friendship with Ford Madox Ford was finally bearing conscious fruit. So that by the time of his meeting with Hemingway, Pound was deeply interested in prose; in fact, in 1923, he helped William Bird bring out the six books of "new prose" that were to reform prose in the same way Imagism had revitalized poetry a decade before. Among those six books were Williams' *The Great American Novel*, Pound's *Indiscretions*, and Hemingway's first book, *3 Stories & 10 Poems*.

Pound's excitement over Hemingway's writing (judging it the best prose he had read in forty years) probably allowed the presence of those ten poems in a series dedicated to prose. By 1922, Hemingway had written more poems than stories,[2] poems easily marked as Imagist. Among others, "Along with Youth" and "Oklahoma" illustrate well the chary use of words, the reliance on free verse, and the emphasis on the observable detail of an "Image."

During the years following 1913, when the essays about Imagism first

*First published in the *Journal of Narrative Technique*, 2, no. 2 (1972): 88–98. Reprinted by permission of the journal.

appeared, the trademark of that poetic movement was concentration. One of the primary aims was "To use absolutely no word that does not contribute to the presentation,"[3] a directive aimed at eliminating from poetry its weak phrases and lines of filler. "Use either no ornament or good ornament," Pound warned; "Don't be descriptive. . . . Go in fear of abstractions." Such axioms demanded that the poet employ his craft consciously, a word at a time, and that he give his impressions the sharp focus of the image.

Pound also defined the image as "that which presents an intellectual and emotional complex in an instant of time." By stressing the wide inclusive powers of the image, he greatly strengthened the Imagist concept; and his emphasis on *speed* gave new life to the post-Victorian poem that was nearly buried in expected details. As he continued, "It is the presentation of such a 'complex' instantaneously which gives the sense of sudden liberation . . . that sense of sudden growth which we experience in the presence of the greatest works of art" —epiphany, if you will.

The Imagists usually worked in free verse forms because they could thus more easily attain organic form, a shape consistent with the mood and subject of the poem being written. Concentration, speed, and the use of the writer's own conversational language—these were the chief means the Imagists chose to present those objects or experiences which would convey the "white light" of full meaning. Concentration, speed, and the use of the writer's own conversational language—these are certainly trademarks of the famous Hemingway style.

Influence studies are impractical unless intrinsic evidence exists in quantity. The montage effect of the highly compressed stories and vignettes of Hemingway's 1924 *In Our Time* is the young writer's most obvious tribute to Imagism itself, and has been noted by several critics. But perhaps the most sustained example of the Imagist method transferred to prose is that maligned novel, *The Sun Also Rises*, 1926. In using the methods of suggestion, compression, and speed within the outlines of traditional novel form, Hemingway achieved a lyric evocation of one segment of life in the 1920's.

Perhaps we should remember that Hemingway was disappointed throughout his life because *SAR* was the novel most often misread; it was the "naturalistic" Hemingway, or at any rate, the "realistic" novel. As he recalled much later, "I sometimes think my style is suggestive rather than direct. The reader must often use his imagination or lose the most subtle part of my thought."[4]

The Sun Also Rises is not, of course, a picture of the "lost generation." Hemingway's poetic method of telling the reader has caused some confusion. His epigraphs to the book and his final title (the book was called *Fiesta* in its European publication) prove that to him Stein's comment is indeed only "splendid bombast."[5] He uses Stein's comment as the first epigraph for the novel, but the second—the quotation from *Ecclesiastes*—follows it, as if in contradiction: "One generation passeth away, and another generation cometh;

but the earth abideth forever. . . . The sun also ariseth, and the sun goeth down, and hasteth to the place where he arose. . . . All the rivers run into the sea; yet the sea is not full; unto the place from whence the rivers come, thither they return again."

By choosing an affirmative phrase as title, Hemingway further reinforces his view, that these characters are not "lost," but merely "beat up." More important, they still have the strength to act against worn out social forms and find truth for themselves. Jake does, when he gives Brett to Romero in order to make her happy; and Brett does when she sends Romero away. But, because society's arbitrary evaluations of these acts would be unsympathetic, Hemingway has to create the organic whole of the novel so that the acts in themselves convey the proper nobility. It is a difficult task, bucking conventional morality; but Hemingway made it even more difficult by using techniques that could easily be called "poetic," at least in relation to Pound's terminology.

One of the most troublesome of Hemingway's techniques was the strict first person narration. Jake Barnes, with his self-effacing terseness, gives the readers of *SAR* only skeletons of action and characterization. We know very little about Bill and Mike, for example, though everything Hemingway tells us about Bill is positive. But in Mike's scenes, interpreting his remarks is sometimes hard. The same kind of ambivalence surrounds both Brett and Jake. Obviously they are the protagonists, but some of the circumstances surrounding them could stand a more sympathetic explanation—or at least a fuller one—than Jake with his assumed stoicism can realistically give them. Hemingway tried rewriting this novel in third person, so that his 1926 audience would have help with the somewhat unconventional characters, but he evidently liked that effect less well. So he returned to the strictly "objective" presentation of Jake's telling his own story, as it occurred, rather than in a past tense, which would at least have allowed for more reflection. This turning loose a character on an audience, reminiscent as it was of Pirandello, was also a manifestation of Pound's principle, "Direct treatment of the 'thing' concerned," with little ostensible interference from the author. How different Jake Barnes' version of his story was from Carrie Meeber's account of hers.

When Pound directed writers to "Use absolutely no word that does not contribute to the presentation," he was implying a sharp selection of detail. Because Hemingway's selection of detail was so accurate, even skeletal presentations are usually convincing. Brett's bowed head as Mike and Robert argue shows well her tired submission to the present situation, just as Jake's drinking too much after Brett leaves with Romero tells us clearly his emotional state. The repetition of mealtime and drinking scenes in the novel is particularly good for showing the slight but telling changes in a few recurring details. It is of course these changes in the existing relationships that are the real center of the novel, rather than any linear plot.

Following the sometimes minute vacillations in a friendship, or the subtle shadings in a conversation, admittedly demands close attention from the reader. As T. S. Eliot was to point out, reading the modern novel requires concentration as intense as reading poetry—as well as training in that kind of skill. "A prose that is altogether alive demands something that the ordinary novel-reader is not prepared to give."[6]

Hemingway also used a somewhat oblique characterization of his protagonists. Jake and Brett are not always present. Jake as narrator usually speaks about others rather than himself, and when he does think about his own dilemma, it is again in the laconic phrases that leave much to the reader's own empathy. Even though Hemingway introduces Jake in the opening chapter, his focus seemingly falls on Robert Cohn. He tells us innocently enough that Cohn was a college boxing champ, although "he cared nothing for boxing, in fact he disliked it." Then Hemingway begins to accumulate related details: later we see that Romero loves his bullfighting, just as Bill and Jake love fishing. We must then be suspicious of a man who devotes himself to something he dislikes. Subsequent chapters continue the parallel descriptions of Jake and Cohn, and less apparently of Frances Clyne with Brett. It is a stroke of genius that Hemingway waits until we have clearly seen what Jake and Brett are not to present them for what they are—sad but honest people—together, in a would-be love scene.

The Sun Also Rises is also filled with passages that could easily be considered images if they were isolated from their context. An image to Pound was to be more than just a pictorial representation: "an image presents an intellectual and emotional complex in an instant of time." The brief moment when Brett enters the café in the company of homosexuals combines a good set of graphic details with the evocation of Jake's sad excitement and anger as he sees her:

> A crowd of young men, some in jerseys and some in their shirt-sleeves, got out. I could see their hands and newly washed, wavy hair in the light from the door. The policeman standing by the door looked at me and smiled. They came in. As they went in, under the light I saw white hands, wavy hair, white faces, grimacing, gesturing, talking. With them was Brett. She looked very lovely and she was very much with them.
> One of them saw Georgette and said: "I do declare. There is an actual harlot. I'm going to dance with her, Lett. You watch me."
> The tall dark one, called Lett, said: "Don't you be rash."
> The wavy blond one answered: "Don't you worry, dear." And with them was Brett.[7]

The policeman's smile, the grimacing, the dancing—Hemingway often worked through actions to reveal character and specific mood. But the touchstone here, as often throughout the book, is Jake's own mood, his astonished sadness, caught in the simple refrain line, "And with them was Brett."

Not only does Hemingway use concentrated descriptive passages, he also moves quickly from one passage to another, sometimes without logical transition. This use of juxtaposition to achieve speed in impressions is another poetic technique, enabling a short piece of writing to encompass many disparate meanings. Near the end of the novel, when the reader's attention should be on Brett and Romero as lovers, or on Jake as sacrificial figure, Hemingway instead moves to the account of a young man killed in the morning bull run. "A big horn wound. All for fun. Just for fun," says the surly bartender, picking up one of the repeated key words in the book—*fun, luck, values*. The bartender's emphasis on the unreasoning fun ends with Hemingway's objective report of the younger man's death, his funeral, and the subsequent death of the bull.

> The coffin was loaded into the baggage-car of the train, and the widow and the two children rode, sitting, all three together, in an open third-class railway-carriage. The train started with a jerk, and then ran smoothly, going down grade around the edge of the plateau and out into the fields of grain that blew in the wind on the plain on the way to Tafalla.
>
> The bull who killed Vicente Girones was named Bocanegra, was Number 118 of the bull-breeding establishment of Sanchez Taberno, and was killed by Pedro Romero as the third bull of that same afternoon. His ear was cut by popular acclamation and given to Pedro Romero, who, in turn, gave it to Brett, who wrapped it in a handkerchief belonging to myself, and left both ear and handkerchief, along with a number of Muratti cigarette-stubs, shoved far back in the drawer of the bed-table that stood beside her bed in the Hotel Montoya, in Pamplona (198–99).

Hemingway follows this already wide-reaching image with the suggestion of Cohn's "death" as Brett leaves with Romero. This brief descriptive sequence, then, has established the deaths of man, bull, man—all at the whim of the fiesta and its larger-than-life hero, the matador.[8]

Another device used frequently in the book is Hemingway's re-creation of natural idiom—in both dialogue and introspective passages—and perhaps more importantly his use of prose rhythms appropriate to the effect of the writing desired. Although the Imagist axiom, "Compose in the sequence of the musical phrase, not that of the metronome," was more liberating to poetry than it was to prose, it also spoke for a kind of freedom in prose—sentences unrestricted in tone, diction, or length because of formal English standards. In passages like this opening to Part III, Hemingway arranges sentences of varying lengths and compositions to create the tone he wants (here, a melancholic nostalgia), a tone which may be at odds with the ostensible facts of such a passage.

> In the morning it was all over. The fiesta was finished. I woke about nine o'clock, had a bath, dressed, and went down-stairs. The square was empty and there were no people on the streets. A few children were picking up

rocket-sticks in the square. The cafés were just opening and the waiters were carrying out the comfortable white wicker chairs and arranging them around the marble-topped tables in the shade of the arcade. They were sweeping the streets and sprinkling them with a hose.

I sat in one of the wicker chairs and leaned back comfortably. The waiter was in no hurry to come. The white-paper announcements of the unloading of the bulls and the big schedules of special trains were still up on the pillars of the arcade. A waiter wearing a blue apron came out with a bucket of water and a cloth, and commenced to tear down the notices, pulling the paper off in strips and washing and rubbing away the paper that stuck to the stone. The fiesta was over (277).

In these two paragraphs Hemingway moves from an emphasis on Jake's feelings and actions to the specific details of his locale, using those details to complete his sketch of Jake—alone, and now numbly realizing only that "it was all over." To open the second section with more description of Jake helps the reader keep his focus on the protagonist. The observable details are significant to the story (here and usually throughout the novel) primarily because they help identify an emotional state. Even the movement within this passage, building from the short rhythms of the opening to the longer phrases of the penultimate sentence, and coming back to the restrained "refrain," suggests a crescendo in feeling.

"The fiesta was over," repeated as it is in varying contexts, is an example of Pound's *organ base*, which term he described as "a sort of residue of sound which remains in the ear" and acts to establish mood.[9] That Hemingway was cognizant of the effects single repeated words or phrases might have is evident not only in his fictional techniques but in his comments about this repetition. Lillian Ross, for one, quotes his saying, "In the first paragraph of *Farewell*, I used the word *and* consciously over and over the way Mr. Johann Sebastian Bach used a note in music when he was emitting counterpoint."[10] It seems unlikely that Hemingway would have missed Pound's later enthusiasms about the "prose tradition in verse." As Pound explained,

Good writing is writing that is perfectly controlled, the writer says just what he means. He says it with complete clarity and simplicity. He uses the smallest number of words. . . . Also there are various kinds of clarity. There is the clarity of the request: Send me four pounds of ten-penny nails. And there is the syntactical simplicity of the request: Buy me the kind of Rembrandt I like. This last is an utter cryptogram. It presupposes a more complex and intimate understanding of the speaker than most of us ever acquire of anyone. It has as many meanings, almost, as there are persons who might speak it. . . .

It is the almost constant labour of the prose artist to translate this latter kind of clarity into the former: to say "Send me the kind of Rembrandt I like" in the terms of "Send me four pounds of ten-penny nails."[11]

Hemingway's emphasis on clarity and seemingly simple diction certainly reflects these kinds of distinctions.

The passage describing the fiesta also provides a good example of Hemingway's failure to use overt symbols (a failure which troubled many critics enough that they began inventing parallels between bulls, steers, and men). In repeating "The fiesta was over," Hemingway suggests broader implications for "fiesta" —a natural expectation of gaiety and freedom, here ironically doomed because of the circumstances of the characters. Through the description, we easily feel Jake's nostalgia, but not because fiesta is a true symbol; it never assumes any existence other than its apparent one. As Pound, again, had phrased the definition, "the natural object is always the adequate symbol. . . . If a man use 'symbols' he must use them that their symbolic function does not obtrude."[12] In one sense, in *The Sun Also Rises*, the amount of liquor a person drinks is symbolic—of both the kind of person he is, and the emotional condition he is in. So too is anger, and various stages of it. But the purely literary symbol—which the unsuccessful fireworks exhibition might suggest—is rare. Even the fireworks sequence is used more to show various characters' reaction to the failure than it is to represent another object or state of being *per se*. That Brett does not want to watch the failure is as significant for her character as the fact that she enjoys the artistry of the bullfights.

A corollary to the principle about symbolism is Pound's warning that the writer "Go in fear of abstractions." Love, hate, grief, religion, death, fear—these are the prime movers of the novel, yet the words scarcely appear. *SAR* is essentially a study of various kinds of love, yet no character ever discusses that passion. We are forewarned of Hemingway's definition to come in *Death in the Afternoon*, that "obscenity" is "unsoundness in abstract conversation or, indeed, any other metaphysical tendency in speech" (95). As Floyd Watkins has capably pointed out, Hemingway characters are nearly always to be mistrusted when they speak in abstract terms, whereas Hemingway heroes identify themselves by their preference for the concrete.[13]

Perhaps more than being a study of kinds of love, *SAR* is the paradigm of Jake's initiation into the fullest kind of that emotion. Jake's self-abnegation is not martyrdom; he knows he can not benefit from Brett's affair with Romero. But his education throughout the book consists in learning just how much his love—and hers—can bear. In Part I, it is Jake who wishes they could marry. By Part III he has learned that any fulfillment of their relationship is impossible. There is no question that he still loves Brett, perhaps even more in her new-found and convincing nobility.[14]

The novel in its three-part division is also the story of Brett's coming to maturity. Although in Part I she considers herself one with the Count and Jake, the men share satisfactions she does not understand. By the end of the novel she has lost the coy femininity that makes her somewhat cloying. She has thought of someone else—Romero—and she continues thinking, of Mike and—always—of Jake. Stanley Edgar Hyman suggests, "The key action of the book is Brett's renunciation of Romero for the boy's own good, the first truly unselfish act of her life."[15] It could well be that her separation from the church is suggested throughout the novel to help build toward the ending, with her turn to Jake. Brett has no suprahuman comforts; she must call Jake, and the reader must see her telegram to him, as he does, as completely natural.

In his first novel, Hemingway appears to have drawn a little on a Hamlet-like situation. The many male characters act as either complements or foils to Jake, and the inevitable comparisons serve to keep Jake before us at all times, whether he is or not. By making him physically less than a competitor, however, Hemingway allows Jake *as person* rather than as male to occupy the center of these relationships, even the peripheral ones with Krum and Woolsey, the Britisher Harris, and the Basques. All of these masculine ties help to substantiate Jake's real if injured manliness (see Hemingway's *Paris Review* comments), and add pathos to his love affair with Brett. Jake's wound is his ironic gift from life, and he has no choice but to live with it—gracefully. Never again will Hemingway create such a sensational wound for a protagonist, even in the more obviously war-oriented novels, but it does serve a powerfully dramatic function in keeping the otherwise normal Jake out of the normal rivalry for Brett's affections.

Yet, for all his anguish, what does Jake say? Hemingway's choice of idiom for his hero could well have been autobiographical, but it also bears the trace of Pound's ideal character, who speaks in his own unliterary voice, speaks in cryptic suggestion, and speaks with truth. "I've got a rotten headache," when he can no longer bear seeing Brett; "I wanted to get home." The leavetaking scene with Brett after the dialogue with Count Mippipopolous has Jake vacillating between "Don't be sentimental" and then, after a kiss, "You don't have to go." But after Brett does go, Hemingway gives us some brief introspection so that we understand the depth of Jake's feelings. When he comes to the more important good-byes at the end of Part I, as Brett is going to San Sebastian, Hemingway relies on our earlier knowledge, and gives us Jake as an objective sketch: "The door opened and I went upstairs and went to bed." We can presumably re-create the rest for ourselves.

Hemingway relies on Jake's silence or near-silence frequently, not only in the love scenes. Jake says only "Wasn't the town nice at night?" trying to reach Cohn through his own foggy bombast. (Jake's method here is Imagist also, bringing Cohn back to one specific experience, one night, one town; and having Cohn react like the most literal-minded of men.) Instead of dialectics, Hemingway here gives us suggestion.

Even Jake's wound is given in a simple declarative sentence, the poignancy of its terseness aided by the opening modifier: "Undressing, I looked at myself in the mirror of the big armoire beside the bed." The only adjective in the sentence describes a piece of furniture; the situation itself needs no description. Hemingway is, graphically, and in mirrorr image, "presenting," as Pound had edicted. The mention of bed also adds pathos to the brief line. The concentration on the furniture offers a moment of deflection also, before Hemingway brings us back to more understatement: "Undressing, I looked at myself in the mirror of the big armoire beside the bed. That was a typically French way to furnish a room. Practical, too, I suppose. Of all the ways to be wounded. I suppose it was funny" (30). The climatic act of the novel, for Jake, his giving Brett to Romero, is another model of suggestive gesture instead of speech: "He looked at me. It was a final look to ask if it were understood. It was understood all right."

The chief danger in reading Hemingway is, I think, to overlook this rather apparent origin of many of his stylistic traits. Simplicity has too often become simple-mindedness, just as Williams' "No ideas but in things" has become "No ideas." For instance, a recent essay by Ihab Hassan equates Hemingway's style with the character of Jake Barnes. I agree with Hassan's summary of Hemingway's remarkable tightness in writing, "Its rigor, terseness, and repetitions, its intractable concreteness and vast omissions, resist rhetoric, resist even statement, and discourage the mind from habitual closure." We cannot read Hemingway with any sense of complacence because we are thrown too much on our own, and the old patterns of expectation do not work. But Hassan goes on to move from seeing style, somehow separated, to seeing style as the only possible means of re-creating any Hemingway hero, any Hemingway theme, because he finds Hemingway very close to a contemporary "blankness and rage. . . . Indeed, Hemingway's fiction makes for itself a place in the tradition of silence that extends from Sade, through Kafka, Genet, and Beckett, to the inverted literary imagination of our day."[16] He continues, "the ethic of Hemingway's characters is not only reductive but also solitary. What they endure, they can never share with other. Existentially, they remain alone; they find momentary communion only in a dangerous ritual. Always they disengage themselves from the complexities of human relations, and simplify their social existence to the primary functions of the body. 'The only thing that could spoil a day was people . . . ' Hemingway writes. 'People were always the limiters of happiness except for the very few that were as good as spring itself' " (91).

While Hassan's thesis in the complete essay is almost convincing, I am bothered by his tendency to overstate—just as Hemingway's use of *always* in the above excerpt is quickly disproved, so can Hassan's be a few lines before. There is a tone of pride here that is misleading; an attitude of "my-knowledge-is-so-dreadful-that-I-cannot-communicate-it." Perhaps the Hemingway protagonist is "alone" in that he is usually limited to a few confidants rather than a menage. But he does have intimates—Bill Gorton, the Count, Montoya, in a sense Romero, and in another sense, Brett. In fact, Jake seems much less isolated than the miserable Cohn, who has literally no one to talk with. And yes, the kind of idiom Hemingway uses is terse and cryptic, but primarily because the emotions are too big to handle in abstract words, not because no emotions exist, or because there is no desire to communicate. *The Sun Also Rises* gives evidence, in its various set scenes, of a great deal of communication. Jake understands perfectly what he must do for Brett, and Brett knows how little she has to say to reach him (in contrast to Francis Clyne who takes an entire chapter to do what Brett can do in three lines). "Let's not talk," Brett tells him. "Talking's all bilge" (25).

The tacit understanding that exists here is better evidence of the author's interest in love, it seems to me, than of his obsession with death. The too-facile equation between death and silence need not shadow every cryptic idiom in American literature. Neither is the prevalent mood in this novel one of terror, as Mr. Hassan later states. (Terror of what? In Jake's eyes, the worst has already happened.) It seems to be rather one of sorrow, of sorrow growing from the unfulfilled love of Jake and Brett which acts in turn as a graphic image for the loves of the many other characters—men with men as well as men with women—which come so seldom to fruition. For those few relationships that had the warmth of the sun in his title, Hemingway was only too grateful. In fact, most of his fiction stands in tribute to just such slight moments.

In his eagerness to present rather than to tell (to render rather than report), Hemingway erred only in following the Imagist doctrines perhaps too closely. *The Sun Also Rises* is a difficult book to read correctly, until the reader understands the way it works; then it becomes a masterpiece of concentration, with every detail conveying multiple impressions, and every speech creating both single character and complex interrelationships. It also takes us back to Pound's 1923 description of the best modern prose, which should "tell the truth about *moeurs contemporaines* without fake, melodrama, conventional ending."[17] There is nothing fake about anything in *The Sun Also Rises*, least of all the writing. And to read it as a masterpiece of suggestion makes one compliment Mark Schorer for his statement that Hemingway had in his career written "the very finest prose of our time. And most of it is poetry."[18]

Notes

1. Quoted by George Wickes in *Americans in Paris* (Garden City, New York, 1969), 162.
2. Throughout his life, Hemingway considered himself a poet, and occasionally talked of bringing out a collection of poems.
3. "Imagism" and "A Few Don'ts by an Imagiste," *Poetry*, I, No. 6 (March 1913), 199–201.

4. "The Great Writer's Last Reflections on Himself, His Craft, Love, and Life," *Playboy*, X, No. 1 (January 1963), 120ff.

5. Carlos Baker, *Ernest Hemingway, A Life Story* (New York, 1969), 179.

6. Introduction to *Nightwood, The Selected Works of Djuna Barnes* (New York, 1962), 228.

7. *The Sun Also Rises* (New York, 1954), 20. Later page references to this edition are given in parentheses in the text.

8. As Hemingway's columns on bullfighting substantiate, the lure of the matador is irresistible, for both sexes. See pp. 90–108, *By-Line: Ernest Hemingway*, ed. William White (New York, 1967).

9. *Poetry*, 205.

10. Lillian Ross, "Ernest Hemingway," *The New Yorker* (May 13, 1950), 60.

11. "The Serious Artist," *Literary Essays of Ezra Pound* (Norfolk, Conn., 1935), 50.

12. *Poetry*, 205.

13. See *The Flesh and the Word* (Nashville, Tenn., 1971).

14. Hemingway's interest in Brett as character—much like his later fascination with Pilar—seems genuine. As he wrote in a 1956 column (*By-Line*, 461): "I have always considered that it was easy to be a man compared to being a woman who lives by as rigid standards as men live by. No one of us lives by as rigid standards nor has as good ethics as we planned but an attempt is made."

15. Stanley Edgar Hyman, *Standards: A Chronicle of Books for Our Time* (New York, 1966), 31.

16. Ihab Hassan, "Hemingway: Valor Against the Void" in *The Dismemberment of Orpheus* (New York, 1971), 80 ff.

17. Pound, *Pavannes and Divagations* (Norfolk, Conn., 1958), 50–51.

18. "With Grace Under Pressure," *New Republic*, 127 (October 6, 1952), 19.

The Affirmative Conclusion of
The Sun Also Rises

DONALD A. DAIKER*

Until a decade ago *The Sun Also Rises* had usually been interpreted as a chronicle of a lost generation, as an expression of nihilism,[1] or as a representation, in Philip Young's words, of "motion which goes no place."[2] Within the past ten years, however, some critics—though still in the minority—have discerned in Hemingway's novel a pattern of development; they have argued that at the end of the story Jake Barnes and Brett Ashley are not back where they started, that Jake has gained in self-mastery and acquired at least a measure of control in his relationship with Brett.[3] Surprisingly, even those who assert that Jake is a developing character pay scant attention to the crucial Book III.[4] Although Hemingway underscores its importance through its positioning and its brevity (it consists of but one chapter), Book III has usually been dismissed with brief mention of Jake's symbolic cleansing at San Sebastian and of his ironic statement which concludes the novel. A close reading of Book III reveals, I believe, that *The Sun Also Rises* is basically an affirmative book. Hemingway's first serious novel affirms through the characterization of Jake Barnes that man can get his money's worth in life, that he can learn how to live in the world. By the end of the story, Jake's sun has risen, and there is no suggestion that it will set.

Book III opens with images of washing and cleansing. The fiesta finally over, waiters "were sweeping the streets and sprinkling them with a hose." One waiter, carrying a "bucket of water and a cloth," began "to tear down the notices, pulling the paper off in strips and washing and rubbing away the paper that stuck to the stone."[5] Since in Pamplona Jake has defiled himself, betrayed Montoya, and profaned his *afición* by acceding to Brett's request to help her sleep with Romero, his description reflects his own need for emotional cleansing and spiritual purification. Jake recognizes the truth of Cohn's calling him a "pimp," making him feel worse at the end of Book II than at any other point in the novel. "I feel like hell," he tells Bill Gorton, and he later adds, "I was drunker than I ever remembered having been." (pp.

*Originally published in the *McNeese Review*, 21 (1974–75): 3–19. Reprinted by permission of the journal.

232, 233) Because Jake, like Hemingway,[6] defines immorality as "things that made you disgusted afterward," (p. 153) Jake's pimping ranks as his most immoral act. The closing of Book II—"The three of us sat at the table, and it seemed as though about six people were missing" (p. 234)—indicates Jake's sense of loss and, in echoing a casualty report, reinforces earlier suggestions that the fiesta has been another war for Jake, wounding him emotionally as World War I had injured him physically. Yet even at the nadir of self-revulsion, there are signs of new awareness growing within Jake. In telling Mike Campbell "I'm blind," (p. 233) he not only acknowledges that he is drunk but more importantly hints that he is beginning to realize the cost to himself and others of his failure to see clearly the nature of his relationship to Brett. When Jake says, "I looked strange to myself in the glass," (p. 234) he vaguely recognizes himself for what he has been: a panderer at least partially responsible for Cohn's bloody beating of Romero, for Mike's increased drunkenness, and for his own self-contempt. It is precisely this "strange" self which Jake seeks to wipe out and which creates his need for washing and cleansing, for the waters of San Sebastian.

Cleaning up the mess, the novel implies, is not easy. For the waiters "washing and rubbing" were necessary to remove the paper that stuck to the stone. It is relatively simple for Jake to empty the liquor glasses when Brett leaves his Paris apartment, but the emotional mess—"I felt like hell again" (p. 35)—remains. In order to recover fully from the "nightmare" (p. 67) of his repeatedly frustrating meetings with Brett, Jake finally finds it necessary to leave Paris altogether, to journey to the idlyllic Burguete countryside for a week of fishing, relaxation, and masculine camaraderie with Bill Gorton.

It might at first appear that Jake's leaving the "nightmares" (p. 232) of Pamplona for the beaches of San Sebastian exactly parallels his earlier movement from Paris to Burguete. This is a crucial consideration, for if Jake's experience in San Sebastian merely duplicates that of Burguete, he becomes not the developing character I believe him to be but instead a static figure who travels in circles and gets nowhere. To be sure, Hemingway consciously links Burguete to San Sebastian, but he does so primarily to invite attention to more important contrasts. There is a qualitative difference between Jake's interlude at Burguete and his self-restoration at San Sebastian that is ultimately explained by the impact upon Jake of Pedro Romero's bullfighting. Although Romero does not appear in person in Book III, Jake travels to San Sebastian, and then to Madrid, with the example of the bullfighter before him at all times. At Burguete, by contrast, Jake had for guidance only the admirable but finally irrelevant figure of Count Mippipopolous.

The Count is the only character in Book I who offers Jake a possible means to achieve his goal of learning how to live. The other lesser characters—Frances Clyne, Robert Prentiss, Harvey Stone, Georgette, Krum and Woolsey—obviously have nothing to teach Jake since their own lives are characterized by falseness, dissipation, or dullness. Of all the Paris crowd, only the Count gets his money's worth.[7] He explains to Jake that "it is because I have lived very much that now I can enjoy everything so well." (p. 63) And Jake notices that the Count does enjoy many things: buying champagne, eating a good meal, smoking cigars that really draw, drinking wine, watching Brett dance, ordering Napoleon brandy. At one point Jake describes the Count as "beaming" and "very happy," (p. 64) a sharp contrast with Jake himself who has been "having a bad time." (p. 57) Before leaving for Burguete Jake thinks about money and is reminded of the Count: "I started wondering about where he was, and regretting I hadn't seen him since that night in Montmartre. . . ." (p. 99) At Burguete Jake consciously emulates the Count in getting his money's worth. In preparation for the trip he buys "a pretty good rod cheap." (p. 92) At the inn in Burguete Jake convinces the innkeeper to include wine in the price of room and board. "We did not lose money on the wine," (p. 114) Jake later comments. The entire Burguete episode demonstrates that Jake has profited from the Count's example, for the bus trip with the Basques, trout fishing in the Irati River, joking with Bill Gorton, and friendship with Harris all give Jake his money's worth of enjoyment.

But finally the Count cannot serve as a meaningful tutor because, unlike Jake, he is not under pressure. Although the Count offers Brett money to go away with him, he is not emotionally attached to her. He appears not to care when Brett and Jake leave the restaurant together, and Jake notices that Brett's place at the Count's table is quickly taken by three girls. (p. 67) Because the Count is "always in love," (p. 63) he is not deeply involved with any one person, and the shallowness of his emotional relationships precludes his being subject to the kind of pressure which, because of his abiding love for Brett, Jake must bear. Thus the Count provides Jake with a code of conduct which functions well only in situations where pressure is not present, only in places like Burguete where there "was no word from Robert Cohn nor from Brett and Mike." (p. 129) But even in Burguete Jake becomes angry when Bill asks about his relationship to Brett, (p. 127) a foreshadowing of his more serious loss of control in Pamplona. Since Jake cannot forever reside in the primitive and isolated man's world of Burguete but must return to the conflicts and tensions of modern society, the Count's example proves irrelevant to Jake's predicament. Finally, the Count's actions are like those of the false bullfighter who works at a distance from the bull's horns: "something that was beautiful done close to the bull was ridiculous if it were done a little way off." (p. 174)

Romero, by contrast, is the true bullfighter; he is "a real one." (p. 170) Unlike the Count, Romero in the bull ring functions gracefully under constant pressure, subject at every moment to goring and possible death. Romero provides Jake with the code of conduct to face and subdue his bull—

Brett—and it is with Romero's example in mind that Jake travels to San Sebastian.

The first detail which suggests that Jake's experience in San Sebastian will significantly differ from that in Burguete is his traveling alone. Although he misses the companionship of Bill Gorton—when Bill's train leaves Jake says, "the tracks were empty," (p. 241) the objective correlative pointing up Jake's sense of loneliness—he emulates Romero in resolving to go on by himself. From the first, Romero's aloneness is emphasized. When Jake is introduced to Romero, he notices that Romero stood "altogether by himself, alone in the room." (p. 169) And later, in the center of the bull ring, Romero performs "all alone." (p. 227) Jake further follows Romero's example in deciding to return to Spain. France, like Burguete, has a "safe, suburban feeling" (p. 242) because everything there has "such a clear financial basis." (p. 243) By contrast "you could not tell about anything" (p. 244) in Spain. Jake's movement to San Sebastian thus exposes him to greater dangers and risks, in part because of the complexity of Spain and in part because it was at San Sebastian that Cohn and Brett had slept together. In the metaphor of the bullfight, Jake is moving closer to the terrain of the bull: "As long as a bull-fighter stays in his own terrain he is comparatively safe. Each time he enters into the terrain of the bull he is in great danger." (p. 222) By choosing to leave France for Spain Jake evinces the bravery and courage that Romero displays in working always within the terrain of the bull. "Each time he [Romero] let the bull pass so close that the man and the bull and the cape . . . were all one sharply etched mass." (p. 226)

Having felt "tragic sensations" (p. 222) by witnessing Romero's performance in the bull ring, Jake takes little interest in the bicycle racers he encounters in San Sebastian.[8] In contrast to the dedicated Romero, the bike riders "did not take the race seriously except among themselves." (p. 246) Whereas the duel between Romero and the bull involved life and death, "it did not make much difference who won" (p. 246) the bicycle race. When Jake has coffee with the manager of one of the bicycle teams, he responds to the manager's overstatements—"The Tour de France was the greatest sporting event in the world" (p. 247)—with ironic enthusiasm. Asked if he would like to be awakened the next morning to watch the start of the race, Jake replies that he will leave a call at the hotel desk. In fact, Jake purposely avoids watching the race begin, awaking fully three hours after the riders have left. After watching Romero give "the sensation of coming tragedy," (p. 222) Jake reacts only with mild amusement to the triviality of a bike race in which the greatest danger seems to be "an attack of boils." (p. 246)

At San Sebastian the activity described in greatest detail is Jake's swimming. It relates to Romero's bullfighting in that each is a ritual act which functions in part to cleanse and purify. His face and body smashed by Cohn's fists, Romero in the bull ring "was wiping all that out now. Each thing that he did with this bull wiped that out a little cleaner." (p. 228) Although Jake, too, wipes out the degrading experiences of Pamplona in the waters of San Sebastian, his task is quite different from Romero's. "The fight with Cohn had not touched his [Romero's] spirit," (p. 228) but Jake has suffered both physical and spiritual defeat. He has been physically beaten by Cohn and spiritually defeated by his inability to resist Brett's appeal for help. Foolishly clinging to the unrealistic notion that he and Brett can somehow develop a meaningful and permanent relationship, Jake moves closer to the position of the romantic Robert Cohn, as suggested by his sleeping in Cohn's room and wearing Cohn's jacket (p. 165). Just as Cohn is prepared "to do battle for his lady love," (p. 184) Jake asks Brett, "What do you want me to do?" (p. 190) and "Anything you want me to do?" (p. 215). Aware of his vulnerability, Jake had accurately foreseen that given "the proper chance" he would "be as big an ass as Cohn." (p. 188) If Cohn is an emotional adolescent throughout the novel—even during his last appearance he sports his Princeton polo shirt (p. 201)—Jake also acts immaturely at Pamplona. His telling Cohn "Don't call me Jake" and his making Cohn take back the name "pimp" (p. 201) represent the same kind of prep-school stuff for which he had earlier chided Cohn. In agreeing to shake hands with Cohn, as Romero would not, Jake tacitly acknowledges that he and Cohn are linked by their falsely romantic attitude toward Brett and by their lack of self-control.

Thus when Jake goes to San Sebastian, he attempts not only to wipe out his degrading experiences in Pamplona but also to recreate his inner self. Because Jake expects eventually to be summoned by Brett, (p. 250) he consciously strives to build a stronger self, one capable of recognizing the self-destructive nature of his relationship to Brett, subduing his passion for her, and resisting her appeals whenever they threaten his manhood. Jake's swimming and diving symbolically represent his efforts toward self-renewal. During the first day at San Sebastian Jake swims out to the raft and tries several dives: "I dove deep once, swimming down to the bottom. I swam with my eyes open and it was green and dark. The raft made a dark shadow. I came out of water beside the raft, pulled up, dove once more, holding it for length, and then swam ashore" (p. 245). In swimming to the bottom of the sea, Jake is figuratively probing depths of his inner self. There he clearly recognizes the darkness and confusion which has motivated his conduct. Although the "dark shadow" of Jake's past hovers over him, he will build upon it, use it as a learning experience, pull himself up by it to create a new self. In this sense Jake's diving deep suggests that his new self will have depth and a sound basis; his holding the second dive "for length" signifies that his new self will last and survive.

When on the next morning Jake sees "Nurses in uniform" and a wounded soldier (p. 248), forcefully reminding him of the conditions under which he met Brett (p. 39), he is not emotionally upset. Yet just as Brett in the past has made it difficult for Jake to preserve his emotional equilibrium, so this recollection makes it more difficult for him to stay afloat while swimming. He encounters rough surf and rollers which force him "to dive sometimes." Although such swimming tires Jake, the water feels "buoyant and cold," making him feel "as though you could never sink." (p. 248) Having gained in self-confidence, Jake thinks he "would like to swim across the bay" but is "afraid of cramp." (p. 249) The swim across the bay represents for Jake the ultimate test; symbolically, it anticipates his next direct encounter with Brett which will take place in Madrid. Although Jake's fear of cramp indicates that the outcome of that encounter, as of a bullfight, is in doubt, his final dive and swim suggest a newly won sense of power, purpose, and self-control: "After a while I stood up, gripped with my toes on the edge of the raft as it tipped with my weight, and dove cleanly and deeply, to come up through the lightening water, blew the salt water out of my head, and swam slowly and steadily in to shore" (p. 249).

When Jake returns to his hotel he is handed a telegram that had been forwarded from Paris: "COULD YOU COME HOTEL MONTANA MADRID AM RATHER IN TROUBLE BRETT." Moments later a postman with a "big moustache" looking "very military" delivers an identically worded telegram that had been forwarded from Pamplona. The military appearance of the postman who brings Brett's telegram suggests a link between Brett and the war. Each is able to wound Jake: the war injures Jake physically; Brett damages Jake emotionally. Moreover, each produces within Jake a loss of self-control, a "feeling of things coming that you could not prevent happening." (p. 151) Jake's receiving two telegrams from Brett forcefully drives home the repetitive quality of their relationship. In Book I Brett had told Jake, "I've been so miserable," (p. 24) implicitly asking him to relieve her misery. In Book II she begged Jake to "stay by me and see me through this." (p. 190) In Book III, again "rather in trouble," Brett again solicits Jake's help. Although Jake had earlier sensed the circular, unprogressive nature of their relationship—"I had the feeling . . . of it all being something repeated, something I had been through and that now I *must* go through again" (p. 67, italics mine)—he had felt impotent to change it. Now he feels differently, and his refusal to tip the concierge for the second telegram as he had for the first (p. 250) indicates his determination to break the pattern of repetition.

If Jake is angered by Brett's telegram—"that meant San Sebastian all shot to hell" (p. 250)—he nevertheless feels responsible for Brett because of his part in arranging her affair with Romero. Thus he wires Brett that he is coming, but his thoughts indicate that it will be a changed Jake who arrives in Madrid: "That seemed to handle it. That was it. Send a girl off with one man. Introduce her to another to go off with him. Now go and bring her back. And sign the wire with love. That was it all right" (p.

250). For the first time in the novel Jake looks with brutal honesty at his relationship with Brett. Frankly admitting to himself that he has been the panderer in Brett's liaison with Romero, he also acknowledges that he has been in part the cause of Brett's going off with Cohn. He realizes that, in Cohn's case, the sense of frustration created within Brett by being with the man she loves but with whom she cannot live causes her to escape an impossible situation by running off with any convenient male. Jake realizes, then, that his relationship with Brett is mutually destructive. Its continuance encourages Brett's promiscuity by allowing her to rationalize her actions even as it condemns Jake to nights spent crying in his room and days filled with feelings of self-revulsion. In repeating "that was it," Jake not only makes clear that he recognizes the irony of a "love" which destroys its participants but also seems to suggest that "this is it," that this is the end.

Jake travels to Madrid to see Brett, then, for three reasons. First, he knows that "the bill always came," (p. 153) that his having to extricate Brett from trouble in Madrid is one way in which he must pay for the pimping that caused it. Second, he realizes that physical escape from Brett provides no solution to his problem; he had earlier told Cohn that "going to another country doesn't make any difference. I've tried all that. You can't get away from yourself by moving from one place to another." (p. 11) Third, he follows Romero's example in subjecting himself to "the maximum of exposure." (p. 174) Jake is fully exposed, of course, only when with Brett.

The image of the bullfight provides the framework for understanding the final encounter between Jake and Brett. The meeting with Brett gives "the sensation of coming tragedy," (p. 222) for Jake risks his emotional life in Madrid as surely as the bullfighter risks his physical life in the bull ring. When Jake reveals that on the train to Madrid he "did not sleep much," (p. 250) recalling his sleepless nights in Paris, his vulnerability is underscored. Arriving in Madrid Jake says: "The Norte station in Madrid is the end of the line. All trains finish there. They don't go on anywhere." (p. 251) Their symbolic significance established through repetition, these sentences hint that Madrid will be the end of the line for Jake. Whether Jake has merely reached "dead end," as Robert W. Stallman contends,[9] or whether he will effectively end his destructive relationship with Brett remains at this point problematic, further building the tension necessary to produce "tragic sensations." (p. 222) In its extreme heat Madrid resembles Paris and Pamplona, testing places where Jake has suffered emotional defeat because he has allowed Brett to dominate him. Moreover, the Hotel Montana where Brett is staying sounds remarkably like Pamplona's Hotel Montoya, the scene of Jake's most recent failure. All the elements necessary to create the impression of imminent tragedy are present.

But Hemingway subtly yet decisively shows through his masterful selection of details that Jake wins a final victory over Brett and over his old, ineffectual, romantic self. The principal technique Hemingway uses is juxtaposition: he carefully contrasts the present and past relationship of Jake and Brett in order to suggest that their roles are reversed, that Jake rather than Brett is fully in control of the situation. For example, in Paris Brett had come to Jake's apartment whereas in Madrid Jake comes to Brett's room. Brett had earlier experienced difficulty getting by Jake's concierge (p. 32), but now Jake finds that the hotel operator is reluctant to admit him to Brett's room. Whereas Brett had found Jake in bed when she visited his Paris apartment, now Jake finds Brett in bed. In Paris it was Jake who kissed Brett when they were alone together for the first time (p. 25); in Madrid it is Brett who kisses Jake (p. 252). Earlier it was Jake who refused to talk about painful subjects—"let's shut up about it," (p. 26) he tells Brett; now it is Brett who exclaims, "Don't let's ever talk about it. Please don't let's ever talk about it." (p. 254) When Brett came to Jake's apartment Jake "lay face down on the bed" because he "did not want to see her" (p. 57); when Jake comes to Brett's hotel room in Madrid it is Brett who "would not look up." (p. 255) In Madrid Brett does the crying that Jake had done in Paris.

What accounts for the radically altered nature of their relationship is that Jake, not Brett, has changed. Brett's greeting to Jake—"Darling! I've had such a hell of a time" (p. 252)—duplicates her earlier "Oh, darling, I've been so miserable." (p. 24) Her lack of self-control in Madrid—"How can I help it?" (p. 256) she asks Jake—corresponds to her previously having told Jake, "I can't help it. I've never been able to help anything." (p. 190) Rather than Brett, it is Jake who has changed and, thanks to the example of Pedro Romero and his self-renewal at San Sebastian, changed dramatically.

Jake's change is best understood in metaphorical terms as his transformation from a steer to a bullfighter in relation to Brett the bull. Brett figuratively represents the menacing and murderous force of the bull in Jake's life because she alone has the power to gore Jake, to reduce him to tears, to sap him of his self-control and self-respect. Appropriately, Brett is frequently compared to a fighting bull. When Brett first sees a bull she explains, "isn't he beautiful," (p. 144) an adjective equally descriptive of Brett herself: when Bill Gorton first sees Brett he exclaims, "Beautiful lady." (p. 76) Mike Campbell, who refers to Brett as "a lovely piece" (p. 82), asks, "Aren't the bulls lovely?" (p. 146) If the bulls are noted for their "breeding," (p. 146) so is Brett for Cohn remarks on her "breeding" (p. 39) and the Count comments that she has more "class" than anyone he knows (p. 60). The unloading of the bulls is an "extraordinary business," (p. 145) and Brett is an "extraordinary wench." (p. 171) Aside from verbal echoes, Brett is likened to a bull in that each becomes an object to dance around. During the San Fermin religious procession a group of dancers "formed a circle around Brett and started to dance." (p. 160) After Romero kills his final bull a group of boys made "a little circle around him. They were starting to dance around the bull." (p. 230) Like the bull, Brett becomes dangerous only when detached from the herd. Jake explains that the bulls want to kill only "when they're alone, or only two or three of them together." (p. 145) In the same way, Brett poses no major problem for Jake when they are part of a larger group. If Mike identifies Brett as a bull when he asks, "*Is* Robert Cohn going to follow Brett around like a steer all the time?" (p. 146), Jake hints that he too recognizes an affinity between Brett and the bull when he says, "I think he [Romero] loved the bulls, and I think he loved Brett." (p. 224)

Through the first two books of *The Sun Also Rises* Jake, as well as Cohn, plays the role of steer to Brett's bull. In the unloading of the bulls, steers function "to receive them and keep them from fighting, and the bulls tear in at the steers and the steers run around like old maids trying to quiet them down." (p. 137) The passage symbolically delineates Jake's relationship to Brett, for he too is kept busy trying to calm Brett when her desires are aroused. Just as the steers are unable to protect themselves because "They're trying to make friends," (p. 137) so Jake, who "had been having Brett for a friend," (p. 153) proves incapable of warding off her assaults. During the unloading Jake points out that the bull has "a left and a right just like a boxer," and Brett sees the bull "shift from his left to his right horn" (p. 144) when he gores a steer, knocking it down. Jake is later identified as a steer when Bill Gorton calls him "the human punching-bag" (p. 207) following his emotional battering by Brett and his being knocked down by Cohn. As long as Jake metaphorically remains a steer, he will obviously be vulnerable to the thrusts of Brett the bull, and his emotional life will be constantly threatened.

By watching Romero subdue the bull Jake learns how to come to grips with Brett. Just as Romero "dominated the bull," (p. 174) so Jake dominates Brett in Madrid. Jake's dominance is shown in a number of ways. He treats Brett almost as if she were a child, stroking her hair, putting his arms around her when she cries and shakes, and comforting her by saying "Dear Brett." (p. 254) Whereas Jake's immaturity was stressed in Book II, in Madrid it is Brett who is portrayed as childlike and Jake as the adult. Jake's dominance is further suggested when Brett echoes Jake's words. After Brett says that Romero really wanted to marry her Jake replies, "You ought to feel set up." (p. 254) Moments later Brett follows Jake's lead in saying, "I feel rather good, you know. I feel rather set up." (p. 254) Earlier it was Jake who had imitated Brett, who even in his thinking had gotten "into the habit of using English expressions." (p. 154) Jake's dominance is also indicated by the emotional detachment which characterizes his attitude toward Brett throughout their final meeting. When Brett kisses Jake he could feel her "trembling in [his] arms. She felt very small." (p. 252) Even while embracing the woman he has loved Jake retains control over himself, his thoughts, and his sensations. Like Romero's bullfighting, Jake's responses are "all so slow and so controlled." (p. 226)

Jake has learned from Romero how to transform his relationship with

Brett from "a spectacle with unexplained horrors" to "something that was going on with a definite end." (p. 173) The end Jake has in mind is the emotional independence of each from the other. Jake's awareness of Brett's psychological dependence upon him is heightened when he finds her hotel room in Madrid "in that disorder produced only by those who have always had servants." (p. 252) Unlike Jake, whose room at San Sebastian is neat and orderly, Brett is unable to clean up the mess which she has created. She sees Jake in part as a servant who can always be counted on to tidy up after her. Jake is concerned, therefore, with both freeing Brett from her dependence upon him and liberating himself from her. Like Romero in the bull ring, Jake acts as he does in Madrid "for himself . . . as well as for her." (p. 224) But also like Romero he does "not do it for her at any loss to himself." (p. 225) As his approaching Brett's room symbolically suggests, Jake has finally come to "the end" of the "long, dark corridor" (p. 252) which represents his past relationship with Brett.

After Jake and Brett leave the Hotel Montana for cocktails and lunch, Jake's words and acts continue to demonstrate his emotional independence of Brett. When Brett tells Jake to think about her having already been attending school in Paris at the time Romero was born, Jake responds with humor and detachment: "Anything you want me to think about it?" (p. 256) Moreover, Jake metaphorically separates himself from Brett through his statements and conduct. When Brett asserts that "deciding not to be a bitch" is "what we have instead of God," Jake challenges her use of the plural pronoun: "Some people have God. . . . Quite a lot." (p. 257)[10] During lunch their emotional separation is further implied by Jake's eating "a very big meal" (p. 257) while Brett, like the sick and defeated Belmonte, eats very little. For the first time in the novel Jake feels "fine" while he is with Brett. He is now able to integrate the lessons of Count Mippipopolous and Pedro Romero, getting his money's worth of life's pleasures in a pressure-packed situation. Like the Count, he can now "enjoy everything so well" (p. 63) because through experience he has gotten to know the values. "I like to do a lot of things," (p. 257) Jake twice tells Brett. Like Romero, he can dominate his bull; it is Jake rather than Brett who controls the action, selecting the restaurant where they dine and deciding to take a carriage ride through Madrid.

Jake's drinking a good deal of wine does not mean, as Brett believes, that he is trying to drown his frustrations in alcohol. In Pamplona Jake may have gotten drunk to "Get over [his] damn depression," (p. 233) but this is a changed Jake. He drinks, as he explains, because he finds it enjoyable. Metaphorically, Jake drinks heavily to drive home the utter necessity of complete emotional severance from Brett, which is yet to come. Through the use of juxtaposition—in Paris Brett had told Jake that he was "slow on the up-take," (p. 33) but in Madrid it is Jake who says, "You haven't drunk much" (p. 258)—Hemingway again underlines the reversal in their relationship. As Brett and Jake are about to leave the restaurant Jake says, "I'll finish this," (p. 258) a remark meaningful on at least three levels. Jake's draining his glass first indicates that he will not leave a mess behind him which he or others must later clean up. Second, by finishing his drink Jake makes sure of getting his money's worth of wine, just as he is now getting his money's worth of enjoyment from life. Finally, "I'll finish this" conveys Jake's intention of permanently ending his romantic relationship with Brett.

The final and crucial test which Jake must pass before his victory is assured begins when he and Brett emerge from the coolness of the restaurant into the "hot and bright" (p. 258) streets of Madrid. Previously, Jake had always conducted himself well in the shaded and breezy settings of Bayonne, Burguete, and San Sebastian, but in the heat of Paris and Pamplona his self-control had been lost. This time, however, Jake is master of himself and the situation. In contrast to the first taxi ride in Paris,[11] Jake does not ask Brett where she would like to drive but instead chooses their destination himself, again signaling a reversal from their earlier positions but more importantly signifying that Jake knows exactly the direction in which he must proceed if he is to "finish this." As the taxi starts Jake is relaxed and confident. He sits "comfortably" (p. 258) even when Brett rests her body against his. He does not stare at Brett as he had during the first ride or as the steers had stared at the bull (p. 143). In fact, the cab ride in Madrid more closely resembles Jake's *fiacre* ride with the prostitute Georgette than the earlier drive with Brett. When Jake had gotten into the *fiacre* with Georgette he had "Settled back" until, as he relates, "She cuddled against me and I put my arm around her." (p. 15) This sequence of events is duplicated in Madrid. Having "settled back" in the taxi, Jake explains that "Brett moved close to me" and "I put my arm around her. . . ." (p. 258) The point is that Brett no more dominates Jake in the present that Georgette had in the past.

When the taxi turns onto the "Gran Via," (p. 258) Jake and Brett are on the "great way," the symbolic highway of life. Their responses, therefore, will reveal with high accuracy their current attitude toward each other and to life: " 'Oh, Jake," Brett said, 'we could have had such a damned good time together.' " Brett's remark is obviously inspired by self-pity. Since her affair with Romero has turned out badly—although Brett claims she made Romero leave, her crying and trembling together with her refusal to "look up" (p. 254) indicate that, as in Pamplona, she "couldn't hold him" (p. 210)—she seems to have no alternative but to go back to Mike who, she honestly admits, is her "sort of thing." (p. 255) But Brett wishes it were otherwise, and her feeling sorry for herself prompts her remark, aimed as it is both to rationalize her own failings by blaming circumstance and to evoke from Jake the sympathy and compassion she feels entitled to.

Jake, by contrast, refuses to indulge in self-pity or to share her illusions: "Ahead was a mounted policeman in khaki directing traffic. He raised his baton. The car slowed suddenly pressing Brett against me. 'Yes,' I said. 'Isn't it pretty to think so?' " (p. 259) In the closing line of the novel Jake suggests, as Mark Spilka has noted,[12] that it is foolish to believe, even had there been no war wound, that he and Brett could ever "have had such a damned good time together." But although Spilka properly recognizes the military and phallic references in the "mounted policeman in khaki" and the "raised . . . baton," his conclusion that war and society have made true love impossible for those of Jake's generation oversimplifies the psychological subtleties of the situation. The reference to the khaki-clad policeman and his erect baton functions primarily to create for Jake the circumstances under which he would be most likely to revert to his old self, to lose control and to allow Brett once again to dominate him. Jake passes the ultimate and severest test of his newly won manhood by resisting the temptation, as Brett could not, to blame the failure of their relationship upon the war or his sexual incapacity. Under maximum pressure, created physically and emotionally by Brett's "pressing . . . against" him, Jake delivers in his final words the *coup de grâce* which effectively and permanently destroys all possibilities for the continuation of a romantic liaison between them.

It is Romero's experience with Brett in Madrid that has rightly convinced Jake that under no circumstances could he and Brett have lived happily together. Brett's unwillingness to let her hair grow out for Romero— he wants to make her "more womanly" (p. 254)—is significant of her more general incapacity to become a complete woman even for the man whose masculinity is beyond doubt. Moreover, Brett tells Jake that Romero wanted to marry her so she "couldn't go away from him," that he "wanted to make it sure [she] could never go away from him." (p. 254) Apparently Brett has given Romero reason to doubt her constancy. Romero's reaction to Brett is important because in Jake's mind Romero represents the epitome of manhood, the kind of man Jake thinks he might have become had he not been injured in the war. Since Romero, surrogate for the unwounded Jake, grows ashamed of Brett's lack of womanliness and fearful of her inconstancy, Jake properly concludes that even were he uninjured there could be no "damned good time together."

Jake's behavior throughout the Madrid sequence but especially during the taxi ride is equivalent to Romero's performance in the bull ring. No longer the defenseless steer, Jake metaphorically functions as the bullfighter in relation to Brett the bull. Jake triumphs over Brett because, like Romero, he held "his purity of line through the maximum of exposure, while he dominated the bull by making him realize he was unattainable, while he prepared him for the killing." (p. 174) Brett's "we could have had such a damned good time together" corresponds to the final charge of the bull; Jake can still be gored if he succumbs to her attempt to revive their romantic love. Jake does not immediately respond to Brett because, like Romero, he is "being very careful," because he does "not want to make any mistake."

(p. 192) When Brett's body presses against Jake, it parallels the moment in the bull ring when "for just an instant he [Romero] and the bull were one." (p. 227) The raised baton of the policeman suggests the drawn sword of the bullfighter. What directly follows in both the bull ring and the taxi is the death blow. Jake's ironic "Isn't it pretty to think so" is the equivalent of Romero's driving the sword between the shoulders of the bull. Jake administers the metaphorical sword to Brett for the same reason that Romero kills the bulls: "So they don't kill me." (p. 193) Although Brett is Jake's "friend" (p. 153) and the bulls are Romero's "best friends," (p. 193) each must be killed—the one figuratively, the other literally—in order that the emotional life of Jake and the physical life of Romero may be preserved. Early in the novel Jake had told Robert Cohn that "Nobody ever lives their life all the way except bull-fighters." (p. 10) In Book III Jake metaphorically becomes a bullfighter, suggesting that he is now living his life "all the way up."

Jake's goal of learning how to live in the world is achieved without real loss to Brett. Although she is the metaphorical bull who must receive the thrust of "Isn't it pretty to think so," Jake's final statement aims not to destroy Brett as a person but to annihilate the romantic illusion which, until recently, had made Jake an emotional cripple and which, arousing Brett's feelings of helplessness and self-pity, has permitted her psychologically to justify her promiscuity and irresponsibility. In dispelling the illusion, Jake gives Brett the opportunity for self-renewal that she herself has been unable to provide. Because her experience with Romero has "wiped out that damned Cohn," (p. 254) Brett now has the chance, thanks to Jake, of beginning afresh. The point is that even in severing the romantic ties that had united them Jake treats Brett with kindness and consideration. Remembering that Brett "can't go anywhere alone," (p. 105) Jake arranges for "berths on the Sud Express" (p. 255) so as not to leave her stranded in Madrid. Hemingway altered what had originally stood as the last line of the story—"It's nice as hell to think so"[13]—apparently because the use of profanity would indicate, as elsewhere in print, Jake's anger. Hemingway wanted to avoid any such suggestion not simply because anger would indicate Jake's lack of full self-control but also because it might imply vindictiveness, Jake's punishing Brett for having made him miserable in the past. Jake does treat Brett with irony but also with a deep sense of pity and concern.

Since manhood for Hemingway is measured not by sexual prowess but by one's ability to master his own life, Jake Barnes has demonstrated, despite his physical incompleteness, that he is fully a man in every sense that matters to Hemingway. He has mastered his life by gaining the strength and self-control to end once and for all his destructive relationship with Brett. For Jake, there will be no more nights spent in tearful longing for the might-have-been. Having known all along that "The world was a good place to buy in," (p. 153) Jake has now learned how to get *his* money's worth of life's pleasures and satisfactions. Most characters in *The Sun Also Rises*, of course, do not learn how to live. The bankruptcy of Mike Campbell and the foolish purchases of Bill Gorton[14] are metaphors for their inability to get their money's worth. Cohn and Brett, both of whom cry during the final scene in which they appear, obviously have not yet learned how to enjoy living. But Jake has, and it is Jake—as narrator, protagonist, and center of vision—who carries the weight of the novel and whose emotional growth and mastery of life make its conclusion quietly but deeply affirmative.

Notes

1. See, for example, James T. Farrell, *The League of Frightened Philistines* (New York: Vanguard Press, 1945), pp. 20–24.

2. *Ernest Hemingway: A Reconsideration* (University Park: Pennsylvania State Univ. Press, 1966), p. 86. In *Hemingway's Craft* (Carbondale: Southern Illinois Univ. Press, 1973), Sheldon Norman Grebstein virtually repeats Young's assessment: ". . . the thematic movement [of *The Sun Also Rises*] is circular and at the end of the novel the protagonists are headed back to where they started." (p. 37) Numerous essays support the views of Young and Grebstein: Minda Rae Amiran, "Hemingway as Lyric Novelist," *Scripta Hieresolymitana*, 17 (1966), 292–300; William L. Vance, "Implications of Form in *The Sun Also Rises*," in *The Twenties—Poetry and Prose: 20 Critical Essays*, ed. Richard E. Langford and William E. Taylor (Deland, Florida: Everett Edwards Press, 1966), pp. 87–91; Robert W. Cochran, "Circularity in *The Sun Also Rises*," *Modern Fiction Studies*, 14 (1968), 297–305; Harold F. Mosher, Jr., "The Two Styles of Hemingway's *The Sun Also Rises*," *Fitzgerald / Hemingway Annual* (1971), pp. 262–273; and Chaman Nahal, *"The Sun Also Rises"* in *The Narrative Pattern in Ernest Hemingway's Fiction* (Rutherford, New Jersey: Fairleigh Dickinson Univ. Press, 1971), pp. 28–48.

3. The most cogent arguments are Earl Rovit, *Ernest Hemingway* (New York: Twayne, 1963), pp. 147–162, and Dewey Ganzel, *"Cabestro* and *Vaquilla:* The Symbolic Structure of *The Sun Also Rises*," *Sewanee Review*, 76 (1968), 26–48. See also Paul B. Newman, "Hemingway's Grail Quest," *University of Kansas City Review*, 28 (1962), 295–303; Daniel J. Schneider, "The Symbolism of *The Sun Also Rises*," *Discourse*, 10 (1967), 334–342; Jackson J. Benson, *Hemingway: The Writer's Art of Self-Defense* (Minneapolis: Univ. of Minnesota Press, 1969), pp. 30–43; and Bruce L. Grenberg, "The Design of Heroism in *The Sun Also Rises*," *Fitzgerald / Hemingway Annual* (1971), pp. 274–289.

4. For example, although Arthur Waldhorn argues in *A Reader's Guide to Ernest Hemingway* (New York: Farrar, Straus and Giroux, 1972) that Jake is an "exemplary hero," he characterizes Book III as "a deliberately anticlimatic vignette of futility." (p. 111) For Delbert E. Wylder in *Hemingway's Heroes* (Albuquerque: Univ. of New Mexico Press, 1969), Book III is no more than an "epilogue." (p. 38)

5. Ernest Hemingway, *The Sun Also Rises* (New York: Scribners, 1926), p. 237. Subsequent references are to this edition.

6. In *Death in the Afternoon* (New York: Scribners, 1932) Hemingway writes that "I know only that what is moral is what you feel good after and what is immoral is what you feel bad after." (p. 4)

7. See Claire Sprague, *"The Sun Also Rises*: Its 'Clear Financial Basis,' " *American*

Quarterly, 21 (1969), 259–266, for a gathering of the novel's many monetary references. Disappointingly, Ms. Sprague reaches few meaningful conclusions.

8.   See Wylder, pp. 45–47, for a perceptive discussion of the significance of the bicycle race.

9.   *"The Sun Also Rises*—But No Bells Ring," in *The Houses That James Built and Other Literary Essays* (East Lansing: Michigan State Univ. Press, 1964), p. 184.

10.   See Rovit, p. 156.

11.   Although Waldhorn, p. 96, and Grebstein, p. 30, see the two taxi rides as essentially repetitive, Grenberg is clearly correct in arguing that the two rides present a "compelling contrast." (p. 285)

12.   "The Death of Love in *The Sun Also Rises*," in *Twelve Original Essays on Great American Novels*, ed. Charles Shapiro (Detroit: Wayne State Univ. Press, 1958), p. 255.

13.   Carlos Baker, *Ernest Hemingway: A Life Story* (New York: Scribners, 1969), p. 155.

14.   In "Bill Gorton, The Preacher in *The Sun Also Rises*," *Modern Fiction Studies*, 18 (1972–73), 517–527, Morton L. Ross contends that Bill is the voice of Hemingway's code but has little to say of Bill's conduct.

The Two Faces of Brett:
The Role of the New Woman in
The Sun Also Rises

Delbert E. Wylder*

It is refreshing to find so much excellent criticism of Hemingway's *A Farewell to Arms*—criticism based *not* on Philip Young's autobiographical theorizing and the perpetuation of the progressive code hero concept in its various forms, but on an examination of Hemingway as an imaginative writer who created works rather than merely going through the process of selective reporting. Michael Reynolds, in *Hemingway's First War: The Making of A Farewell to Arms*,[1] broke new ground in Hemingway criticism by his careful analysis of manuscript materials and by his discovery and analysis of materials Hemingway had used to describe those areas Hemingway had never seen and the battles that were fought before Hemingway had even arrived in Italy. Bernard Oldsey, in his work with almost the same subtitle, *The Writing of A Farewell to Arms*,[2] follows with an even more detailed analysis of the "making" of both the introduction and the conclusion of the novel. It is unfortunate that the same attention to Hemingway's artistry has not been given to *The Sun Also Rises*. However, with materials now being made available in the Hemingway Collection of the John F. Kennedy Library, work should be appearing that will be as illuminating about Hemingway's technique as it is destructive of some of the shibboleths of previous Hemingway schools of criticism.

Yet, a critically objective approach to Hemingway's first "serious" novel will be extremely difficult, more so now than if scholars had had the manuscript materials available to them immediately after the publication of *The Sun Also Rises*. Even then, the task would have been almost impossibly complicated by the "autobiographical" element and that marvelous gossipy attempt to identify each one of the characters involved in the scandalous behavior "reported" in the novel. Now, with years of mistaken identification and curiously related "facts" about the characters who peopled that novel, and with critical pronouncements promulgated and then perpetuated on

*Reprinted by permission from the *Kentucky Philological Review* (1980): 27–33.

misinformation (some of it produced by Hemingway himself), biography and character development have been almost inextricably mixed. For no character is this more true than for Lady Brett Ashley, or Mary Smurthwaite Stirling Duff Twysden King.

What is immediately apparent, but not at all surprising, is that all of the people Bertram D. Sarason interviewed for his *Hemingway and the Sun Set* had quite different attitudes about the woman who served, at least, as some kind of touchstone for the development of the character of Brett Ashley. And though Sarason's book has a tendency to confuse some of the issues involved in identification of character, it at least should help strip away the dependence of Hemingway criticism on misinformation. He concludes that "The book was not mere reporting . . ." but must then, unfortunately, add "Yet much of it was drawn from actual events, actual conversations, actual relationships."[3] He goes on to explain that this is not unnatural for a *roman à clef*, and Bernard Oldsey, I'm sure, would agree with that classification, since he is careful to place Hemingway in the category of *mimetic* writers. Yet, much of the criticism of *The Sun Also Rises* clings to the concept some people had of Duff Twysden, and few are willing to point out the differences between her and Lady Brett Ashley that made *The Sun Also Rises* a novel rather than biographical reportage.

Furthermore, a number of Hemingway-hating feminist critics have taken this novel to task, along with most of his other works, because of Hemingway's male chauvinistic attitudes. Most of the condemnation of Hemingway's attitudes might well be true, but again what is important, critically, is the novel itself, where we are more concerned with Jake Barnes' attitudes than we are with Hemingway's. One of the things, it seems to me, which makes this novel an exceptionally fine one is the subtlety with which Hemingway treats some of the deeper aspects of Jake's and Brett's rather complicated relationship, and particularly the characterization of Lady Brett Ashley.

Years ago, commenting on *A Farewell to Arms*, Allen and Irene Cleaton (*Books and Battles: American Literature, 1920–1930*) reported that "Bertrand Russell, on a lecture tour in America soon after it was published, denounced it as Victorian."[4] They continue to defend particularly the type of Victorianism in Hemingway's World War I novel, but I am most concerned here with transferring the charge of Victorianism to *The Sun Also Rises*, with specific reference to Brett Ashley. Much criticism by American males has treated Brett Ashley with a great deal of condescension and very little sympathetic understanding. One of the more frequently anthologized and quoted essays on *The Sun Also Rises*, for example, is Mark Spilka's "The Death of Love in *The Sun Also Rises*." Spilka correctly recognizes that both males and females are responsible for the "death of love," but his very concept of love is determined by a Victorian attitude, as when he categorically states that, "when men no longer command respect, and women replace their natural warmth with masculine freedom and mobility, there can be no serious love."[5] Evidently, there is a distinction made here between "love" and "serious love," and it is also made quite clear that "freedom and mobility" automatically destroy the "natural warmth" of women. We are to suppose, then, that once a woman leaves the cave in primitive society, or the drawing room in Victorian society, she is no longer capable of loving or of being loved. She loses all of her "natural warmth." Obviously, then, there is no hope from the very beginning of the novel that Brett could love anyone until she settles down, so to speak, a curiously Victorian attitude on the part of Mark Spilka and, I would suggest, most of the males in the novel.

I think that it is time, now, to look closely at Lady Brett. When Brett is introduced in the novel, there are a number of things to note. "Brett was damned good-looking. She wore a slipover jersey sweater and a tweed skirt, and her hair was brushed back like a boy's. She started all that. She was built with curves like the hull of a racing yacht, and you missed none of it with that wool jersey."[6] She is dressed like a woman (perhaps slightly *declassé* or bohemian, just as later in the bar Jake notes that she is not wearing stockings), but her hair is combed like a boy's, and she enters with a group of homosexuals. On the other hand, as Jake enthusiastically notes, her breasts make it quite clear that she is a woman. She is obviously, the "new woman" or the "twentieth century woman," breaking from the strictures of Victorianism as much as most of the expatriated males in the novel. Spilka seems quite convinced that "Brett does have some respect for Barnes, even a little tenderness, though her actions scarcely show abiding love" (p. 130). Yet, when Jake and Brett leave the dance, and cling together in the cab, Brett is the more desperate of the two. "Love you?" she says, "I simply turn all to jelly when you touch me" (p. 26). And then, "But, darling, I have to see you. It isn't all that you know" (p. 26). And when Jake tells her that being in love is an enjoyable feeling, she responds, "No. I think it's hell on earth" (p. 27). She also tells him that, although she doesn't think it is good for them to see each other, she *has* to see him.

Now, if this is merely a display of "respect" and "tenderness," I am at a loss. It is perhaps true that she is incapable of an abiding love with Jake, but that is the fault of the war wound. Their possibilities for an abiding love without sexual relationships are hopeless, unless Spilka is suggesting that Brett should have an abiding love by denying her own sexuality, much like the woman in the A. E. W. Mason story Jake is reading on the fishing trip, where a woman and her true love were going to wait twenty-four years for the man who had been frozen in the Alps to thaw out and move down out of the mountains with the morraine. The story is a curious Victorian adaptation of the courtly love tradition, but at least there was a time restriction on the waiting period. There is no time restriction on the impossibility of Jake and Brett's relationship.

Spilka recognizes that the males of the novel are all adolescents, as does

Leslie Fiedler. But in Fiedler's examination of the novel (in *Love and Death in the American Novel*), he, too, comes to the conclusion that "Brett never becomes a woman really; she is mythicized rather than redeemed."[7] It is certainly true that she is mythicized, especially in the famous passages where the Spanish *riau-riau* dancers want her as an image to dance around. Fiedler correctly recognizes this as the celebration and worship of the bitch-goddess, certainly part of Brett's personality. But she is also worshipped by others of her own crowd, and there she shows another face. The essential adolescence of the males leads Brett to assume the role of Mother and protector. She spends a good deal of time in this novel comforting Jake. She soothes him in his apartment, and she takes care of him at various points in the novel. There is something almost maternal in the way she listens to his explanations of the bullfight, and Jake is as proud of conveying his knowledge as any young lad telling his mother what has happened that day in school. And Brett uses rather amazing maternal skills in taking care of Mike, and of keeping fights from breaking out among her sons and lovers. Her escapade with Cohn was at least *partly* prompted by her belief that she would be "good for him." And when it has not been good for him, she treats him like a spoiled child. She deftly manipulates all of the males in the novel, and finally, at the age of thirty-four, she runs away with a nineteen-year-old bullfighter who is the epitome of the tradition-directed male with some strong inner-directed qualities. I think that enough has been said of Romero as a strong, principled, courageous, self-disciplined character who is extremely attractive sexually to Brett, who thinks he must have to use a shoehorn in order to get himself into his bullfighter's pants; thus, there is no need to develop that point here. However, I do think it necessary to comment on some rather Victorian and, I believe, rather unfair statements about Brett's relationship with men, and especially with Jake.

Fiedler, in his diatribe against this "bitch-goddess," says, "Incapable of love except as a moment in bed, Brett can bestow on her worshippers nothing more than the brief joy of a drunken ecstasy—followed by suffering and deprivation and regret. In the end, not only are her physical lovers unmanned and degraded, but even Jake, who is her priest and is protected by his terrible wound, is humiliated."[8] Spilka thinks that, by forcing Jake to introduce her to Romero, Brett has, indeed, reduced him "to a slavish pimp."[9] The emphasis is quite clearly on Jake. He has been humiliated and reduced. At least Spilka will admit that Jake's own lack of integrity and Jake's own lack of masculinity are responsible for his humiliation. I would be willing to go even a bit farther.

Jake's motivation for introducing Brett to Romero is, I believe, far more complicated than it appears on the surface. As we know from his treatment of Cohn, Jake is usually able to conceal his feelings. He is, in many respects, the adolescent that Spilka recognizes, and his wound has made him unmanly. But he is also very human, and he can be vicious. As

I have already suggested in *Hemingway's Heroes*, I believe that part of the reason that he capitulates so easily to Brett's request is that he wishes to punish her for her infidelities. He is, in a sense, "getting back" at her for "trompering" him with Cohn. Even more than this, however, I believe that Jake, along with critics like Spilka and Fiedler, must have had a very strong faith in that Victorian masculine belief, often expressed in rather blunt language, that "all any woman needed, including Brett, was a good lay." That was what would make a woman of her.

It didn't, of course. Romero wanted her to fit the stereotype—he wanted her to let her hair grow long. And long hair, particularly in the Victorian era (as well as in many primitive eras) was the symbol for woman. Although Brett assures Jake that Romero would have become used to the way she looked, most critics will not. For Spilka, "when Brett refuses to let her hair grow long for Pedro, it means that her role in life is fixed: she can no longer reclaim her lost womanhood."[10] I suppose it is a womanhood lost even before the beginning of the novel, or perhaps Spilka believes that she at least became a woman when she was living with the masculine, dominating figure of Pedro Romero. And I suppose that Spilka would also believe that no woman with short hair could have a "natural warmth." What becomes clear is that Brett is not just a bitch-goddess figure, and a Mother figure (both Jung's "terrible" emasculating mother figure and his "loving" mother figure), but she is the "new woman," "the emancipated woman," "the Twentieth-century woman." Though she is tremendously attractive and sexually stimulating, she is also a threat, and no one, least of all the critics, has been able to forgive her for that.

It is true that, in the role of the new woman, Brett does not understand herself very well. But the same can be said for all the rebellious males. They do not understand themselves very well, either. They have entered the twentieth century, have suffered through and from the catastrophe of World War I, and are now in rebellion against the Victorian attitudes that they blame, generally, for the catastrophe. They are all at sea. For a balanced criticism of *The Sun Also Rises*, critics must be aware of this, and it would be best, perhaps, to stay within the novel itself for character analysis. There are tremendous subtleties in the novel. As George Snell said, in *The Shapers of American Fiction*, many years ago, "*The Sun Also Rises*, while it does skillfully create character, and reports brilliantly the surface of conversation and somewhat hectic action, is an interesting novel by reason of its investigation of submerged meanings, and for what is symbolic in the relationships of its strangely assorted personnel."[11] Perhaps more than any of Hemingway's novels, what is submerged has much to do with the characters he has *created*—not just reported.

Those who return to the biographical, especially if they are preconditioned to the progressive hero concept, must be cautious in their approach. There are already speculations that Hemingway was viciously attacking Duff

Twysden because he wished to have an affair with her; however, because of her loyalty to Hadley, she would have nothing to do with him beyond a casual flirtation that did not lead to the bed. Such a theory seems to have grown largely out of the attention he paid to her at Pamplona and in Paris, plus a remark to prove the viciousness of Hemingway, a remark he made to Kitty Cannell. He told her that he was writing a novel, and then pointed to Harold Loeb and Bill Smith, and said, "I'm tearing those bastards apart," indicating that Loeb would be the "villain." (This is reported in both Carlos Baker's *Ernest Hemingway: A Life Story*, p. 154, and Bertram D. Sarason's *Hemingway and the Sun Set*.) In Sarason, it is made clear that Hemingway says this loudly enough for Loeb and Smith to hear, *perhaps* indicating that this was a joke. Indeed, Bill Smith is not torn apart at all. He, as Bill Gorton to the biographically-oriented critics, comes off quite well as Jake's loyal friend, a wise and sympathetic man with a magnificent sense of humor and a clever mind, drunk or sober. And Duff Twysden, we find, *was* capable of romantic love. She left Pat Guthrie (Mike Campbell) for the artist Clinton King when they fell in love at the first sight of each other in a mirror in a bar. She married him, went with him to America—first in the East and then to Texas. Evidently, they had an abiding love, for they lived through some rather hard times, financially, before she died, a tubercular, in Santa Fe eleven years after their marriage. No one has reported whether she allowed her hair to grow long during the marriage.

Notes

1. Michael S. Reynolds. *Hemingway's First War: The Making of A Farewell to Arms* (Princeton: Princeton University Press, 1976).

2. Bernard Oldsey, *Hemingway's Hidden Craft: The Writing of A Farewell to Arms* (University Park: Pennsylvania State University Press, 1979).

3. Bertram L. Sarason, *Hemingway and The Sun Set* (Washington, D. C.: National Cash Register Co., Microcard Editions, 1972), p. 90.

4. Allen and Irene Cleaton, *Books and Battles: American Literature*, 1920–1930 (Boston: Houghton-Mifflin Co., 1937), p. 244.

5. Mark Spilka, "The Death of Love in *The Sun Also Rises*," in Robert P. Weeks, ed., *Hemingway: A Collection of Critical Essays* (Englewood Cliffs, N. J.: Prentice Hall Inc., 1962), p. 130.

6. Ernest Hemingway, *The Sun Also Rises* (New York: Charles Scribner's Sons, 1926), p. 22. All future references are to this edition.

7. Leslie Fiedler, "Men Without Women," in Robert P. Weeks, ed., *op. cit.*, p. 89.

8. *Ibid.*, p. 90.

9. Spilka, p. 135.

10. *Ibid.*, pp. 136–137.

11. George Snell, *The Shapers of American Fiction* (New York: E. P. Dutton, 1947), p. 162.

Why Robert Cohn? An Analysis of Hemingway's *The Sun Also Rises*

ROBERT E. MEYERSON*

Hannah Arendt, in her brilliant analysis of anti-Semitism, that "outrage to common sense" as she so aptly characterizes it, recounts the old story about the anti-Semite who claims that the Jews caused the First World War. "Yes," his foil replies, "the Jews and the bicyclists." "Why the bicyclists?" asks the anti-Semite. "Why the Jews?" responds the foil.[1]

Arendt tells this old joke in order to introduce us to the scapegoat theory of anti-Semitism, a theory which she not only cracks but rather demolishes by way of explaining the role of anti-Semitism in the theory and practice of National Socialism. Basically, Arendt argues that the anti-Semites did not take aim at the Jews arbitrarily, as the facetious foil of the joke does in order to make his point and as the scapegoat theorists do in order to make theirs. Rather, the anti-Semites chose their Jewish target quite deliberately as a means, first, of facilitating the destruction of the old European state system and, second, of introducing their new method of political rule: terror.[2] Annihilation of the Jews and of traditional political life went hand in hand for the particular reasons whose skeletal history Arendt records.

Of course, the historical fallout radiating from Arendt's analysis with all its implications of ideology, Nazism, terror, and genocide has nothing to do with Ernest Hemingway. But Arendt's suggestion that anti-Semitism in politics must be regarded as rational, as deliberately chosen, at least for the lessons it hopes to impart, has much to do with Hemingway and with a proper understanding of his first great success, *The Sun Also Rises*.[3] It would be all too easy to write off Hemingway's portrait of the Jew Robert Cohn as an inconsequential by-product of a then-fashionable upper middle-class anti-Semitism or as a fictional insult aimed at a real-life model. It might even be argued, as is so often the case with Shakespeare's *Merchant of Venice*, that what appears at first sight to be the portrait of a despicable cad turns out upon closer examination to be an analysis of a pathetic loser, drawn for purposes of eliciting sympathy in the spirit of modern humanitarianism and ecumenism.

*Reprinted from the *Liberal and Fine Arts Review* 2, no. 1 (1982): 57–68, with the permission of Eastern New Mexico University.

It is always possible to interpret evidence in a manner directly opposite to the ostensible appearance, thereby suggesting a motive of satire or even entrapment. There is no fail-proof method of deciding the issue; one can only summon the relevant testimony and bring the best judgment to bear. In the case of Hemingway's Robert Cohn, it would seem that the relevant testimony consists of the text itself, Hemingway's collected works, and the biographical facts upon which the fiction is based. With this evidence in hand, it should become clear that Hemingway's nasty portrait of Cohn was deliberate and that Hemingway chose to highlight the Jew in Robert Cohn for the definite, if limited purpose of strengthening the sentimental message of his story.

Politically speaking—as opposed to that omnivorous chatter according to which every position on every matter must ultimately translate into a political equivalent, a chatter which sometimes passes for political discourse—Hemingway was an unequivocal anti-Fascist. He opposed Mussolini at an early date, helped produce an anti-Fascist propaganda play and film, and encouraged a heroic identification with the Republican, or leftist, side of the Spanish Civil War in *For Whom The Bell Tolls*. To be sure, Hemingway was not a Marxist either. In fact, he very definitely rejected the demands of ideology, or "class consciousness" as the chic and insidious popular frontism of leftist aesthetics would have had it in the late 1930s. Responding to a chiding Communist-admirer, Ivan Kashkeen, Hemingway archly confessed: "I believe in only one thing: liberty. . . . I believe in the absolute minimum of government. . . . A true work of art endures forever; no matter what its politics."[4] And that was that. Hemingway, for all his scoffing at academic and philosophic critics, was sufficiently irritated by his Communist critic to fashion a crude philosophical tool to help him work his way out of the unjust criticism of being socially irresponsible. But his senses were not so pained as to make him try his hand "at a sustained theory of art and politics— after all, Hemingway was the kind of artist who regards criticism as just another form of parasitism."[5] If he could draw a one-paragraph distinction between the two without sacrificing the one to the other, he felt he had done quite enough. Politically speaking, his position was classically liberal, and, so far as his belief in liberty signified a respect for the value of political life rather than an anarchistic and therefore sentimental rejection of the value of all political action, many will agree that Hemingway's judgment was sound. But even if we do not grant Hemingway the benefit of the doubt, we must concede that anarchism is scarcely compatible with fascism—nihilism, perhaps, but anarchism most definitely not.

If Hemingway's judgment of the relationship between art and politics was basically sound, or at any rate anti-ideological, how then do we explain the fact of Robert Cohn? Cohn is the Black Sabbath Rabbi of Hemingway's *The Sun Also Rises*, an individual who, by virtue of his lack of character, helps orchestrate both the story's celebration of hopelessness and Hemingway's dialectically unresolved aesthetic, namely, the cosmic battle between the choices dictated by fate and desire. It would not be proper to label Cohn the villain of the piece because he is not the root cause of the rottenness that destroys the souls of Hemingway's lost generation expatriate gang. It is clear that that role is played by The War, the First World War, which is directly responsible for everything from Jake Barnes's emasculation and the Lady (Brett) Ashley's sexual unmooring to the perpetual drunken binging of veterans Mike Campbell and Bill Gorton who have no good reason not to drown in drink. If Cohn is therefore not the villain, then neither is he the anti-hero, for anti-heroes, however they transvalue the traditional, nevertheless remain heroic in some redeemed sense, whereas Cohn is more a devalue-er rather than a transvalue-er of tradition.

To be precise, Cohn's role in the unfolding plot is actually that of a strong accompanist helping to underscore the piece played by the leading men and the primadonna. On the one hand, Cohn is the negative to the picture of Hemingway's unabashedly perfect hero, the bullfighter Pedro Romero. Where Pedro enters the story to the instant acclaim of a Hemingway gang impressed by his great looks and relentless potential, Cohn is introduced in terms of a dubious badge-of-courage broken nose and a rather pathetic insistence on cultivating his meager literary talents. Where Pedro is all grace and effectiveness in the bull ring and in front of his numerous admirers, Cohn is a cloying pest stumbling around a circle of nauseated fellow expatriates. Where Pedro stoically endures and even masters the physical pain suffered at Cohn's skillful fists by proceeding to triumph over the menacing bull, lending his life meaning and accomplishment, Cohn mawkishly opens up his psychological wounds for public display until at last he fades out of view and into oblivion. If on the one hand Cohn therefore helps to set off the true picture of heroism, on the other hand he helps bring out the worst in the group of lost souls whose depths only seem to well up in the service of some small-time decadent purpose, such as Bill's impetuous and ill-advised bet regarding the time of Brett's arrival in Pamplona or Mike's accelerating cuckold rage resulting in an overturned dinner-laden table. Cohn thus proves to be both a bad example and a bad influence. Or, as Allen Tate put it in the heat of his first impressions as book reviewer for *The Nation* in 1926, "Robert Cohn [is] a most offensive cad."[6]

But if Cohn's function in Hemingway's tale is clear, what is not so clear is the purpose of rendering Cohn a Jew. To be sure, Cohn, like all the characters in the novel, is based on a real-life individual, Harold Loeb. Loeb, like Robert Cohn, was the scion of rich New York Jewish families, a Princeton graduate, a formidable boxer and tennis player, a dabbler in affairs literary, and a short-lived lover of Lady Duff Twysden,[7] the real-life woman model for Hemingway's Lady Ashley. Like Cohn, Loeb sneaked off with his

Duff Twysden / Lady Ashley just as he was scheduled to fish in Spain with Hemingway and other friends. Many of the melodramatic details of this real-life tryst and the subsequent regrouping during the holiday approximate those related in *The Sun Also Rises*, even to the extent of the falling-out between Barnes and Cohn, with the exception that in real life the fight between Hemingway and Loeb ended by mutual consent without a blow having been struck,[8] whereas in the novel Jake gets knocked on his prat. While both Hemingway's biographer, Carlos Baker, and Loeb himself record the fact that Hemingway and Duff Twysden were drawn to each other, neither seems to think that anything much came of it.[9] A further distinction between fact and fiction appears to be the purely literary involvement of the expatriates with the young bullfighter; there were no such corresponding events in the history of the real-life Hemingway entourage. And most certainly, the emasculated Jake Barnes was no literal transcription of author Hemingway, who liked to wear his manhood on his sleeve, so to speak— although the critic with a taste for psychological interpretation might prefer to see a kind of emasculation in the fact of Hemingway's first marriage, given Hemingway's natural inclination to ride the range and his sullen rejection of those who tried to pen him in.

The upshot of all this is that Hemingway's novel is, to be sure, based on Hemingway's experience but with important exceptions that serve the demands of his sense of significance and poetic justice. Just as so much of the rest of Hemingway's fiction expresses a sentimental daydream renovation of his real-life encounters—for example, there is early in Hemingway's career the Frederic Henry of *A Farewell To Arms* who actually gets the nurse that the real-life Ernest Hemingway, convalescing in Milan, chased but never hooked; and in his posthumous novel, *Islands in the Stream*, hero Thomas Hudson actually does perform some useful patrolling duties along the Cuban coast during the Second World War, by contrast to Hemingway, the itchy would-be buccaneer whose volunteer World War II sailoring ended in an inglorious scoff and fizzle[10]—so does *The Sun Also Rises* comprise a mix of wish fulfillment, literary purpose, and evened scores. Robert Cohn is only one unflattering portrait in a gallery of tailed donkeys, all based on acquaintances that the Parisian Hemingway made and betrayed in the mid-1920s. Hemingway was therefore being either true to the mood of his characters or perhaps effectively irritating as well in his attacks on "That kike!," Robert Cohn, as the novel's Bill Gorton puts it. Model Harold Loeb, it may not be too farfetched to assume, might have been pained by Hemingway's attempt to boil his personality down to a merely Jewish marrow, although to judge by the absence of any comment on the Cohn portrayal in Loeb's memoirs and much else in that work as well, the real-life Loeb was as dizzily nit-witted as his fictionalized counterpart who, commenting on the rousing "Hurrah for the Foreigners" banner erected during the novel's

Pamplona fiesta, naively asks his friends: "Where are the foreigners?"[11] Perhaps Harold Loeb did not realize that he was Hemingway's donkey; more likely, he did not regard the jibe as vicious. Anyone who ends his memoirs, as Loeb does, with the statement (a statement much in the same tone as the rest of his book): "but at least ours was a generation that had set out to discover, a generation that had chosen to dare,"[12] just has to have lived a very sheltered emotional life.

Irrespective of the real-life accuracy of Hemingway's characterization of Loeb / Cohn, there is no doubt that Hemingway personally was not very fond of Jews as Jews. While he did have an occasional Jewish friend, such as the improbable General Morris Abraham Cohen, a pistol-packing, Cantonese-fluent former bodyguard of Sun Yat-sen, Hemingway more typically regarded Jews as did his character Bill Gorton, that is, as "kikes." Biographer Carlos Baker, in discussing the Loeb-Hemingway relationship, recognizes that Hemingway was subject to unexpected and "occasional anti-Semitic outbursts,"[13] much like an epileptic seized by an unanticipated fit. In Hemingway's published work outside of *The Sun Also Rises*, the few references that are made to Jews are generally unflattering or demeaning. For example, Jack Brennan, the salvaged boxer hero of "Fifty Grand," refers to his former opponent as "Kid Lewis . . . That Kike!" Again, in an unpublished Nick Adams story entitled "On Writing," passing reference is made to one Young Asch (Yiddish writer Scholem Asch's son), who "Had something but you couldn't tell. Jews go bad quickly." The most sinister Jew Hemingway ever portrayed is Al, one of the killers in the story by that name, whose rough-jibing partner banters about the "kosher convent" in which Al was schooled in order to let the reader in on Al's background. There are several other minor references to Jews in Hemingway's fiction, including a positive portrait of the sensitive Jewish doctor in "God Rest You Merry, Gentlemen," but none sheds much light on the author's attitude towards Jews.[14] Indeed, even the above references may better be understood as attempts at fleshing out fictional characters than gratuitous calumnies launched by a bigoted author. There are probably as few references to Jews throughout the Hemingway literary corpus as there are to any other people or nationality, far fewer than there are to, say, Spaniards, Italians, Negroes, or even the English; that is, except in *The Sun Also Rises*.

Appositive and parenthetical-like allusions to Cohn's Jewishness and Jews in general are numerous, indeed all too numerous in *The Sun Also Rises*. Early in the story, narrator Jake Barnes sets the tone by snorting out his disgust over his inability to deflect Cohn from an ill-conceived plan to travel to South America: "He had a hard, Jewish, stubborn streak."[15] Later, Jake takes a humorous poke at Cohn by describing his impressions of Cohn's first glimpse of Lady Ashley: "He looked a great deal as his compatriot must have looked when he saw the promised land."[16] The other characters follow suit. Bill Gorton and Mike Campbell frequently raise the Jewish question throughout the novel:

BILL TO JAKE:	"Well, let him not get superior and Jewish."[17]
BILL TO JAKE:	"Haven't you got some more Jewish friends you could bring along?"[18]
MIKE TO JAKE:	"No, listen, Jake. Brett's gone off with men. But they weren't ever Jews, and they didn't come and hang about afterward."[19]
BILL TO JAKE:	"He's got this Jewish superiority so strong that he thinks the only emotion he'll get out of the fight will be being bored."[20]
MIKE TO JAKE:	"I gave Brett what for, you know. I said if she would go about with Jews and bullfighters and such people, she must expect trouble."[21]

Even Brett finally learns how to play the game when, in exasperation, she refers to "that damned Jew" by way of trying to evoke sympathy from the ever compliant Jake. This list, while not exhaustive, is sufficiently tedious to make the point. But the tedium is Hemingway's characters'; it is not accidental. Hemingway was far too meticulous and demanding a craftsman for all this anti-Semitism to be accidental.

For the most part, references to Cohn's Jewishness or to Jews in general are just the mindless pot shots of trigger-happy loose tongues. The impetus behind them is not specific. They do not serve to convey information about Cohn or Jews. Rather, they are a measure of the mood of the characters who utter them. They are also another indication of the abandonment of that polite social pretense that these honest casualties of the Great War can no longer abide, a measure of the gone-to-seed indulgence of a generation without values, a generation with only its personal pleasures and pains. Novel hero Jake Barnes, while sharing in much of this bitter convalescing, nevertheless does try to get hold of himself—his return to San Sebastian and vigorous swimming toward the end of the story may be understood not so much as the cold shower that cools down his passion for Brett, nor the baptism that washes away his sins in order to open up the opportunity for new life but, rather, as the conscious effort to break through the syndrome of drunkenness and boorishness that characterizes the expatriate fling in Pamplona. Of course, Brett's emergency telegram quickly pulls Jake back into the suicidal world of his peers, thus undermining the possibility of his fully breaking with fate. But Jake never foreswears the possibility of salvaging something from his life, only the reverie that things might be fundamentally different. Given this aesthetic / moral dialectic that plays itself out within Jake's soul—a struggle between his better, because intentional, but emasculated self and his indulgent, because irresolute, but also passively resigned self—Jake's expressions of anti-Semitism and occasional enjoyment of Cohn's discomfiture may well be regarded as the antithesis to his more sober and balanced moments. Indeed, just before the stormy fiesta is to begin and just after a fresh and cool evening rain has calmed all nerves, Jake as narrator tells us: "We all felt good and we felt healthy, and I felt quite friendly to Cohn."[22] Thus attitudes toward Cohn rise and fall according to the health and welfare of those around him. This, as well as those several instances, more numerous in the early pages, where Jake the narrator describes Cohn's virtues and likeable traits, is the best evidence for Hemingway's contention, seconded by one critic who reads into Robert Cohn a restrained heroism, that "If you think the book is anti-Semitic you must be out of your mind. . . ."[23]

But the fact that Cohn is not a complete villain and the fact that he has his better moments does not mean that he thereby joins the ranks of Hemingway's heroes. And the fact that Cohn serves as a barometer of the moral health of the novel's cast of characters does not mean that he himself is without further significance. Indeed, it is this very quality of Cohn's as human lightening rod, as the salient figure who draws the vicious energies out of a charged social environment, which leads us to the more likely explanation of Hemingway's purpose in including a Jew as a key figure in this work. Two of the more articulate references to Cohn and Jewishness are especially telling. In one, Mike Campbell speaks of the heavy interest payments that Brett must make to her creditors, "to Jews." But then he immediately sets the record straight by adding, "They're not really Jews. We just call them Jews. They're Scotsmen, I believe."[24] The reader is unequivocably informed that the matter of alleged Jewish niggardliness and Shylockian business practice is not at stake here. The real issue, however, is revealed when Brett officially divests herself of the last trace of consideration for Cohn and figuratively bares her breast: "I hate him, too. . . . I hate his damned suffering."[25]

Admittedly, there is no specific mention of Cohn's Jewishness here. But by this point in the story there is no need for it. Cohn has been coupled with the designation so often that the two, Cohn and Jew, become inseparable. It is Cohn's suffering as the particular manifestation of a more generalized Jewish characteristic that Hemingway is after. And by the time Brett confesses that she is sick of it, the reader is ready to agree with her.

Suffering is an issue of major proportions in *The Sun Also Rises*. It is the source of the initial problem of the book: how can Jake Barnes, veteran of the First World War, try to fashion a life for himself as a writer in the face of the horrible wound he received in combat. That wound is, indeed, so basic that it need not even be described. Its consequences are clear, however: Jake is incapable of consummating the love he can still feel, like any other normally endowed male, for Lady Brett Ashley. Jake nevertheless does his best to detour his appetite by way of sport, as both participant and observer. He also tries to master his psychological and physical pain by detaching himself from the human involvement which would require either another disclosure of his problem or an abandonment of that easy simpering which substitutes for a facing-up to responsibility. In his negative moments, Jake, true to the model of the eunuch, is therefore eminently passive in his relationships with others. He does nothing to encourage or discourage the attentions of those he loves, like Brett, those he often hates, like Cohn, or those for whom his feelings are less pronounced, like Bill and Mike. At the same time he obliges everyone, reconciled as he is to his role as high priest officiating at the funeral service of a Lost Generation. If he can console Brett by pimping out a liaison with the emotionally untried bullfighter, Pedro Romero, so be it; if Cohn needs a shoulder to cry on, Jake obliges; if the boys want another drinking partner, then Jake is their man. Jake's mission is to minister to the incurable psychological wounds of his generation, preferably with strong prescriptions of sex and booze. Where the others are pathetic, however, Jake is tragic; where the others have lost their nerve, Jake has lost his manhood. All seem reconciled to their fate; all refuse to damn their luck. Mike takes his bankruptcy without bitterness; Bill accepts his geographical buffeting-about as the way of nature; Brett keeps trying out the fit of different masculine replacement parts as a temporary surrogate for Jake. It is only Robert Cohn who still believes in the possibility of a happy ending and in his ability to effect it; only Cohn refuses to believe that their brief love affair meant nothing to Brett; only Cohn believes that the world should listen to his sad lament; only Cohn refuses to find a substitute solution, insistently acting as if fate had not fulfilled its part of the bargain, as if the promised land of Lady Ashley were owed to him as his part of the ancestral Covenant.

While all the expatriates in the book suffer, Cohn's case is qualitatively different. All the expatriates with one exception are veterans of the war. Even Brett qualifies by virtue of having lost her fiancée. The exception, of course, is Robert Cohn—at least there is no mention of his war record (Harold Loeb did serve in the United States Army during World War I but never made it to the European front). It is this reason, as much as any other, which lends deeper meaning to Mike's taunting Cohn: "Do you think you belong here among us? . . . Why don't you see when you're not wanted, Cohn?"[26] It is not only Cohn who is not wanted, but Jews in general, as Mike indicates when describing the whole freakish affair to Jake: "Brett's gone off with men. But they weren't ever Jews. . . ."[27] Brett at first tacitly, and later explicitly, agrees. The veterans who fought on the winning side, who entered the war hopefully and saw it through successfully, discover themselves to be losers after all, castrated like Jake, infertile like Brett, homeless like Bill, emotionally and financially bankrupt like Mike. Only Cohn, of all the central figures in the story, was unscathed by the most devastating war of all history to that date. Only Cohn refuses to acknowledge defeat after losing his personal battle for the love of Brett. More than Jake's admitted jealousy of Cohn's affair with Brett, it is Cohn's inability to comprehend and recognize tragedy that galls Hemingway / Barnes. The ultimate tragedy in the sense of the novel, of course, is that of an entire lost generation; and the ultimate jealousy is that of the Lost Generation for the champion sufferers of all time, the Jewish people.

Hemingway's book is both a celebration and a lament. What is celebrated is the loss of innocence, the pre-war innocence that still believed in ideals and covenants. What is lamented is the very same thing. It is this that constitutes Hemingway's sentimentality, his effort to paint a group portrait in colors both stylish and pathetic. It is, indeed, a sentimentality that would attempt the ultimate by raising its subject to the historical level, as indicated by the book's prefatory quotation from Ecclesiastes, the source of the book's title. However, there is one thing standing in the way of this apotheosis, and that is that the most coveted niche in the pantheon of suffering is already occupied by the all-time scapegoat: the Jewish people. Hemingway had to remove the Jewish bust from this niche in order to make room for his replacement: the Lost Generation.

As if to prove that the Lost Generation is the more worthy subject of historical sentimentality, Hemingway shows that its superiority lies in knowing when to accept defeat. By contrast, Robert Cohn and presumably the Jewish people as well never know when to quit. Indeed, the mark of the Lost Generation, as well as the Hemingway hero in general, is that only in defeat does it truly triumph: Jake Barnes and even Brett, by their unillusioned acceptance of the impossibility of consummated love; Frederic Henry and Robert Jordan by their successful completion of missions that end in personal disaster; Santiago the fisherman by his stubborn retaliation against an undoubtedly superior foe[28]—it is as if true character is only achieved in the recognition of one's personal tragedy. Robert Cohn is the antithesis of such self-recognition. "What do you think it's meant to have that damned Jew about? . . ."[29] Brett asks her Father Confessor Jake Barnes. It means that Robert Cohn and the Jewish people, with their illusions of Divine Favor and Divine Justice, refuse to go away and accept defeat gracefully and thereby clutter up everyone else's life. When they finally insist on causing a scene, Hemingway as the literary bouncer throws them out: Cohn, out of the story, and the Jews, out of history or at least out of their niche in the pantheon. By quoting from Ecclesiastes to the effect that "One generation passeth away, and another generation cometh; but the earth abideth forever, . . ." "Jesse James" Hemingway robs from the rich to give to the poor by stealing the epitaph from those who have outlived it and conferring it upon those who have most recently earned it. If it seems as if the suffering Jews contradict their prophet's moral by their longevity, they only do so relatively speaking in comparison with other, more short-lived, generational losers. But in comparison with the abiding earth, they too will pass away in the end.

According to critic William White, *The Sun Also Rises* was not only Hemingway's first literary success, it was also a prefiguring of the hero, style, and theme that Hemingway was to repeat and enlarge upon in everything he wrote subsequently.[30] Whatever the truth of White's observation with respect to the major concerns of the Hemingway aesthetic, it most certainly does not apply to his attitude toward the Jewish people as developed in *The Sun Also Rises*. While I am not trying to argue that this first great Hemingway success is a secret tract on Jewish history, a literary version of the then ever so popular "exposé," *The Secret Protocols of the Elders of Zion*, I am suggesting that Hemingway's treatment of Cohn's Jewishness was deliberate and that it fits in exceedingly well with the sentimental epitaph he was trying to sell to the reader. For the most part, the exit or ejection of Robert Cohn from *The Sun Also Rises* marks the dismissal of the Jewish question from Hemingway's literary presence. Perhaps this was due to the fact that what had been an acceptable bias in Hemingway's social set in the 1920s became a vicious weapon for his political enemies by the 1930s. Or perhaps it was due to the fact that Hemingway's "successful" exorcising of the spectre of Judaism freed him for the kind of Christian Paganism *sans* Divine Law that constituted his cosmic faith in subsequent works. Or perhaps, finally, Hemingway simply had the good sense to stay away from a theme and a point of view which he had thoroughly exhausted for his own purposes and which could only have locked him into a forced logic. There is, after all, a difference between personal prejudice and the attempt to raise such bigotry to a philosophical or political principle. Hemingway apparently knew the difference between the two just as he was later to know the difference between art and politics.

Notes

1. Hannah Arendt, *The Origins of Totalitarianism* (Cleveland and New York: The World Publishing Company, 1958), p. 5.
2. Ibid., pp. 5–10: "The point for the historian is that the Jews, before becoming the main victims of modern terror, were the center of Nazi ideology. And an ideology which has to persuade and mobilize people cannot choose its victims arbitrarily." (pp. 6–7) "If in the final stage of disintegration, anti-Semitic slogans proved the most effective means of inspiring and organizing great masses of people for imperialist expansion and destruction of the old forms of government, then the previous history of the relationship between Jews and the state must contain elementary clues to the growing hostility between certain groups of society and the Jews." (pp. 9–10)
3. Ernest Hemingway, *The Sun Also Rises* (New York: Charles Scribner's Sons, 1970), paperback edition. All page numbers from this story used below refer to this edition.
4. Carlos Baker, *Ernest Hemingway: A Life Story* (New York: Charles Scribner's Sons, 1969), p. 277.
5. Ibid., p. 280: "He had defined critics as the lice that crawl on literature. . . ."
6. Allen Tate, "Hard Boiled," in William White, compiler, *The Merrill Studies in "The Sun Also Rises"* (Columbus, Ohio: Charles E. Merrill Publishing Co., 1969), p. 18.
7. Or Twitchell, depending on whether one reads Carlos Baker's biography of Hemingway or Loeb's memoirs.

8. Baker, ibid., p. 151.

9. Ibid., p. 145. Loeb is somewhat obscure about this. Reference is made to a "black eye" that Duff sported the morning after one of the Pamplona drinking bouts, the implication being that Hemingway may have been its author. More to the point, perhaps, is the following: "Duff must have asked him [Hemingway] to promise good behavior because he, too, had got himself involved. I had suspected he liked Duff. She had implied as much when she told me that she was careful to have little to do with him because of Hadley." Harold Loeb, *The Way It Was* (New York: Criterion Books, 1959), p. 283.

10. Baker, ibid., pp. 372–75, 380.

11. Hemingway, *The Sun Also Rises*, p. 154.

12. Loeb, ibid., p. 300.

13. Baker, ibid., p. 133.

14. The following is a list of those stories referred to: "Fifty Grand," in *Men Without Women* (New York: Charles Scribner's Sons, 1927), pp. 115–161; "On Writing," in *The Nick Adams Stories* (New York: Bantam Books, Inc., 1973), pp. 213–220; "The Killers," in *Men Without Women*, op. cit., pp. 78–96; and "God Rest You Merry, Gentlemen," in *Winner Take Nothing* (New York: Charles Scribner's Sons, 1933), pp. 41–50.

15. Hemingway, *The Sun Also Rises*, p. 10.

16. Ibid., p. 22.

17. Ibid., p. 96.

18. Ibid., p. 101.

19. Ibid., p. 143.

20. Ibid., p. 162.

21. Ibid., p. 203.

22. Ibid., p. 151.

23. Arthur L. Scott, "In Defense of Robert Cohn," *College English*, XVIII (March, 1957), p. 310.

24. Hemingway, *The Sun Also Rises*, p. 230.

25. Ibid., p. 182.

26. Ibid., p. 177.

27. Ibid., p. 143.

28. Frederic Henry in *A Farewell to Arms* and Robert Jordan in *For Whom the Bell Tolls*. Santiago in *The Old Man and the Sea*.

29. Hemingway, *The Sun Also Rises*, p. 184.

30. White, ibid., p. 3.

The Writing of the Manuscript of *The Sun Also Rises*, with a Chart of Its Session-by-Session Development

William Balassi*

Ernest Hemingway began the manuscript of *The Sun Also Rises* either on or within a few days of his twenty-sixth birthday, July 21, 1925; he finished it two months later on September 21. A variety of manuscript clues makes it possible to reconstruct the session-by-session writing so that for most of the estimated sixty-seven sessions, one can tell precisely where Hemingway began and ended each session. When the manuscript is subdivided in this manner, it reveals a great deal about the genesis and growth of the novel and about Hemingway's growth as a novelist. It shows his thinking, discoveries, and choices as they occurred, thereby allowing unusually close access to the mind of the writer in the act of creation, leading to a clearer understanding of both the novel and its author.

Recognizing these daily segments is especially valuable since Hemingway—by training and by temperament—tended to think of his writing in terms of one-day tasks, many of which formed units that he focused on as though they were short stories. Because these daily units are frequently embedded within longer chapters, their special quality may be overlooked in the printed text. When the novel is divided into its component parts, however, their importance becomes apparent. And because this writing took place during two concentrated and intensely creative months, such a reconstruction of the day-by-day writing reveals a great deal about the development of the manuscript, about what Hemingway may have been thinking as he wrote, and about his artistic development as he learned how to be a novelist.

The accompanying chart is based on a collation of the manuscript and the Scribner's text that I put together in 1981–82. This collation indicates all additions, deletions, ink-color changes, skipped lines, punctuation differences, name changes, mistakes, idiosyncracies, notes written on front and back covers—in short, everything in the manuscript but not in the published text, everything in the published text but not in the manuscript, and every-

*First published in *The Hemingway Review* 6 (Fall 1986): 65–78. Reprinted by permission of the journal.

thing common to both the manuscript and text. One discovery I made while constructing this collation is that there are surprisingly few major revisions, a conclusion borne out by numerical evidence.

There are 83,364 total words in the manuscript, including 3,024 words added and 6,130 words deleted, leaving a net total of 77,234 words. The Scribner's text contains 67,920 words. The revised opening—which, since it was not deleted until the galley stage, should be included because it presents a clearer account of the main revision process—contains an additional 3,616 words, for a total of 71,536 words. Seventy-nine percent (56,676 words) of this total came directly from the manuscript; 21% (15,117 words) was added in revision. Of these 15,117 words, 832 words consist of name changes (e.g., from "Duff" to "Brett"); 1,004 words are single-word additions; 4,527 words were added as phrases (that is, additions of less than a sentence); 1,801 words were added as single sentences; and 6,953 words were added in passages of two or more sentences, nearly half of which (3,059 words) were added in five sessions. Seventeen sessions contain no revisions longer than a sentence. Not a single scene was added in revision, and only three manuscript sessions (7, 8, and 27) were altogether eliminated. These figures indicate that, despite later statements to the contrary, Hemingway learned how to write a novel not by revising the manuscript but by writing the manuscript itself. The struggle to find form, direction, tone, point of view, focus, method, and significance occurred during the writing of the manuscript.

The germ of the novel is contained in a first-person narration, paraphrased below, that Hemingway wrote during the first four sessions. Using real-life names, he began this thirty-two page narration by recounting the first time he met Cayetano Ordoñez, nicknamed "Niño de la Palma," whose name Hemingway used as his title:

It is twenty minutes before the *corrida* is to begin. Hem is impressed by this strikingly handsome *torero*. Later, after watching him fight that day, Hem and Quintana (the hotel owner and fellow *aficionado*) agree that Niño is the best bullfighter either has seen. Both men are excited by the prospect of witnessing the emergence of a potentially great matador. After their talk, Hem returns to the fiesta for a night of drinking and dancing until three in the morning.

At 6:00 the next morning, three men, carrying a fourth, probably Niño, mistakenly bang open Hem and Hadley's door before going to Room 8, that is, Niño's room.

Later that day, at the urging of the others in his group, Hem is cajoled into greeting the American ambassador because no dignitary is there to welcome him. In the ambassador's entourage is Mrs. Carleton, a short, sensuous woman, whose specialty is taking husbands away from their wives. She worships bullfighters, has apparently been intimate with at least one, and expresses an interest in Niño. The entire time she is talking, she is openly flirting with

Hem, who becomes angry with himself for *not* being immune to the sexual advances of someone he clearly does not admire.

The next night a worried Quintana tells Hem that he has just received a message from the American ambassador requesting Niño's company later that evening. He asks Hem's advice. Together, they decide not to give Niño the message, a decision that stirs their passions because—at least for the time being—they have protected Niño from "people [who] would wreck him to make a nymphomaniacs [sic] holiday" (193.19)[1] Hem refers to their emotions as "drunk feelings," but then comments that Quintana wasn't drunk: only he himself was drunk.

After talking to Quintana, Hem joins the others, who are even drunker than he is. They are having a boisterous time as Don (Donald Ogden Stewart) keeps buying shoe shines for Pat (Pat Guthrie). Niño, sitting at the next table, invites Hem to have some wine with him and a friend, a bullfight critic from Madrid. After the three of them have been talking for a while, Duff (Duff Twysden) calls from the next table and, without taking her eyes off Niño, asks Hem to introduce his friends. Niño comes over to join them, is given a large glass of cognac, and finds himself barraged by drunken non sequiturs. The climax of the story occurs when Quintana walks into the room and sees Niño sitting between Hem and two women in evening dresses at a table full of drunks, a large glass of cognac in his hand. Without nodding, Quintana walks out, disgusted by what he sees and dismayed that Hem would be sitting in the middle of it all, doing nothing, this man with *afición*, who only an hour before had felt so moved because he had shielded Niño from a similar situation.

The story concludes with a coda that shifts the attention to the group of expatriates: Pat tries to propose an insulting toast, but Hem, seeing it coming, interjects a toast of his own, enabling Niño to exit gracefully. Duff comments on Niño's good looks, and, alluding to an earlier line by Pat, agrees that she would indeed love to see Niño get into his tight-fitting clothes. Pat tells Hem he is angry with him for interrupting and, declaring that he wants things settled, suddenly turns on Harold (Harold Loeb), *not* Hem. This is the first reference to Harold, who had been sitting there not saying a word. During the previous month, he had had an affair with Duff: since she is engaged to Pat, Harold's presence at the fiesta has created a great deal of tension. Distraught with anger jealousy and alcohol, and nearly crying, Pat demands that Harold leave. When he refuses, Pat goes after him but is grabbed by Hem, who tells him that he can't fight there in the hotel and leads him out. The story ends as Harold is putting his glasses back on, Pat is stumbling on the stairs, and—if Hem remembers correctly—Hadley and Duff are talking about their mothers.

The more one looks at the conflicts within this opening story—especially those concerning alcohol, sexuality, and modes of life—the more it appears that the real subject is not the potential ruination of Niño, but the conflicts and turmoil within Hem as he tries—unsuccessfully—to resolve the tensions and contradictory values of two mutually exclusive worlds: the *aficionado* world he preferred and the expatriate world he inhabited. Further complicating this turmoil is Hem's (and later Jake's) conflicting emotions concerning women such as Mrs. Carleton and, more importantly, Duff Twysden, whose sensuality draws him almost against his will and yet whose values he cannot admire. In the novel, this conflict is intensified. Whereas Hem is caught in the middle of a situation not of his making, Jake knowingly becomes an accomplice in the possible ruination of Pedro Romero when he acts as the go-between for him and Brett, and, in so doing, he unforgivably violates the values he most wants to live by. To use Hem's words about the ambassador's group, Jake becomes one of those people who "would wreck him to make a nymphomaniacs holiday and start him away from being a bull fighter" (193.19).

Thus, the climax of this initial story prefigures the climax of the novel and provides a key for reading it. In the same way that the opening story is Hem's story, not Niño's, so the novel is Jake's story, not Brett's, despite Hemingway's opening galley comment, "This is a novel about a lady." The people, the subject matter, and the conflicts touched upon in this initial story so intrigued Hemingway that he decided he had to explore them further, and in doing so, he transformed the story into his first—and perhaps best—novel.

TRANSFORMATION   This transformation from non-fiction to novel took place during the next five days. On July 23, in Session 5, Hemingway continued the story in a notebook, the first of seven. At this point he apparently intended to write one-sentence descriptions of each of the expatriates. When he got to Duff, however, he was either unwilling or unable to confine her to one sentence. He wrote about her for the next two days. Though he presents a thoroughly negative picture of her as an aimless drunkard, he is nevertheless clearly attracted to her. This dilemma and his decision to write at length about her changed the shape of the novel by introducing the material that would evolve into Jake's approach-avoidance conflict regarding Duff. The following day, July 25, he abandoned the last vestige of his former plan of briefly describing each expatriate. Instead, the narrator, who on this day becomes "Jake," the first fictionalized character, tells about his boyhood experience of attending the funeral of a favorite uncle. His mother, during a period of religious fervor, had told him that she would rather see him in his grave than do certain things, such as smoke, gamble, or drink, things that this now-dead uncle had been guilty of. At the funeral, Jake kept looking for the uncle, when suddenly he saw his uncle's purple nose amid the mass of flowers directly in front of him, the sight of which froze him with a sudden awareness of death. Afterwards, whenever his mother said she would rather see him in his grave than do these things, he thought of his uncle, but saw himself in the casket. This shocking awareness of death caused him to reject his mother's arbitrary, inflexible, and compassionless moral code, so that Jake will not say that it would be better for Niño to be in his grave than to drink with the expatriate crowd. But then the anecdote turns upon itself as Jake goes on to say that if Niño continues to accompany them, he will be dead soon enough. These contradictory conclusions—the rejection of arbitrary values and yet the need for them—reflect the conflict that Hemingway, or at least Jake, was experiencing as someone who belonged both to the world of the Paris expatriates, in which drinking and rejection of middle-class values were *de rigueur*, and to the world of the *aficionados*, in which "quite unimportant" things, such as drinking, could prove fatal. Such contradictory messages suggest that Hemingway was touching upon a significant moral dilemma that he himself had not fully resolved.

At the end of the anecdote, there are two illuminating editorial paragraphs, one concluding the writing for July 25 and the other beginning the writing for July 26. (The manuscript page containing these two paragraphs has been reproduced in Frederic Svoboda's *Hemingway and The Sun Also Rises* [37], which contains a number of other manuscript passages as well.) In the first, Hemingway says that he is sick of clear, restrained writing, that he is going to try to tell the whole story, and that he will not use literary signs to mark the significant things; the reader will have to decide upon these for himself. At this point Hemingway may not have been at all sure what the significant things were going to be; first he had to be free to try "to get in the whole business." In the second paragraph, after noting that his friends—he mentions Gertrude Stein by name—will probably not like what he is writing, he announces his freedom to write in his own way, declaring that if what he is writing is not literature, he never claimed it was.

This declaration is followed by a major shift in the direction of the novel. Stating that in order to understand what happened in Pamplona the reader has to understand the Quarter in Paris, Hemingway shifted the setting from Spain to France. He then spent the rest of the session writing a negative sketch of life in the Quarter; however, dissatisfied with what he was writing, he stopped mid-sentence, crossed out the description, and rewrote it the next day, going beyond the point where he had stopped. By this time, he had decided that Gerald Cohn (the character based on Harold Loeb) would be the ironic hero of the novel, thereby providing himself a means of continuing the story while obliquely probing the conflicts within Jake. This choice of Gerald as ironic hero completed the basic transformation from story to novel. The next day, July 28, Hemingway wrote the material corresponding to Chapter 1 of the Scribner's text.

THE REST OF NOTEBOOK I   Much of the writing early in Notebook I relies on anecdotes and remarks, rather than on character and incident. As Hemingway continued to write, however, his technique began to change—from illustrative anecdotes to interrelated incidents, from narration through remarks to narration through dialogue, from generalized settings and unspecified chronology to identifiable places and specific times. In effect, he was adhering to Stein's edict: "Remarks are not literature," but he did so by rediscovering the principle for himself as he wrote, thereby making it his own.

As these changes brought him closer to his story, they also took him away from his declared hero. Though he did write another chapter about Gerald (text: Chapter II), Hemingway shifted the focus to Jake only three days after stating that Gerald is the hero. On July 30, he described the first part of Jake's evening in the Quarter, pairing him with Georgette, the Belgian *poule*; the next day, he paired Jake with Duff, a juxtaposition that invites us to see her as Georgette's moral double. This is Duff's first appearance since Hemingway had decided that she and Jake would be involved in a long-standing relationship that could never be consummated, and Hemingway chose to surround her with negative associations. Nevertheless, Jake is irresistibly drawn to her, and therein lies the basic conflict that informs the novel.

In Session 14, on August 1, Hemingway described Jake and Duff's taxi ride to the Café Select where they meet Count Mippipopolous; on August 2, he wrote about Jake's walk back to his flat where he cried himself to sleep only to be awakened by Duff; and on August 3, Hemingway finished Notebook I by describing Jake's walk to work the following morning.

By the end of Notebook I the story was going well, and Hemingway had the right to feel pleased. It is fitting that the last page of the notebook reads like an apostrophe in praise of work. As Jake put it: "It felt pleasant to be going to work." Hemingway, the disciplined craftsman, by sitting down day after day to work on his task, had begun to create something truly worthwhile—and he knew it.

NOTEBOOK II   But there were still problems facing him, most significantly the question of whose story he was telling. Though he had earlier announced that Gerald was the hero, it was becoming clear that the story was moving away from him, just as earlier it had slipped away from Niño. The writing of Notebook II is the story of Hemingway's search for a hero and his eventual choice of Jake through the process of elimination.

Early in the notebook, at the end of Session 17, there is the following passage that Hemingway later crossed out (the ms. page on which this appears is reproduced in Svoboda 32): "Now you can see. It looked as though I were trying to get to be the hero of this story. But that was all wrong. Gerald Cohn is the hero. When I bring myself in it is only to clear up something. Or maybe Duff is the hero or Niño de la Palma. [But] He never really had a chance to be the hero. Or maybe there is not any hero at all.

Maybe a story is better without any hero" (194.II.7). As though to investigate these possibilities, Hemingway examined the potential first of Gerald and then of Duff to be the hero.

In Session 18 he tried to return the focus to Gerald. The session originally had an ironic balance to it; it began with Duff's not showing up for her date with Jake and ended with an explanation of why she didn't show up: she has a date with Gerald. But by the next day, having changed his mind about Gerald's date with Duff, Hemingway rewrote the last part of this scene, this time leading up to Gerald's date with Frances, not Duff. Instead of returning the focus to Cohn, however, this new plan resulted in Gerald's being so thoroughly annihilated by Frances during the next two sessions, that there was little chance after this for him to be the hero, ironic or otherwise.

In Session 21, Hemingway turned his attention to Duff, and within three days she, too, had been all but eliminated from consideration as the hero. Her elimination occurred through the contrast between her and the Count. When one considers that the scenes with Gerald and Frances and those with Duff and the Count would not have occurred if Hemingway had not changed his mind about Gerald's having a date with Duff, then it appears as though Hemingway might have been testing the potential of each to sustain the story, and he found each wanting.

Without Niño, Gerald, and Duff, the choices for hero had been narrowed to either Jake or no one. In a sense, Hemingway chose both. That is, he may have tried not to have a hero, but because the story is located within the consciousness of the narrator, it is the narrator's story that Hemingway is telling. By claiming to have no hero, however, Hemingway was free to focus on different characters in various sections of the novel: Gerald in Notebook I, Duff in Notebook II, Bill in Notebook III, Guerrita in Notebook VI. But while these come and go, Jake remains.

NOTEBOOK III   This notebook can be thought of as the Men-Without-Women Notebook. Not only does it center on the friendship between Jake and Bill, but it was also primarily written during the week that Hemingway was by himself in Hendaye after Hadley had gone ahead to Paris on August 12. However, whereas Jake's world became calmer without Duff, Hemingway's became less peaceful without Hadley to help regulate the non-working hours. On August 15, after four straight days of multiple writing sessions, Hemingway wrote to Howell Jenkins that he was "working harder than he had ever worked in his life, often until three or four in the morning. Then he would fall asleep, his head feeling like a frozen cabbage, only to jump awake again a few hours later, with the words already stringing themselves into sentences, clamoring to be set down" (Baker 199).

Notebook III is marked by the presence of Bill, the general absence of Duff, the removal of Gerald from the center of things, and the presentation of the friendship between Jake and Bill. Together, they show what life can be like without people like Duff and Cohn. These men-without-women enjoy themselves, living deliberately and taking pleasure in the physical world. Together, they show how to live the good life that the Count and Jake had talked about in the previous section. Bill is such an important character that Hemingway twice tried to make him the first-person narrator, once at the Ledoux-Kid Francis fight, which is described in the manuscript, and later at Burguete.

On the back of Notebook III, Hemingway outlined his plan for the rest of the novel (reproduced in Svoboda, 24). The outline generally corresponds to what Hemingway was to write, though some things were either modified or altogether left out. For instance, Hemingway had planned to devote only one chapter to the Burguete section; but it grew as he wrote. He left out several characters mentioned in the outline: "the South American" and Noel Murphy, who was to have shown up with the Count in Pamplona. And the Count was to have refused Mike a job. Despite such differences, the outline indicates that by the middle of August, Hemingway had a good idea of the shape of his novel. It is probable that about this time he chose his working title—"Fiesta"—which he kept throughout the rest of the manuscript.

NOTEBOOK IV   Written in Paris in twelve sessions from August 20 to 29, this notebook begins with the hiking and fishing at Burguete and ends with the description of the opening of the fiesta. Unlike earlier notebooks in which Hemingway was discovering his hero, his focus, and his procedure, this one is characterized by fewer discoveries and more experimentation, much of which took the form of one-day writing challenges that can be identified with particular days.

For instance, on August 22 Jake retells the A. E. W. Mason story, "The Crystal Trench," which he follows with an Alpine story of his own (not in the Scribner's text), almost as though Hemingway used this day to show that he could tell a better story than Mason. On August 23 he experimented for a second time with making Bill the first-person narrator and he created a one-day character, the Englishman, Wilson-Harris, who appears only in Session 38.

On Monday, August 24 Hemingway wrote what amounts to a preface to the Pamplona section of the novel; that is, he postponed continuing the action of the story for a day in order to discuss the nature of *aficion*, that deeply-felt passion for bullfighting that carries with it a way of apprehending the world and an unstated code of behavior. This discussion provided a context against which to measure Jake's subsequent actions.

On successive days, August 24, 25, 26, and 27, Hemingway created "literary signs" for each of the four main characters: *aficion* for Jake, bankruptcy for Mike, the gored and segregated steer for Gerald, and the Circe myth for Duff. And on August 28 he wrote Jake's late night interior mono-logue, which is considerably longer in the manuscript. (See Svoboda, 20–21, for Hemingway's typescript revision of a portion of this monologue.)

These and later experiments indicate that in the second half of the manuscript Hemingway was less concerned with verisimilitude and more concerned with creating precisely the kinds of literary signs that in Notebook I he had declared he would not use. This means that Hemingway wrote the second half of the novel using a different principle of meaning than the one he had used in the first half. At first he was trying to get the whole story in, refusing to impose a meaning and trusting that the events themselves—if presented with sufficient precision—might be made to yield their own meaning, a meaning that had to be discovered before it could be articulated. But by the second half of the manuscript, he knew much more about where his story was going and what it meant, so that he was in a position to suggest meaning through the use of various figures of speech. The diversity of the writing that characterizes the second half of the manuscript is much more apparent when the novel is divided session by session.

THE FINAL NOTEBOOKS   Notebook V, written in eleven sessions from August 29 to September 9, covers the period from the beginning of the fiesta to the lunch scene on its final day. In this notebook Hemingway continued to experiment with one-day writing challenges, and as he became increasingly sure of where his story was going and how it was going to get there, his writing became more cryptic, especially in terms of what Jake was thinking and feeling. Through the shorthand of symbolism and the presentation of events without comment in such a way that the reader can and must infer what is not stated, Hemingway was able to achieve a remark-able degree of compression.

One curiosity of Notebook V—perhaps the results of the emphasis on compression—is that it contains a number of internal inconsistencies. For instance, after acting as go-between for Duff and Guerrita, Jake finds Bill, Mike, and Edna at the Bar Milano where they had been "festival-ing" the English, yet in an earlier session, Jake told us that it was the too-quiet Bar Milano that they had *left* in order to do their "festival-ing." In the next session Jake returns to the hotel shortly after his fight with Gerald, who is already there in his room; Hemingway simply did not allow sufficient time for Gerald's protracted fight with Guerrita. And in the story of Vicente Girones, the peasant who had been killed during the running of the bulls, Jake describes a funeral procession that he couldn't possibly have witnessed, having left Pamplona before the funeral took place. Finally, he describes the contents of a drawer in Mike and Duff's room, though it is improbable that Jake could have known these details since it is unlikely that he would actually have looked there. The fact that these inconsistencies, and earlier ones such as conflicting dates, went into the published novel undetected suggests that during the revision Hemingway may not have been as close to the material as he later indicated.

Notebook VI, written from September 9 to 21, begins with the last day of the fiesta and concludes with the scene between Jake and Duff in the bar of the Palace Hotel in Madrid; Hemingway then completed the manuscript three pages into Notebook VII.

In Notebook VI there is a 633-word passage, almost all of which Hemingway later crossed out in pencil, that provides a key for making sense of Jake's subsequent erratic behavior in Madrid. In this passage (portions of which are reproduced in Svoboda 84–85) Jake responds to Duff's telegrams. Her call for help dissipates the hard-won growing sense of tranquility that he had been able to achieve in his two days at San Sebastian. Clearly annoyed, Jake decides that he will act hard-boiled, deal with Duff as quickly as possible, and get back to his retreat. Then all of a sudden he launches into a lengthy tirade against Braddocks, indicating to the reader and perhaps to himself just how difficult it is going to be for Jake to maintain his controlled, hard-boiled pose.

According to the manuscript, Jake sleeps well on the Sud Express, apparently an indication of how Jake was trying not to let Duff get to him, but when Hemingway revised this passage, he apparently decided that since Jake was thoroughly upset, he would not be able to sleep. This one change, as Svoboda points out, allowed him to eliminate the entire passage about Jake's response to Duff's telegrams, since his internal state could be inferred by his not being able to sleep. However, in eliminating this passage, Hemingway also eliminated the clues that explain Jake's otherwise baffling behavior in the closing scenes of the novel.

Jake's apparently inconsistent behavior begins to make sense if we see it as the product of his unsuccessful attempt to maintain his hard-boiled exterior, to act like one of the "good people" (Braddocks' phrase), and to convince himself that he can live deliberately even with Duff around. Jake's wide and rapid mood changes, often shifting from one line to the next, and his excessive drinking in this last section of the novel only make sense if we see this behavior as the result of the conflict between how Jake tries to act and how he feels. Despite his two days at San Sebastian and despite the fact that he knows how he wants to live, at the end of the novel there is no assurance that he will be able to change. Though he has achieved a transforming awareness, Jake has yet to become transformed. This change, if it is to come, will be won slowly, day by day, as the sun rises and sets.

THE CHART OF THE SESSION-BY-SESSION WRITING

Each item in the Hemingway Collection at the Kennedy Library has been assigned a library number which is written on photocopies of the originals.

The thirty-two loose sheets on which Hemingway began the manuscript have one number: JFK 193. The seven notebooks in which the rest of the manuscript was written are designated as JFK 194; the library has assigned an additional number to each notebook (e.g., 194.IV), except the last notebook which is numbered as though it were a continuation of Notebook VI. Page numbers are based on photocopies rather than on the originals. Each photocopy contains two manuscript pages—the verso and recto of an open notebook page. Thus, a hundred-page notebook will result in about fifty JFK Library page numbers.

Each entry in the chart contains the following: the session number; probable date and place of composition; page references for both the manuscript and the Scribner's text, including an indication of precisely where the break between sessions occurred; and word counts for both the manuscript and the text. *Net* = total ms. words minus deletions; *omitted* = ms. words not in the Scribner's text; and *added* = text words not in the manuscript. (Note: one would expect that net ms. words minus omitted words plus added words would be equal to the number of words in the text; however. Hemingway wrote certain words, such as "anybody" and "everything," as though they were two words, and he did not usually hyphenate compound adjectives; thus, some words have been counted as two words in the manuscript and as one in the text, thereby accounting for the discrepancy.) Some entries also include one or more of the following: *omissions*, that is, indications of manuscript material not in the printed text; *additions*, that is, indications of printed material not in the manuscript; and *comments*.

The chart can be used to subdivide the Scribner's text into its component parts, thereby making it possible to retrace the step-by-step emergence of Hemingway as a major novelist.

Session 1, July 19, 20, or 21, 1925; Valencia, Spain.
    Manuscript: 193.1–12 (1805 total; 1713 net); ends at ink-color change to darker black that occurs shortly after the scene between Hem and Mrs. Carleton.
    Text: pp. 162–64 (483 words; 1489 omitted; 262 added), beginning "I'm going over to the hotel . . ." and ending ". . . and went down-stairs."
    Omissions: Paragraph in which Hem and Quintana agree that Niño is the best bullfighter either has seen; paragraph describing how Hem's door was banged open at 6:00 a.m.; and seven pages containing the scene with Mrs. Carleton.
    Additions: 99-word transitional passage on p. 162, beginning "I'm going over to the hotel . . ."; numerous changes in phrasing and details.
Session 2, July 20 or 21, Valencia.
    Manuscript: 193.12–19 (1140 total, 1118 net).
    Text: pp. 171–72 (444 words; 1100 omitted; 425 added), beginning "I left the crowd at the café . . ." and ending ". . . in the down-stairs dining-room."

Omissions: Three paragraphs about the bullfight; paragraph about the fashionable tourists arriving for the fiesta; paragraph about Belmonte; paragraph indicating that the entire group is intoxicated and that Don's girlfriend (later called Edna) is an awful person; references to Mrs. Carleton, except obliquely: "There's one American down here now that collects bull-fighters" (172).

Additions: 69-word prefatory section, beginning "I left the crowd at the café; 56-word transitional paragraph at the end of the scene between Jake and Montoya: "I went down-stairs . . ." (172).

Session 3, July 21, Valencia.

Manuscript: 193.20–25a (869 total; 843 net). Note: there are two pages numbered "25."

Text: pp. 172–175 (824 words, 228 omitted; 218 added), beginning "They were well ahead of me" and ending "He had very nice manners."

Additions: 100-word passage, beginning "Have you seen the bulls for tomorrow?"

Session 4, July 22, Valencia.

Manuscript: 193.25b–31 (1044 total: 1008 net).

Text: pp. 175–78 (844 words; 333 omitted; 171 added), beginning "I introduced them all around . . ." and ending "Brett was sitting looking straight ahead at nothing."

Comment: This completes the story on the unbound pages.

Session 5, July 23, Valencia.

Manuscript: 194.I.2–4 (545 total; 516 net); ends at a skipped line in the manuscript.

Text: Not in the Scribner's text; corresponds to first half of Galley 1 (ending ". . . obviously one of us") of the unpublished opening of *The Sun Also Rises* (382 words; 370 omitted; 230 added); the three galleys of this deleted opening are reprinted in Svoboda 131–37.

Omissions: 325-word paragraph primarily about Duff: her boredom, her posing for portraits, and her prodigious daily drinking.

Additions: 83-word opening paragraph; first two sentences of the next paragraph; last 90 words of the second paragraph, beginning "Brett always declared. . . ."

Session 6, July 24, Valencia.

Manuscript: 194.I.4–6 (848 total; 811 net); ends at a skipped line in the manuscript.

Text: Svoboda 132–33 (942 words; 175 omitted, 333 added), beginning "They arranged the whole business . . ." and ending ". . . something of the sort."

Additions: 149-word paragraph beginning "Brett was very different from Mike about drinking"; this paragraph is a revision of material on 194.I.2–3.

Session 7, July 25, Valencia.

Manuscript: 194.I.6–9 (807 total; 763 net); ends at a skipped line in the manuscript.

Text: Not in Scribner's text or in galleys.

Omissions: All of Session 7, most of which describes the uncle's funeral.

Session 8, July 26, Valencia.

Manuscript: 194.I.9–10 (413 total; 49 net); ends mid-sentence in a crossed-out description of the Quarter in Paris.

Text: Not in Scribner's text or in galleys.

Session 9, July 27, Valencia.

Manuscript: 194.I. 10–15 (1337 total; 1256 net): ends one sentence before passage corresponding to the beginning of the Scribner's text.

Text: Svoboda 133–137 (2292 words; 482 omitted; 1495 added)

Omissions: Six sentences from the description of the Quarter; references to Dos Passos, who had become "Alec Muhr" in revision.

Additions: Last paragraph of Chapter I; first part of Chapter II, including Jake's biography, ending ". . . had spent two years there"; and from "Alec, who thereafter took no part . . ." to "My word."

Session 10, July 28, Valencia.

Manuscript: 194.I.15–20 (1428 total; 1331 net); ends with the end of the chapter.

Text: Chapter I. pp. 3–7 (1349 words; 296 omitted: 302 added).

Session 11, July 29, Valencia.

Manuscript: 194.I.20–25 (1756 total; 1651 net).

Text: Chapter II, pp. 8–13 (1509 words; 296 omitted; 186 added).

Session 12, July 30, Valencia.

Manuscript: 194.I.26–31 (1575 total; 1518 net)

Text: pp. 14–19 (1298 words; 516 omitted: 304 added); ends as they leave for Braddocks' dancing club.

Session 13, July 31, Valencia.

Manuscript: 194.I.32–37 (1650 total; 1568 net)

Text: pp. 19–24 (1525 words; 307 omitted; 255 added); to end of chapter.

Session 14, August 1, Valencia.

Manuscript: 194.I.28–42 (1240 total; 1102 net); ends after a deleted passage in which Duff said she would drop in at Jake's office around cocktail time. Hemingway probably crossed this out at the beginning of the next session when he decided that Duff would plan to meet Jake at the Hotel Crillon.

Text pp. 25–29 (1132 words: 195 omitted: 222 added); ends with the line "I've got a rotten headache."

Additions: 124 word passage regarding Jake's wound (replacing a 78-word ms. passage), beginning "Don't talk like a fool" and ending ". . . for the person possessing them" (26–27).

Session 15, August 2, Valencia.

Manuscript: 194.I.42–48 (1724 total; 1661 net): to end of chapter.

Text: pp. 29–34 (1782 words; 229 omitted; 359 added).

Additions: most of paragraph on p. 31. beginning "I never used to realize it, I guess," including references to Brett and to Catholicism (Hemingway didn't decide to make Jake a Catholic until Session 29 on August 14); he also added the last sentence of the chapter.

Session 16: August 3, Valencia.

Manuscript: 194.I.48–49 and II.2–4 (723 total; 705 net).

Text: pp. 35–37 (672 words; 86 omitted; 58 added); probably ends with the line: "They've got good hors d'oeuvres."

Session 17, August 3, Valencia.

> Manuscript: 194.II.4–7 (702 total; 606 net); ends with ms, passage about who the hero is.
>
> Text: pp. 37–40 (648 words; 61 omitted; 103 added); to end of chapter.
>
> Comments: Probably written in a second session on August 3; August 4 was a travel day, on which Hemingway probably did not write.

Session 18, August 5, Madrid.

> Manuscript: 194.II.7–15 (1945 total; 1665); net); ends after a 183-word passage, crossed out by the next day, leading up to Gerald's announcement that he has a date with Duff.
>
> Text: pp. 41–44 (979 words; 1199 omitted; 522 added); ends with the words ". . . slowly sure of himself in the traffic."
>
> Omissions: anecdote about using Hotel Crillon stationery; 370 words of dialogue between Jake and Henry Stone (text: Harvey), about H. L. Mencken, writers becoming rich and famous, and Gerald Cohn: 280 more words of dialogue after Gerald joins them, regarding intelligence and Gerald's lack thereof: the session-ending scene mentioned above.
>
> Additions: The omitted ms. scenes were considerably rewritten and reduced.

Session 19, August 6, Madrid.

> Manuscript: 194.II.15–19 (1268 total; 1209 net); ends at a skipped line, one sentence before ms. Chapter IX, a chapter designation later crossed out.
>
> Text: pp. 44–48 (1190 words; 204 omitted; 141 added); ends "Yes Come on."
>
> Comment: August 7 was a travel day, on which Hemingway probably did not write.

Session 20, August 8, San Sebastian.

> Manuscript: 194.II.19–24 (1301 total; 1207 net).
>
> Text: pp. 48–51 (1215 words; 108 omitted; 115 added); to end of chapter.

Session 21, August 9, San Sebastian.

> Manuscript: 194.II.24–32 (2251 total; 2125 net); ends at a skipped line after the sentence, "Now I'll open it."
>
> Text: pp 52–59 (2000 words; 271 omitted; 193 added).
>
> Omissions: Six lines of dialogue between Jake and Duff (the ms. page on which these lines appear is reproduced in Svoboda 47).

Session 22, August 10, Hendaye.

> Manuscript: 194.II.32–35 (650 total; 592 net); ends prior to ink-color change to light blue that follows the sentence. "I'm not dead at all."
>
> Text: pp. 59–61 1532 words; 92 omitted; 23 added).

Session 23, August 11, Hendaye.

> Manuscript: 194.II.35–39 (1015 total; 980 net); to end of chapter.
>
> Text: pp. 61–65 (1003 words; 184 omitted; 203 added).
>
> Comment: Unlike the printed text, the manuscript is not divided into books.

Session 24, August 12, Hendaye.

> Manuscript: 194.II.39–42 (782 total; 769 net); completes Notebook II.
>
> Text: pp. 69–72 (813 words; 136 omitted; 264 added); ends with the line. "Let's eat."
>
> Omissions: In the manuscript Bill shows Jake a letter that the boxer sent; Hemingway left space for the letter to be written later.

Additions: From "Brett was gone" to ". . . the end of June." p. 69.

Session 25, August 12, Hendaye.

Manuscript: 194.III.2–6 (1017 total; 969 net); probably ends after the line, "Why not?"

Text: pp. 72–78 (1610 words; 373 omitted; 1030 added).

Additions: From "We walked down the Boulevard" through "I'm a nature writer" (72–74).

Comments: In a deleted ms. line Jake tells Bill that Duff is Mike's second cousin (194.III.6).

Session 26, August 13, Hendaye.

Manuscript: 194.III.6–9 (703 total; 687 net); ends prior to an ink-color change to brighter blue.

Text: pp. 78–80 (610 words; 256 omitted; 178 added): to end of chapter.

Additions: From "I'm sorry I can't go" to end of the chapter.

Session 27, August 13, Hendaye.

Manuscript: 194.III.9–11 (693 total; 674 net); to end of chapter.

Text: Not in text.

Comments: In this description of the Ledoux-Kid Francis fight, probably written in a second session on August 13, Hemingway briefly made Bill the first-person narrator. Ledoux, who serves as a model for Jake of how to live well, is a veteran bantamweight who has lost his punch and now fights on skill and courage. Both Jake and Bill become emotionally caught up by Ledoux's performance and don't even wait around to hear who won, not wanting to spoil what they've experienced. On their way back to Jake's flat, Jake tells Bill that in his own way Bill is as good a man as Ledoux is.

Session 28, August 14, Hendaye.

Manuscript 194.III.12–15 (732 total; 709 net); probably ends as Jake and Bill are about to take the train.

Text: pp. 81–84 (879 words; 86 omitted; 269 added).

Session 29, August 14, Hendaye.

Manuscript: 194.III.15.20 (1374 total: 1332 net): ends one sentence prior to the end of the chapter.

Text: pp. 84–89. (1387 words; 83 omitted; 152 added).

Comments: Probably written in a second session on August 14; during this session Hemingway decided to make Bill a Catholic, then changed his mind and instead made Jake a Catholic.

Session 30, August 15, Hendaye.

Manuscript: 194.III.20–26 (1648 total: 1574 net); probably ends after the driver ". . . started back to Bayonne."

Text: pp. 89–94 (1603 words; 91 omitted; 144 added).

Session 31, August 15, Hendaye.

Manuscript: 194.III.26–33 (1856 total, 1799 net); probably ends with the line "I was asleep when they came in."

Text: pp. 94–99 (1842 words; 421 omitted; 413 added).

Additions: From "and about something funny . . ." to ". . . I felt them dry in the sun" (97).

Comments: Probably written in a second session on August 15. Sometime between this session and the next, on the back cover of Notebook III, Hemingway wrote the outline for the rest of the novel.

Session 32, August 16, Hendaye.

Manuscript: 194.III.33–36 (942 total; 920 net); to end of chapter.

Text: pp. 99–102 (919 words; 63 omitted; 72 added).

Session 33, August 17, Hendaye.

Manuscript: 194.III.36–46 (2653 total; 2509 net); to end of chapter.

Text: pp. 103–111 (2560 words; 248 omitted: 323 added).

Comments: This was probably the last of the material written during Hemingway's Spanish vacation; the next day. August 18, he traveled back to Paris.

Session 34, August 19, Paris.

Manuscript: 194.III 46–52 (1482 total: 1456 net); probably ended with the completion of the notebook: ". . . and went towards the woods on the slope of the first hill."

Text: pp. 112–116 (1322 words; 432 omitted; 279 added).

Omissions: 120 words of dialogue after Jake says "I wanted to start him again," III.50–51; 160-word conversation in which both Jake and Bill shyly admit that they are happy most of the time. III.51–52.

Additions: From "It wasn't a bicycle" to "It'd mean I was a faggot." pp. 115–16.

Session 35, August 20, Paris.

Manuscript: 194.IV2.7 (1354 total; 1292 net); probably ends as Jake settles down "to read until Bill should come up for lunch."

Text: pp. 116–120 (1228 words; 162 omitted; 95 added).

Session 36, August 21, Paris.

Manuscript: 194.IV.7–11 (921 total; 902 net); probably ends in the middle of a ms. scene as Bill goes to sleep and Jake returns to his book.

Text: pp. 120–24 (1165 words; 294 omitted; 547 added); the revision of this ms. session ends with the line, "Utilize a little of this," p. 122; Hemingway added everything from "We uncorked the other bottle" to "I carried the other," pp. 122–24.

Omissions: 215-word discussion between Jake and Bill about Mencken and the Puritanical intolerance of both evolutionists and creationists concerning the Scopes Monkey Trial.

Session 37, August 22, Paris.

Manuscript: 194.IV.11–15 (1140 total; 1033 net); ends one paragraph before the end of the chapter.

Text: pp. 124–25 (97 words; 937 omitted; 4 added).

Omissions: In the ms. Hemingway recounted the A. E. W. Mason story, "The Crystal Trench," presumably as a foil for an Alpine story that Jake then tells. Unlike Mason's fantastic tale, Jake's story is realistic and gathers its force from ironic juxtaposition. Jake tells about seeing a man who had been doubled backwards by the force of an avalanche; when Jake, who had gone ahead for a blanket, entered the lodge, the unsuspecting and now-widowed wife looked up and was disappointed to see Jake instead of her husband; Jake delivered the blanket, then skied off in the other direction, staying away until darkness forced him to return.

Session 38, August 23, Paris.

Manuscript: 194.IV.15–21 (1498 total; 1330 net); probably ends as Jake and Bill are riding the bus back to Pamplona, probably after the line, "I suppose not."

Text: pp. 125–30 (1289 words; 135 omitted; 119 added).

Comments: Wilson-Harris appears only in this session; since he was not mentioned in the outline on the back of Notebook III, his inclusion may have been a recent choice, perhaps within the previous day.

Session 39, August 24, Paris.

Manuscript: 194.IV.21–25 (956 total; 905 net); probably ends as Bill says, "Must be swell being a steer."

Text: pp. 130–133 (926 words; 108 omitted: 143 added).

Session 40, August 25, Paris.

Manuscript: 194.IV.25–30 (1149 total; 1064 net); ends mid-paragraph as the group is walking" . . . to the corrals."

Text: pp. 133–37 (1100 words; 218 omitted; 233 added).

Comment: In the middle of this scene, Hemingway ran out of ink and used pencil to finish the session.

Session 41, August 26, Paris.

Manuscript: 194.IV.30–34 (1217 total; 1129 net); ends prior to their climbing down from the wall at the *descencajonada*.

Text: pp. 137–40 (1105 words; 122 omitted; 102 added).

Session 42, August 27, Paris.

Manuscript: 194.IV.34–39 (1282 total; 1217 net); ends at a skipped line prior to the sentence beginning "They went upstairs."

Text: pp. 140–44 (1176 words; 174 omitted; 127 added).

Omissions: In the ms., after Cohn leaves, Jake, Mike, and Duff converse about one of Duff's former lovers, a polo-playing American named Tom. The manuscript session ends with a comment by Jake that all the fun was going out of the fiesta.

Session 43, August 27, Paris.

Manuscript: 194.IV.39–41 (454 total; 406 net); to end of chapter.

Text: pp. 144–46 (399 words; 70 omitted; 73 added).

Comments: Probably written in a short second session on August 27.

Session 44, August 28, Paris.

Manuscript: 194.IV.41–46 (1616 total: 1554 net); ends as Jake is going to sleep.

Text: pp. 147–49 (817 words; 1142 omitted; 388 added).

Omissions: 885 words of Jake's monologue in which he says he is finished with Duff. He speculates that her going off with Gerald has made her ashamed, which, in turn, has caused her to act vulgar. But though he was losing his fondness for her, he also admits that her tryst with Gerald hurt him as badly as she had ever hurt him when she married Lord Anthony or when she went off with Michael. Jake hates Gerald even though Gerald's problem stems from his ignorance of social rules. In another omitted passage, Jake says that he is thirty years old. (For Hemingway's typescript revision of part of this material see Svoboda 21–22.)

Additions: This monologue appears in greatly revised and reduced form on p.

148, from "There is no reason . . ." to ". . . you could count on";
Hemingway also added the rest of the paragraph on p. 148 from "Perhaps
as you went along. . . ."

Session 45, August 28, Paris.

Manuscript: 194.IV.46–49 (713 total; 674 net); to end of chapter.

Text: pp. 149–51 (644 words; 89 omitted; 72 added).

Comment: Probably written in a second session on August 28.

Session 46, August 29, Paris.

Manuscript: 194.IV.49–52 and V.2–3 (1163 total; 947 net); probably ends
with the sentence "It was a fiesta and it went on for seven days."

Text: pp. 152–55 (878 words; 144 omitted; 88 added).

Comments: In the ms. Hemingway deleted a 138-word passage about the
nature of a seven-day fiesta, which can be dangerous, causing people to
act reckless as though there were no consequences. Nevertheless, he concludes that it was the people themselves and not the fiesta that caused
the trouble in Pamplona.

Session 47, August 30, Paris.

Manuscript: 194.V.3–9 (2005 total; 1936 net); ends as they are going to
sleep.

Text: pp. 155–161 (2011 words; 249 omitted; 297 added).

Session 48, August 31, Paris.

Manuscript: 194.V.9–14 (1274 total; 1187 net); ends with the line, "Just
imagine it."

Text: pp. 161–67 (1212 words; 203 omitted; 177 added).

Comments: In this session, Hemingway caught up chronologically to the opening scene of Session 1; he did not, however, rewrite any of the opening
scene, since he still intended to use it to begin his story; not until after
he had begun to revise the novel did he recast the opening. After the last
line of Session 48, Hemingway wrote an editorial directive to continue
writing about Niño, but by the time he began the next session, "Niño"
had become "Guerrita."

Session 49, September 2, Paris.

Manuscript: 194.V.14–18 (1349 total; 735 net); probably ends with the sentence, "Oh, you'll get a drink."

Text: pp. 167–69 (686 words; 252 omitted; 225 added).

Comments: In the ms. Hemingway wrote a 660-word passage, later deleted,
about Guerrita and the impossibility of capturing in words the emotions
inspired by his bullfighting. In the last paragraph of this deleted material,
Jake tells us that for a time Guerrita will be the hero and that Gerald,
who had been the hero, has been dropped.

Session 50, September 3, Paris.

Manuscript: 194.V.18–25 (2048 total; 1922 net); ends at an ink-color change
after the sentence concluding ". . . that led into town."

Text: pp. 169–71 and 178–84 (1877 words; 507 omitted; 491 added).

Comments: For pp. 171–78, see Sessions 2,3, and 4.

Session 51, September 4, Paris

Manuscript: 194.V.25–28 (777 total; 751 net); to end of chapter.

Text: pp. 184–87 (774 words; 89 omitted; 116 added).

Additions: Last two sentences of the chapter.

Session 52, September 5, Paris.

Manuscript: 194.V.28–33 (1393 total; 1325 net); ends with the waiter sitting ". . . with his head in his hand."

Text: pp. 188–92 (1138 words; 372 omitted; 272 added).

Session 53, September 6, Paris.

Manuscript: 194.V.33–36 (833 total; 806 net); ends as Jake goes to bed.

Text: pp. 192–95 (852 words; 64 omitted; 120 added).

Session 54, September 7, Paris.

Manuscript: 194.V.36–40 (1371 total; 1319 net); ends with the sentence about the bull's ear being left in the drawer.

Text: pp. 195–99 (1397 words; 127 omitted; 118 added).

Session 55, September 8, Paris.

Manuscript: 194.V.40–46 (1842 total; 1751 net); to end of chapter.

Text: pp. 199–204 (1586 words; 279 omitted; 133 added).

Session 56, September 9, Paris.

Manuscript: 194.V.46–48 and VI.2–7 (1948 total; 1803 net); ends after a crossed-out passage prior to the sentence beginning "When the fiesta boiled over. . . ."

Text: pp. 205–11 (1636 words; 289 omitted; 136 added).

Session 57, September 10, Paris.

Manuscript: 194.VI.7–13 (1833 total; 1695 net); ends with the words, ". . . It did not make bull-fighting wonderful to him any more."

Text: pp. 211–16 (1666 words; 134 omitted; 132 added).

Session 58, September 11, Paris.

Manuscript: 194.VI.13–20 (2145 total; 2079 net); ends with the sentence, "The crowd, running, went out the gate with him."

Text: pp. 216–221 (1940 words; 508 omitted; 401 added).

Comment: For a discussion of how Hemingway revised this material, see Svoboda 61–79.

Session 59, September 12, Paris.

Manuscript: 194.VI.20–24 (864 total; 830 net); ends mid-paragraph prior to ink-color change to black after Jake ". . . looked at the wall to make it stop."

Text: pp. 221–24 (759 words; 233 omitted; 160 added).

Session 60, September 13, Paris.

Manuscript: 194.VI.24–29 (1256 total; 1210 net); ends at an ink-color change after the sentence, "Let's drive down toward Hendaye."

Text: pp. 224–30 (1163 words; 135 omitted; 85 added).

Session 61, September 14, Paris.

Manuscript: 194.VI.29–33 (1227 total; 1194 net); probably ends as Jake arrives in San Sebastian.

Text: pp. 230–34 (1162 words; 168 omitted; 150 added).

Session 62, September 15, Paris.

Manuscript: 194.VI.33–38 (1730 total; 1676 net); ends as Jake says good night.

Text: pp. 234–37 (1310 words; 578 omitted; 214 added).

Session 63, September 16, Paris.

Manuscript: 194.VI.38–43 (1446 total; 838 net); ends with the line, "I went in to lunch."

Text: pp. 237–39 (761 words; 221 omitted; 128 added).

Comment: In the ms. Jake responds emotionally to the telegrams from Duff and decides that he will act hard-boiled and in-control when he sees her.

Session 64, September 17, Paris.

Manuscript: 194.VI.43–46 (919 total; 703 net); ends after dialogue, later crossed out in pencil, prior to an ink-color change, which begins, "She was trembling."

Text: pp. 239–41 (606 words; 214 omitted; 152 added).

Session 65, September 18, Paris.

Manuscript: 194.VI.46–47 (435 total; 418 net); ends at an ink-color change after the line, "Good."

Text: pp. 241–243 (343 words; 144 omitted; 67 added).

Session 66, September 19, Paris.

Manuscript: 194.VI.47–48 (244 total; 200 net); ends at an ink-color change at the end of the manuscript chapter (no chapter division in the printed text), as Duff asks that they ". . . never talk about it."

Text: p. 243 (184 words; 76 omitted; 63 added).

Session 67, September 21, Paris.

Manuscript: 194.VI.48–55 (1044 total; 1022 net); end of novel.

Text: pp. 243–47 (959 words; 238 omitted; 227 added).

Comment: The three pages of Notebook VII are numbered as though they were an extension of Notebook VI.

Works Cited

Baker, Carlos. *Ernest Hemingway: A Life Story*. New York: Scribner's, 1969.

Hemingway, Ernest. "Fiesta" (the manuscript title of *The Sun Also Rises*). Unpublished manuscript in the Hemingway Collection at the Kennedy Library.

―――. *The Sun Also Rises*. New York: Scribner's, 1926.

Svoboda. Frederic Joseph. *Hemingway and The Sun Also Rises: The Crafting of a Style*. Lawrence: The UP of Kansas, 1983.

Toreo: The Moral Axis of *The Sun Also Rises*

ALLEN JOSEPHS*

"Let the others come to America who did not know that they had come too late. Our people had seen it at its best and fought for it when it was well worth fighting for. Now I would go somewhere else" (*GHA* 285). Alfred Kazin cites this passage from *Green Hills of Africa* as an epigraph for the chapter on Hemingway in his new book *An American Procession*. Hemingway, he tells us, "at every stage of his life . . . found himself a frontier appropriate to his fresh needs as a sportsman and his ceremonial needs as a writer." And Hemingway differed from other "American writer-wanderers," such as Melville and Twain, because "Hemingway for the most part chose where he wanted to go" (357). I have started with the same passage to point out the same things but also to point out Hemingway's dissatisfaction with what was happening in America, much of which, in his view, had been "spoiled." Earlier in the same passage Hemingway wrote, "Our people went to America because that was the place for them to go then. It had been a good country and we had made a bloody mess of it . . ." (285).

In the long section which John Dos Passos got Hemingway to cut from the last chapter of *Death in the Afternoon*, Hemingway explained his peculiar odyssey in terms of the three peninsulas—Michigan, Italy and Spain—he had loved, lived in, and written about. He had loved Michigan very much when as a boy he had spent summers there, but each time he returned he found it changed more and more. The forests were cut and the streams were ruined and the fishing was no longer any good. Roads had been built everywhere, the tourists had caught all the fish and the farms had been abandoned. He cared about parts of northern Italy the way he had cared about northern Michigan, and he thought that when Michigan was ruined he could go to Italy as a solution to the problem. It was a matter of finding new good country in an old country. But Italy had been ruined too and made impossible by a tyranny he would not accept. So, via Paris he came to Spain where he liked the bull fights and the people and where he found some things being practiced he believed in (JFK, item 49; *Letters* 310).

*First published in *The Hemingway Review* 6 (Fall 1986): 88–99. Reprinted by permission of the journal.

Hemingway's correspondence from 1923–1925 makes it clear that he considered Spain a new "frontier," that is, that he found it still unspoiled. His letters show that he transferred his psychic allegiance from Michigan, via Italy, to Spain. "Spain is the very best country of all. It's unspoiled and unbelievably tough and wonderful," he wrote to James Gamble in December 1923 (*Letters* 107). "There is swell fishing. Like the Black when we first hit it," he told his old fishing buddy Howell Jenkins in 1924. Pamplona was the "greatest country you ever saw and right on the edge of the only trout fishing that hasn't been ruined by motor cars or railroads. . . . The people have any people in the world skinned. . . . You can only live once, Carper, and this is as good as the best of the best days we ever had on the Black and Sturgeon. . . . But Spain is the only country left that hasn't been shot to pieces. They treat you like shit in Italy now. All post war fascisti, bad food and hysterics. Spain is the real old stuff" (*Letters* 130–131).

Fishing, of course, was only part of the attraction. After his first trip to Pamplona in 1923, he sent a long letter to his old roommate and fellow veteran, William D. Horne, claiming that he had "just got back from the best week I have ever had since the Section. . . . You'd be crazy about a really good bullfight, Bill. It isn't just brutal like they always told us. It's a great tragedy—and the most beautiful thing I've ever seen and takes more guts and skill and guts than anything possibly could" (*Letters* 87–88). In the letter to Howell Jenkins about how great Spain was, he reiterated his enthusiasm: "Honest to Gawd Carper there never is anything like it anywhere in the world. Bull fighting is the best damn stuff in the world" (*Letters* 131). The *toreros* themselves were exactly the kind of people he had been looking for, as he wrote to Edward J. O'Brien: "Do you remember me talking one night . . . about the necessity for finding some people that by their actual physical conduct gave you a real feeling of admiration like the sealers, and the men off the banks [Georges Bank] up in your country [Boston]? Well I have got ahold of it in bullfighting. Jesus Christ yes" (*Letters* 117). *Toreros* were the most admirable artists of all, he told Ezra Pound: "The Plaza is the only remaining place where valor and art can combine for success. In all the other arts the more meazly and shitty the guy, i.e., Joyce, the greater the success in his art. There is absolutely no comparison in art between Joyce and Maera—Maera by a mile . . ." (*Letters* 119). In a letter to Scott Fitzgerald, written from Burguete in 1925—he had just been fishing in "wonderful country" and was headed for Pamplona and the fiesta he would fictionalize in *The Sun Also Rises*—he made his ultimate pronouncement on the whole subject: "To me heaven would be a big bull ring with me holding two barrera seats and a trout stream outside that no one else was allowed to fish in . . ." (*Letters* 165). Thirty-five years later Hemingway would describe Spain—in the second sentence of *The Dangerous Summer*—as the "country that I loved more than any other except my own. . . ." For the young Hemingway it was a matter of the last good country, to transfer the title of a Michigan story to Spain. And at the heart of that country were two of the things he loved best—unspoiled fishing and *toreo*, which, Hemingway's use of the term notwithstanding, we somewhat erroneously call bullfighting.

Trout fishing and *toreo*, of course, figure prominently in *The Sun Also Rises*, as well. In a long, rambling, discarded section of "Big Two-Hearted River," published posthumously as "On Writing," Hemingway revealed through his most autobiographical character, Nick Adams, the extent to which both these activities concerned him. Nick's feeling about fishing was explicit: "All the love went into fishing and the summer. He had loved it more than anything" (*NAS* 235). But for Nick, just as for Hemingway, *toreo* would later become paramount: "His whole inner life had been bullfights all one year. . . . Maera was the greatest man he'd ever known" (*NAS* 236–237).

In an article on *Death in the Afternoon* in the *Hemingway Review*, I have attempted to explain how the "explanation and exaltation of the pristine savagery of the *plaza de toros* was tantamount to Hemingway's embracing an ancient mystery and iconoclastically rejecting much of what passed for modern Western values" (16). Now I want to explore how and why *toreo* lies at the heart of *The Sun Also Rises*. In order to do so, we need to keep in mind something Hemingway wrote to Maxwell Perkins shortly after the book's publication: "The point of the book to me was that the earth abideth forever—having a great deal of fondness and admiration for the earth and not a hell of a lot for my generation and caring little about Vanities . . . I didn't mean the book to be a hollow or bitter satire but a damn tragedy with the earth abiding forever as the hero" (*Letters* 229). I can think of no classic of modern literature that has had as many and as varying interpretations as *The Sun Also Rises*, Comedy, tragedy, even Divine Comedy. Jake Barnes as the Fisher King of the Wasteland. Jake Barnes as a *cabestro*, as a steer, that is, as a gelding. Jake as the matador. Brett as a *vaquilla*, a fighting cow. Brett as a, yes, symbolic *toro*. Brett as an alcoholic nymphomaniac, as the bull-goddess, as the fertility goddess, and as her modern avatar, the bitch-goddess. The *corrida* as a Punch and Judy show; Jake as Don Quixote; Cohn as Don Quixote; Romero as Don Quixote; Jake as Sancho Panza. And this is only the tip of the iceberg.

Many of the critical problems derive from an improper or forced interpretation of the meaning of the *corrida de toros*—the bullfight. It is perhaps not surprising, then, to find that one of the best interpretations comes not from a book of literary criticism but from a critical book on the bulls, John McCormick's erudite study *The Complete Aficionado*.

McCormick makes a number of good points about this novel he judges "a masterpiece in small that might be considered as the only war novel in which no shot is fired but the rocket setting off the fiesta of San Fermín at Pamplona." All the "sympathetic characters have either been in the war or are toreros. Their shared experience has given them a common view, a common set of values, and even a private language. Cohn . . . is outside the charmed circle" (237).

McCormick has also understood that *The Sun Also Rises* is a novel of manners: "Although morality as such is almost never on the surface of the page, conduct, whether moral or immoral, is Hemingway's exclusive subject. The moral problems of an immoral world occupy his fullest attention . . ." (238). And he was the first (1967) to understand how we were supposed to grasp this exclusive—but elusive—subject: "We know this not from the moralizing of either writer or characters but through the symbolical burden placed upon *toreo*. The fiesta at Pamplona occupies the center of the novel, just as the characters' response to *toreo* is a measure of their human value in the eyes of Jake Barnes . . ." (238). The war and *toreo* as shared experience, the moral nature of the novel, *toreo* as the moral measure of these characters— McCormick's views, with no quixotic attempts to equate *The Sun Also Rises* and previous masterpieces, form the necessary foundation for what follows.

In a quite different vein, H. R. Stoneback has taken a very careful critical look at the geography of *The Sun Also Rises*, much of which, as Stoneback has demonstrated, Hemingway rearranged to suit his own purposes. In Stoneback's reading, the novel becomes a "quest, the pilgrimage undertaken in order to grow in grace" ("Hemingway and . . ." 144). Glossing Bill and Jake's walk through Paris and explaining the significance of the places they pass, Stoneback explores the figurative and symbolic journey they make, a journey which begins "in the shadow of Notre Dame, on the Ile Saint Louis, with its suggestions of the great crusading king and saint" (142), along the rue Saint-Jacques which is not at all in actual fact the "rigid north and south" that Jake proclaims, past the Val de Grace and through the "Port Royal district with its many associations with Pascal, another 'wounded' quester" (142). What does Hemingway intend with this "paysage moralisé"? In Stoneback's words, it was "the crucial historical importance of the rue Saint Jacques as the road which led south on the long pilgrimage to Santiago de Compostela, in northwestern Spain. Santiago was well known to Hemingway and for someone aware of the importance of this historical highway as a pilgrimage route it might indeed seem, symbolically, a "rigid north and south" (192). Stoneback goes on to explain much more about religious allusions and purposely rearranged geography in *The Sun Also Rises*, and he demonstrates quite convincingly the spiritual nature of Jake's quest "to know the 'values' " (149) through the "careful practice of ritual and discipline" (145) and, indeed, the spiritual design of the entire novel. Calling for "a moratorium on the old, weary circular discussions of the 'code' " (151), Stoneback concludes that "the deepest thrust of this novel is radically spiritual, and it is addressed directly to the radically 'secular age' . . . which has seemed for the most part incapable of deep engagement with Hemingway's vision" (151).

I have quoted Stoneback's article at some length for two reasons: one, because I think it is the most important article to date on *The Sun Also Rises*; and, two, because his decisive groundwork obviates any necessity on my part to prove the "radically spiritual" nature of the work.[1] Citing what is surely the most important passage in *Death in the Afternoon*, in which Hemingway equates the ecstasy produced by a great matador's work with religious ecstasy, Stoneback affirms that in *The Sun Also Rises* "the bullfight is meant to convey an emblem of moral behavior. For conduct to be moral, then, it must be rooted in courage, honor, passion, and it must exhibit grace under pressure. . . . Measured by these rigorous standards, the behavior of every important character except perhaps Romero is found wanting" (149). Both McCormick and Stoneback agree—the former on a secular plane, the later on a more spiritual one—that *toreo* is the measure of all the characters in the novel.

A significant change in the name Hemingway gave his matador bears out Stoneback's more spiritual interpretation. When Hemingway gave the characters fictional names, Antonio Guerra, "Guerrita," was the name he chose for his young artist, a name which echoed the name of the great nineteenth-century matador, Rafael Guerra, "Guerrita." *Guerra*, of course, means war and the diminutive sobriquet, the nom de guerre as it were, "Guerrita," has the effect of "warrior." When Hemingway rewrote the novel in Austria in the winter of 1926, however, he changed "Guerrita" to Pedro Romero, the name of the eighteenth-century matador who was almost indisputably the greatest of all time. He also rewrote the description of Romero's killing his second bull, changing the method of killing from the usual method to the far more difficult and dangerous way of killing *recibiendo*, or receiving the bull's charge, a method of which the historical Romero was the unchallenged master. The effect of these changes, which I will discuss in more detail later, is to remove the suggestion of war and to enhance the stature and artistry of Romero's work precisely at the climax of the novel.

Notice, please, that I said Romero's *work*, not Romero. And let us remember that both McCormick and Stoneback pinpoint *toreo*—the bullfight, rather than the bullfighter—as the measure of the men and women in this book. In a passage in the original manuscript, which was titled *Fiesta*, Hemingway wrote that for a while "Guerrita" was the hero. Then he cut the passage. Earlier on he had written that perhaps the matador was the hero of the story. Then he added, "He never really had a chance to be the hero. Or maybe there is not any hero at all. Maybe a story is better without any hero" (Svoboda 31).[2] This passage originally ended chapter five, and although Hemingway later cut it too, it probably revealed his original intention. In any case, it is *toreo* itself, the *art of toreo*, that is at the core of *The Sun Also Rises*.

To be sure, Romero creates that art, but a close look at the language Hemingway uses shows us that the work, the "it," is what matters: "Romero's *bullfighting* gave real emotion, because he kept the absolute purity of line. . . . Romero had the *old thing* . . ." (168, my emphasis throughout). "The crowd felt *it*, even the people from Biarritz, even the American ambassador saw it, finally" (215). "Pedro Romero had the *greatness*. He loved bullfighting. . . . Never once did he look up. He made *it* stronger that way, and did it for himself, too, as well as for her . . . and did *it* for himself inside, and *it* strengthened him. . . . He gained by *it* all through the afternoon" (216). "Each thing he did with this bull wiped [the fight with Cohn] out a little cleaner" (219). The artistic performance at the center of the *plaza de toros* is not merely the center of attention, it is also the source of moral amelioration and physical antidote.

As Romero's work, his *faena* with his second bull, continues, it becomes clear that he is achieving the kind of great performance that Hemingway would equate with religious ecstasy in *Death in the Afternoon:* ". . . the crowd made him go on. They did not want the bull killed yet, they did not want it to be over. Romero went on. It was like a course in bull-fighting. All the passes linked up, all completed, all slow, templed and smooth. . . . And each pass as it reached the summit gave you a sudden ache inside. The crowd did not want it ever to be finished" (219–220). Although Hemingway's technical descriptions of the bulls were not yet at their peak in 1925–26, he was obviously trying to describe, to quote the description from *Death in the Afternoon*, the *faena* "that takes a man out of himself and makes him feel immortal while it is proceeding," that is capable of "moving all the people in the ring together and increasing in emotional intensity as it proceeds . . . in a growing ecstasy of ordered formal, passionate, increasing disregard for death . . ." (206–7).

This moral, spiritual, even ecstatic dimension of *toreo* ought not surprise us, especially if we bear in mind Stoneback's injunction to desist from seeking heros and codes and to concentrate instead on the spiritual. The art of *toreo* is at the center of *The Sun Also Rises* precisely because it is spiritual. In taurine circles great young performers are not entirely facetiously known as Messiahs. Hemingway used that very term—"Messiah" as well as "Resurrexit"—in his original draft of the novel, and he attempted to describe the effect of great art in the *plaza*, the great art of "Guerrita" Romero, by comparing it to the consummation of a first love together with the feeling of death, a combination which returns us to ecstasy. It is probably just as well he cut that passage, too, but the attempt, however overly romanticized, again reveals explicitly the effect he was after.

All the characters who make the pilgrimage to the fiesta at Pamplona are measured—morally or spiritually—around the axis of the art of *toreo*. Romero, the creator of that art, because he is an innocent and a creator in the face of punishment and death, comes closest to perfection. Montoya and the true aficionados are the keepers of the faith. The morally undiscerning American ambassador and company are splendid examples, by contrast, of what Alfred Kazin meant when he wrote that Hemingway "knew that, morally, the bourgeois world was helpless" (364). They do not know the values, especially not the value of *toreo*. As Montoya, whom Hemingway once called "a highly moral hotel keeper" (*Letters* 240), puts it: "People take a boy like that. They don't know what he's *worth*. They don't know what he *means*" (172, my emphasis). Jake knows perhaps better than anyone, even though he betrays him, and Brett, in her finest moment, comes to understand. Cohn, on the other hand, understands nothing and worries that the *corrida* may bore him. Loveless lover of Brett, vanquished victor of Romero, Cohn is devoid of moral content, a moral bankrupt who is completely out of place at the fiesta, outside, in McCormick's phrase, the charmed circle.

Jake understands better than anyone because only Jake moves freely and knowingly in both the profane world of the Lost Generation and the sacred world of *toreo*. The very reason for the fiesta is, of course, to stop profane time, clock time, historical time. Jake understands perfectly: "The things that happened could only have happened during a fiesta. Everything became quite unreal finally and it seemed as though nothing could have any consequences" (154). A fiesta is time out of time, sacred time, original time, primal time, *illud tempus* to use Mircea Eliade's term. In fact, the "rituals or important acts" which Eliade lists in *The Myth of the Eternal Return* as abolishing profane time—"alimentation, generation, ceremonies, hunting, fishing, war, work" (35)—read virtually like a catalog of Hemingway's only subjects: eating and drinking; love and sex; hunting and fishing; war; writing; and ritual ceremonies, of which *toreo* is a clearly supreme example. On the following page Eliade continues as though he were writing on *toreo* in *The Sun Also Rises:* "Insofar as he repeats the archetypal sacrifice, the sacrificer, in full ceremonial action, abandons the profane world of mortals and introduces himself into the divine world of the immortals" (36).[3]

I have no doubt that Hemingway had a full intuitive understanding of what he was doing with *toreo* at the center of his novel. In a letter to Max Perkins in 1926 he called *toreo* "the one thing that has, with the exception of the ritual of the church, come down to us intact from the old days . . ." (*Letters* 237). *Toreo* is not just the moral axis of *The Sun Also Rises*, it is the *axis mundi* of Hemingway's artistic vision, and it is not accidental that the rituals of the *plaza de toros* and of the church are joined in Hemingway's mind as they are in much of Spanish art.[4]

In order to see how Hemingway went about sacralizing the fiesta with Romero's great *faena* and kill *recibiendo*, how he constantly pared away the trivial and the profane, we need only to compare sections of the original manuscript of the novel in the JFK Library with the published text, concentrating on the fictional changes he made in the morally central character of Pedro Romero. Sixty years ago in Schruns, Hemingway did the ". . . most difficult job of rewriting I have ever done . . . in the winter of 1925 and 1926, when I had to take the first draft of *The Sun Also Rises* which I had written in one sprint of six weeks, and make it into a novel" (*MF* 202).

Interesting phrase that last one: ". . . and make it into a novel." But anyone who reads that rough draft he completed in six weeks alongside the published version will understand precisely how Hemingway went about converting an often journalistic and autobiographical account, especially at the beginning, into a classic of modern literature that in the intervening sixty years has lost none of its fascination.

When Hemingway began writing the novel in Madrid and in Valencia in the second half of July, 1925, within days of the actual events that had inspired it, he used real names. It began *in medias res* in Pamplona:

> Cayetano Ordonez
> "Nino de la Palma"
> Fiesta
> I saw him for the first time in his room in the Hotel Quintana in Pamplona.
> (Svoboda 6)

The characters are called Hem, Don, Duff, Pat, Hadley, Harold or Loeb, Quintana and Nino. What started as a more or less factual account began to evolve into a more fictional account as he continued to write the first draft, and, of course, changed radically in the rewriting as he began to "make it into a novel."

Even though he originally based the characters in part on real people, "inventing from experience," as he often called it, the final creation transcended altogether the historical facts of the summer of 1925. As Hemingway somewhat overstated the case to Max Perkins, ". . . the only stuff in the book that was not imaginary . . ." was the "Brett biography," which of course he cut out at Fitzgerald's urging (*Letters* 224).

That being the case, what are we to make of this statement from *The Dangerous Summer*? "I had known Cayetano years before and had written a portrait of him and an account of his fighting in *The Sun Also Rises*. Everything that is in the bull ring in that book is as it was and how he fought. All the incidents outside the ring are made up and imagined. He always knew this and never made any protests about the book" (50). What concerns me most are the phrases "a portrait of him" and "Everything that is in the bull ring in that book is as it was and how he fought." Those statements need to be taken with a grain of salt since Hemingway transformed Cayetano Ordóñez, "Niño de la Palma," as much or more than he did anyone else, within the *plaza de toros* as well as without. Hemingway's facts about Spain are frequently not correct, but the myths that he makes from the shards of history are far more satisfying than any accurate reconstruction. "Everything that is in the bull ring in that book" is not as it was, and Pedro Romero is, fortunately, not a portrait of Cayetano Ordóñez. To watch the transformation from Cayetano Ordóñez, who fought as "Niño de la Palma," the kid from the Palm (the Palm was the name of Ordóñez's father's shoe shop which failed,

Oag 64–65), into Antonio Guerra, "Guerrita," and finally into Pedro Romero is to begin to understand how Hemingway turned the base metal of banal facts into *The Sun Also Rises*.

In the *in medias res* beginning, which was later moved to its chronological position in Chapter XV, the matador is called "Nino de la Palma" and then just "Nino." "Cayetano Ordóñez" is never used after the first line of the rough draft. It was as though Hemingway had started with and then immediately abandoned the real man, choosing to use fictionally only the artistic persona, "Nino de la Palma." In fact his matador and Cayetano Ordóñez were nothing alike. Cayetano was called "gay, impulsive and warmly generous" by his admirers (Oag, 66), but his detractors spoke of him as a hard drinker, a womanizer, and a spendthrift, in short the classic Andalusian *señorito* who thrived, for a while, on all-night flamenco parties (his wife, Consuelo, whom he married in 1927, was a half-gypsy flamenco dancer, Oag 68). His admirers said he lost his *afición*, his desire to fight bulls (Oag, 69; Cossío III 684 ss.), but his detractors claimed he lost his nerve. Hemingway went on at length about Cayetano Ordóñez's cowardice in *Death in the Afternoon*, calling it, among other things, "cowardice in its least attractive form" (88), and he described his season of 1926 as "the most shameful season any matador had ever had up until that year in bullfighting. What had happened was that the horn wound, the first real goring, had taken all his valor. He never got it back" (89–90; see also 167, 171, 222, 434). It was not actually Cayetano's first goring, nor was it the worst season a bullfighter had ever had. Still, Hemingway's judgment was somewhat justified after having watched Cayetano be disastrously bad four times running in Pamplona in 1926, so bad that he had failed to kill one of his bulls and had had to be protected from the crowd by the police and later smuggled ignominiously out of the Hotel Quintana's backdoor to escape on the train (Iribarren 94–96).

In 1925, however, he "looked like the messiah who had come to save bullfighting if ever any one did," as Hemingway put it in *Death in the Afternoon* (88). In the *in medias res* beginning the narrator and Quintana agree that "Niño" was the best they had ever seen, with the finest and purest style and the greatest authority in the *plaza*, a description which echoed contemporary accounts of "Niño de la Palma" that year (e. g., Iribarren 57). When Hemingway again turned his attention to the Pamplona section, now in its proper chronological place, he kept the name "Niño de la Palma" and "Niño" through the description of the first *corrida*. Then he went back and changed the matador's name to "Guerrita" and added a passage about "Guerrita's" background. Hereafter in the rough draft the matador is called Antonio Guerra, "Guerrita," and "Niño de la Palma" has disappeared.[5]

The real matador, that is, has disappeared altogether and a fictional one named "Guerrita" has taken his place. "Guerrita" is—as the real Cayetano Ordóñez was—from Ronda, and his name—as Cayetano's had—echoes that of a great nineteenth-century matador. As Hemingway would explain some years later in *Death in the Afternoon*, Cayetano Ordóñez had the same name as a matador from Madrid famous a hundred years before, Cayetano Sanz; and he was from Ronda, the cradle of the art (89). In what became one of the most famous phrases in the annals of the bulls, the critic, Gregorio Corrochano, wrote, "Es de Ronda y se llama Cayetano," (He is from Ronda and is named Cayetano), making "Niño de la Palma" famous at once, a kind of instant myth, the newest messiah come to save the *corrida* (*DIA* 89). Hemingway tried to use this bit of propagandistic myth-making for his own purposes to make his fictional "Guerrita" into a "messiah" and also to try to suggest a kind of mythic greatness about him by giving him the same name as the late nineteenth-century master from Córdoba, Rafael Guerra, who, as we have seen, was also called "Guerrita." All of Spain, the narrator in the rough draft tells us, was with him for two reasons: he had the same name as one of the greatest matadors of all time; and he was from Ronda which was the birth place of the art. With the creation of Antonio Guerra, "Guerrita," we are yet another step removed from the historical Cayetano Ordóñez.

The final steps in the evolution from the historical Cayetano Ordóñez to the fictional Pedro Romero occurred in the major rewriting in Schruns the next winter. Now he had become simply Pedro Romero, dedicated, serious and dignified; and the messianic propaganda and the too pointed partial coincidences in names, and the *apodos*, the artistic names, such as "Niño de la Palma" or "Guerrita" were cut.

In their place Hemingway used a far more effective device. On the surface there was merely a fictional matador whose artistic ability and integrity suited Hemingway's purposes perfectly. Beneath the surface lay a historical reality which is never mentioned or alluded to in the published text of *The Sun Also Rises*. Submerged beneath the fictional character lay the real Pedro Romero.

Son and grandson of *toreros*, the serious, dignified matador from Ronda was unquestionably the greatest taurine artist of those waning years of the eighteenth century in which the Romero dynasty became the virtual founders of the modern art of *toreo*. Goya painted an exquisite portrait of him in his prime which reflects Romero's genius with no exaggeration or flourishes. To examine Goya's portrait of him—the assured grace, the understated elegance, the paradoxical delicacy of the prominently displayed right hand that dispatched 5,600 bulls in his long and unmarred career—is to encounter in Romero the prototype of the matador as the Spanish Romantic artist and popular hero. John Fulton, who is the only American to have written knowledgeably about the bulls from the unique vantage of a professional life as a matador, appraises Romero succinctly as "the most impressive matador in bullfighting history" (Fulton 14; Josephs, *White Wall of Spain*, 148–149)[6]. The name Hemingway chose for his young matador as the measuring stick for the modern misfits of the Lost Generation was perfect. And Hemingway's device was as brilliant as it was unobtrusive. The average reader would not be beleaguered by intrusive technical details, yet the aficionado would immediately perceive Hemingway's full meaning.

One final detail assures us that Hemingway was consciously inventing from experience to create a superbly crafted work of art. In the rough draft, "Guerrita" kills the last bull in the usual manner, *volapié*, that is going to the bull. Yet in the finished version, with the descriptions of the *corrida* much augmented and revised, Romero kills in the far more difficult and dangerous manner called *recibiendo* or receiving the bull. The early version probably corresponds to the way "Niño de la Palma" actually fought and killed in Pamplona in 1925.

Why, then, did Hemingway revise it? In *Death in the Afternoon* he tells us that "Niño de la Palma" killed *recibiendo* "once in Madrid" (238). And on July 16, 1925, Hemingway saw one of Cayetano Ordóñez's greatest afternoons in the Madrid *plaza* (*Letters* 167). He did not see him in Madrid again before the rewriting, so it is probable that the revisions in the *corrida* scene do not reflect what happened "as it was" merely in Pamplona but rather comprise an invention from experience based on a conflation or a distillation of the artistic success of Cayetano Ordóñez that Hemingway saw in Pamplona, Madrid and Valencia that year.

But, Cayetano notwithstanding, there is a more compelling reason to explain the change. The historical Pedro Romero, as Hemingway knew, killed all the 5,600 bulls of his career *recibiendo* (*DIA* 239). It was only fitting, then, that the historical figure's newly created fictional avatar kill in the same manner. The aesthetic purity, the inherent danger and the historical reverberation of Romero's kill *recibiendo* fittingly and elegantly enhance the climactic moment of the fiesta and of the novel. The changes, in effect, become important elements in the "making of the novel," and the metamorphosis of Cayetano Ordóñez into Pedro Romero becomes a splendid analogue for the transformation of certain events of the summer of 1925 into *The Sun Also Rises*. All that is left of Cayetano Ordóñez are a few brilliant moments of the season of 1925, moments that had originally inspired Hemingway to begin the novel. It is hardly accidental that he began with Cayetano but no less fortuitous that he ended with Pedro Romero, a fictional matador who, *mutatis mutandis*, owed much more to his legendary eighteenth-century namesake than to the benighted and already dissolute young man who, with no ruining from a Brett or a Duff, disappointed all Spain the following year.[7]

The fictionalizing of Pedro Romero, once we have seen Hemingway's revisions, allows us to return to a mythic consideration of *toreo* as the moral or spiritual axis of the novel. In the process of fictionalizing him, Hemingway made Romero into an idealized or moralized figure. We are not only dealing with a *paysage moralisé*, but with a *figure moralisé*, a kind of exemplar whose perfect sacrifice of the bull is the precise center and climactic moment of *The Sun Also Rises*. In fictionalizing his matador, Hemingway purified him (by contrast, all the other matadors mentioned in *The Sun Also Rises* are historical, real *toreros*), which is not to say that Romero is perfect—only that he is more worthy of being the sacrificer, more worthy that is of projecting us into sacred time. As Eliade put it:

> A sacrifice . . . not only exactly reproduces the initial sacrifice revealed by a god *ab origine*, at the beginning of time, it also takes place at that same primordial mythical moment; in other words, every sacrifice repeats the initial sacrifice and coincides with it. All sacrifices are performed at the same mythical instant of the beginning: through the paradox of rite, profane time and duration are suspended. And the same holds true for all repetitions, i.e., all imitations of archetypes; through such imitation, man is projected into the mythical epoch in which the archetypes were first revealed . . . insofar as an act . . . acquires a certain reality through the repetition of certain paradigmatic gestures, and acquires it through that alone, there is an implicit abolition of profane time, of duration of "history": and he who reproduces the exemplary gesture thus finds himself transported into the mythical epoch in which its revelation took place. (35)

Hemingway, of course, had not read Eliade, but his subtle re-naming of the matador and his intentional change to the exemplary kill *recibiendo* have quite the effect Eliade describes and transport us at once to that mythical epoch, to that first Golden Age, of the original Pedro Romero when modern *toreo*, the archetypal and paradigmatic art of *toreo*, was first created. Beyond that, *toreo*, at its deepest level, goes back much further and recapitulates as spectacle and as rite the oldest myths of the Western world. It is the art that structurally comes closer to the origin of art—the bull must still actually die—than any we know.[8] Hemingway clearly understood, albeit somewhat intuitively, that *toreo* was at the still center of sacred time, and that it was *still* at the center of sacred time, still a part of the eternal present. His revisions provide rather irrefutable proof of his understanding and of his intentions.

Octavio Paz has written very lucidly about this eternal present in his penetrating essay, *The Labyrinth of Solitude*. "The fiesta," he tells us, "becomes the creator of time; repetition becomes conception. The golden age returns. . . . As Van der Leeuw said, 'all rituals have the property of taking place in the now, at this very instant' " (210). According to Paz, rituals and fiestas allow us to participate in mythical time: "Thanks to participation, this mythical time—father of all the times that mask reality—coincides with our inner, subjective time. Man, the prisoner of succession, breaks out of his invisible jail and enters living time: his subjective life becomes identical with exterior time, because this has ceased to be a spatial measurement and has changed into a source, a spring, in the absolute present, endlessly re-creating itself. Myths and fiestas, whether secular or religious, permit man to emerge from his solitude and become one with creation" (210–211).

Paz concludes his essay by reminding us that contemporary man has rationalized these things but not destroyed them. "Modern man," he warns, returning to his central image of the labyrinth, "likes to pretend that his thinking is wide-awake. But this wide-awake thinking has led us into the mazes of a nightmare in which the torture chambers are endlessly repeated in the mirrors of reason" (212). It may be pretty to think that reason is our way and our light, but Paz and Eliade, and Jung and company, and Ernest Hemingway do not believe it.[9] Beneath the nightmarish maze of pure reason lies a deeper and subliminally profound labyrinth, the archetypal labyrinth of so many ancient myths, one which has on rare occasions an extraordinarily exact ritual recapitulation in the arcane and sacrifical art of *toreo*. I once equated that ancient archetype and the art of *toreo*—rare perfect *toreo*, the most exact living configuration of the labyrinth and the most radical entry into sacred time we have left in the Western world—this way: "And in the unchanging utopia of my mind's eye, *in illo tempore* of memory, I can still see—as once I actually did—a lone man, a motionless matador, standing in the center of an ecstatic *plaza* as a great white bull charges and charges again, and the man, the matador, winds him and winds him again in inconceivably slow and successively longer arcs around his waist, spinning a lair for their common minotaur, through the sunlight, through the shadow, as though possessed of some ageless thread of Ariadne" (*White Wall of Spain* 160).

What but such an entry into sacred time could Hemingway have had in mind when he described "the faena that takes a man out of himself and makes him feel immortal while it is proceeding, that gives him an ecstasy, that is, while momentary, as profound as any religious ecstasy" (*DIA* 206)? What when he placed such a *faena* at the very center of *The Sun Also Rises*, a *faena* that the crowd did not ever want to be finished, but which was finished in Romero's exemplary, perfect, and paradigmatic kill *recibiendo*?[10] And why if not to point up the sacred nature of this mythical novel of manners did he change his title from *Fiesta* (with its secondary English connotations of festivity, as opposed to Octavio Paz's use of the word in its Spanish sense, that is, a religious celebration such as the one celebrated in honor of San Fermín at Pamplona) to *The Sun Also Rises*? Why if not to contrast the sacred and the profane did he use as opposing epigraphs Gertrude Stein's otherwise utterly banal dictum "you are all a lost generation," which in context becomes a virtual maxim of historical and profane time, and the poignant and poetic quote from *Ecclesiastes*, the poetic, cyclical and repetitive nature of which denies the importance of the individual or the individual generation and affirms the essence of sacred time in which, as Octavio Paz wrote, man emerges from his solitude and becomes one with creation?

At the still sunlit center of the book is the art of *toreo*, Romero's great *faena* and kill *recibiendo*, and around that in concentric circles, every one at a greater remove from the Promethean fire at the center, revolve first Romero himself, the mystagogue; then Montoya and the true aficionados, the priests; after that at varying distances Jake and Brett and the foreign aficionados, the not altogether faithful converts who make the pilgrimage to Pamplona seeking momentary solace in the fiesta; then farther away in near darkness the uninitiated American Ambassador and his entourage; and finally, altogether blind to the rising sun at the heart of the novel, alone and uncomprehending, Cohn. It was, as Hemingway said, a damn tragedy, the tragedy of his generation inescapably imprisoned in history, irredeemably lost in profane time, with the earth abiding forever as the only possible hero. *The Sun Also Rises*—his first, finest and most profound novel—is Hemingway's tragedy of modern man's fall from primordial grace. If we fail to heed his prophetic admonition to our radically secular age, we only incur the graceless risk of accompanying Cohn in outer darkness.

Notes

1. Stoneback's article is only surpassed by his new article which appears in this issue of *The Hemingway Review*, greatly amplifying his views on the spiritual nature of *SAR*. Rather than quoting at length, I will merely refer the reader to his new piece, "From the rue. . . ."

2. I am greatly indebted to Professor James Hinkle who lent me a copy of his own collation of the original manuscripts (from which I have paraphrased) and the published version of *SAR*.

3. This article, as well as much of my other work, would have been greatly diminished without benefit of Professor Eliade's lifetime dedication to the world of the sacred. I am much indebted to his brilliant insights and would like herein to express formally my appreciation of the work of the recently deceased historian of religion.

4. I discuss in more detail the sacred nature of *toreo*, especially in Hemingway's mind, in my article on *Death in the Afternoon* (cited above); and in much greater detail in general terms in *White Wall of Spain* (cited below), especially in Chapter Six, "Matador."

5. In the original beginning of the novel there is a curious passage in which three men carrying another man come into the hotel at 6:00 a. m., open "Hem's" door by accident and then depart. "Hem" cannot quite see who it is but he thinks it was "Nino." That passage sounds like the real Cayetano, and the implication is, of course, that he was dead drunk. In any case, the drunk disappears with the historical Cayetano.

6. The description of Romero is adapted from *White Wall of Spain*. On p. 132, I reproduced Goya's splendid portrait of Pedro Romero, which is unfortunately printed backwards. The original is in the Kimbell Art Museum in Fort Worth.

7. Stoneback points out in his current article ("From the rue . . .") another dimension to Pedro Romero—that *romero* in Spanish means "pilgrim." Did Hemingway know that or is it merely fortuitous? We will probably never be able to prove it either way, but in Stoneback's reading, *romero* gives Romero even greater resonance (Stoneback 28).

8. For a comparison of the origins of tragedy and the origins of *toreo*, see McCormick (24). It is important to understand, I think, that the *corrida* is actually *less* developed

structurally than Greek tragedy "since it never evolved beyond the stage of the sacrifice and became fixed on the sacrifice itself. Tragedy may echo sacrifice but in tragedy all is mime and symbolic action. The *corrida* on the other hand is quite real" (Josephs, *White Wall of Spain*, 150–151). There is no "otherness" quite like the *toro bravo*.

9. It is interesting to note that after the great *corrida* when everything becomes anticlimatic, Bill and Jake agree that the fiesta was "like a wonderful nightmare" (222). And Jake says he feels "Low as hell . . . like hell . . . [and again] like hell" (222–223). Sacred time is evidently giving way to profane time. To escape "the mazes of a nightmare in which the torture chambers are endlessly repeated in the mirrors of reason," Jake gets "drunker than I ever remembered having been" (223).

10. I am reminded here of another seminal passage: "Now the essence of the greatest emotional appeal of bullfighting is the feeling of *immortality* that the bullfighter feels in the middle of the great faena and that he gives to the spectators. . . . He gives the feeling of his *immortality*, and, as you watch it, it becomes yours. Then when it belongs to both of you, he proves it with the sword" (*DIA* 213, my emphasis).

Works Cited

Cossío, José María de. *Los toros*. Madrid: Espasa-Calpe, 1969.

Eliade, Mircea. *The Myth of the Eternal Return*. Trans. Willard R. Trask. Princeton: Princeton UP, 1971.

Fulton, John. *Bullfighting*. New York: Dial, 1971.

Iribarren, José María. *Hemingway y los sanfermines*. Pamplona: Editorial Gómez, 1970.

Josephs, Allen. "*Death in the Afternoon*: A Reconsideration." *The Hemingway Review* II. 1 (Fall 1982): 2–16.

———. *White Wall of Spain: The Mysteries of Andalusian Culture*. Ames: Iowa State UP, 1983.

Kazin, Alfred. *An American Procession*. New York: Random House, 1984.

McCormick, John (with Mario Sevilla Mascareñas). *The Complete Aficionado*. Cleveland: World, 1967.

Oag, Shay. *In The Presence of Death: Antonio Ordóñez*. New York: Coward-McCann, 1969.

Paz, Octavio. *The Labyrinth of Solitude*. Trans. Lysander Kemp. New York: Grove, 1961.

Stoneback, H R. "Hemingway and Faulkner on the Road to Roncevaux." *Hemingway: A Revaluation*. Ed. Donald R. Noble. Troy, New York: Whitston, 1983, 135–163.

———. "From the rue Saint-Jacques to the Pass of Roland to the 'Unfinished Church on the Edge of the Cliff.' " *The Hemingway Review* VI, 1 (Fall 1986): 2–27.

Svoboda, Frederic Joseph. *Hemingway and The Sun Also Rises: The Crafting of a Style*. Lawrence: U P of Kansas, 1983.

The Importance of Count Mippipopolous: Creating the Code Hero

ROBERT E. FLEMING*

One of Hemingway's most interesting minor characters is Count Mippipo-polous, who appears only in the Paris section of *The Sun Also Rises*. Critics have been little interested in the Count, tending to lump him together with a host of other minor characters who people the Paris scene. However, the Count seems to have had a certain importance for Hemingway, who, at an early stage of the book's composition, had intended to have him reappear in the Pamplona section of the novel.[1] It is possible that Count Mippipopolous is one of the early prototypes in Hemingway's fiction of the character type known variously as the "code hero" or the "tutor,"[2] a type whose minor character flaws are outweighed by his strict observation of a code.

The Count may at first seem to be an unlikely heroic figure. He is overawed by Brett when he first meets her, has a rather unpleasant appearance, tends to show off by conspicuous spending, and although he has a thin veneer of good manners, he often reverts to the kind of bad grammar that is probably more natural to him than the overly correct English which he uses most of the time. Certain facets of his appearance and behavior suggest that he might have fit in well with the principal characters of two other famous novels of the 1920's, Sinclair Lewis's *Babbitt* (1922) and F. Scott Fitzgerald's *The Great Gatsby* (1925). Mippipopolous's elk's tooth, his habit of ordering champagne and expensive brandy, and his suggestion that he knows many important people would endear him to George F. Babbitt and other denizens of Zenith, while his business, a string of sweetshops in the States, may well be like Jay Gatsby's drug stores, the cover for some kind illegal activity such as a bootleg operation or bookmaking; like Gatsby the Count likes to throw parties for other people and then watch them enjoy themselves without actively participating. Nevertheless, Hemingway seems to be groping in the early pages of *The Sun Also Rises* toward the creation of a type that would serve him well in the latter part of the novel and in his future work as well.

*Reprinted by permission from the *Arizona Quarterly* 44 (Summer 1988): 69–75. Copyright © Arizona Board of Regents.

The Count is characterized in a total of three scenes in *The Sun Also Rises*. By examining these scenes, the reader can follow the process of Hemingway's own discovery of what he meant the Count to be.

Scene one is so brief as to suggest that Mippipopolous was intended simply as one of the gallery of odd characters who peopled the Left Bank of the twenties. A fat man "who wore an elk's tooth on his watch chain," the Count appears in the company of "the little Greek portrait-painter, who called himself a duke, and whom everyone called Zizi."[3] He is impressed by Brett, addressing her as "your Ladyship," and assuming that Paris is not so impressive to her as it is to others because "I guess you have pretty big doings yourself over in London" (28). When Jake leaves the Select, the Count is buying champagne, probably in an ostentatious manner, though he has adopted his most gentlemanly style of speech: "Will you take a glass of wine with us, sir?" (29) he asks.

The second scene concerning the Count is merely a conversation about him between Brett and Jake. Here Brett identifies Mippipopolous as "quite one of us" (32). Jake seems to have doubts about him, since he asks, "Is he a count?" Jake is probably drawing a parallel between the Count and Zizi, who "called himself a duke." The juxtaposition with Zizi, however, adds to the stature of the Count; while the titles of both may be questioned, either the Count's is real or it should be. In effect, Brett suggests that it doesn't matter, because the Count has a genuineness of his own: " 'I rather think so, you know. Deserves to be, anyhow. Knows hell's own amount about people. Don't know where he got it all. Owns a chain of sweetshops in the States. . . . He's one of us, though. Oh, quite. No doubt. One can always tell' " (32). Brett goes on to tell how the Count propositioned her, offering her ten thousand dollars to go to Biarritz, Cannes, or Monte Carlo with him. The difference between the Count and Robert Cohn is apparent in the way the former took Brett's refusal to sleep with him: "He was damn nice about it" (33) and when Brett tells him she's in love with Jake, he offers to take the two of them to dinner.

This second scene establishes the Count as perhaps more important than his first appearance suggested. Brett's recognition of him as "one of us" may be cryptic, leading the reader to wonder which of her various cliques the Count fits into—those with titles, those who have been wounded by the war, those who maintain a certain stoicism in the face of tragedy and chaos? But his importance obviously goes beyond that of a Braddocks, a Robert Prentiss, or a Harvey Stone. A man of mystery who combines a title with a mundane occupation, the Count may even suggest diabolic associations, since he knows *"hell's* own amount about people" (emphasis added). Does one become so insightful running candy stores? On the other hand, in manuscript Hemingway suggested that the Count might represent supreme good by depicting him sitting in the bar looking like Buddha.[4] What has been disclosed so far is enough to pique the reader's curiosity.

The Count's final scene satisfies that curiosity, at least as far as Hemingway was willing to satisfy it. The Count, in his most gentlemanly guise, arrives at Jake's flat with Brett, bearing a huge bunch of roses, and Brett reveals that he has made peace with the concierge, whom Brett awakened late the night before, by overtipping her to the tune of 200 francs. The Count is obviously flaunting the ostentatious side of his character again, and he continues in that vein when Brett sends him out for champagne, for he brings back not a bottle or two but an entire basket, carried in, complete with ice, by his liveried chauffeur. Furthermore, he suggests that it is good wine, because "I got this from a friend of mine that's in the business. . . . This fellow raises the grapes. He's got thousands of acres of them. . . . He's a baron" (57). When Brett teases the Count about his title and his titled friends, however, he modifies his boastful speech. "I assure you, sir, [he tells Jake] . . . It never does a man any good. Most of the time it costs you money" (57). Yet a moment later, Mippipopolous slips back into his Babbitt-like role, showing off a gold cigar cutter that he wears on his watch chain and proudly offering Jake "a real American cigar" (58).

During this final scene including the Count, he continues to slip back and forth between his two personae—the social climbing American gangster who is brash, ungrammatical, and crude, and the man of the world who is self-effacing, soft-spoken, and polite. On the one hand he tells Brett, "You got class all over you" and "You got the most class of anybody I ever seen. You got it. That's all" (58). On the other hand, his sophistication and detachment are often most apparent, as when he tells Brett that a fine wine should not be diluted by mixing it with emotion and drinking toasts.

But the Count's last scene culminates in an event which establishes his true role in the novel. When Brett suggests that the Count is a bumpkin from the United States who has not "been around much," he replies, "Yes, my dear, I have been around very much. I have been around a very great deal" and then elaborates on this statement: "I have been in seven wars and four revolutions. . . . And I have got arrow wounds" (59–60). Like the reader, Brett is skeptical and asks to see the arrow wounds: "The count stood up, unbuttoned his vest, and opened his shirt. He pulled up the undershirt onto his chest and stood, his chest black, and big stomach muscles bulging under the light. . . . Below the line where his ribs stopped were two raised white welts. 'See on the back where they come out.' Above the small of the back were the same two scars, raised as thick as a finger" (60).

These scars, incurred during the course of "a business trip" to Abyssinia when the Count was just twenty-one, are his stigmata, which identify him as a character who knows what he is talking about in the postwar era just as surely as Christ's nail holes and spear wound identified him as the risen God-man in the New Testament. From this point on, it is clear that he is to be regarded as a wise man, whose pronouncements are not merely the opinions of a fat old man from a sweetshop empire, but a sort of prophet who has been tested in the fire and who has remained intact.

What lessons does the Count impart to Jake and to the 1926 reader who may still be wandering in the postwar wasteland? Not the final lessons that will be taught by Pedro Romero, whose ultimate role in the novel was probably still unclear to Hemingway when he created the Count, but lessons that will help Jake toward a philosophy of life. The Count likes quiet in spite of the fact that he is currently sampling Paris nightlife; he insists on getting good value for his money (as he does when he buys old brandy); he serenely observes the frantic lives of members of the lost generation rather than getting caught up in them personally; and he maintains his self-respect, not allowing Brett to manipulate him as she does most of the men in her life.

Jake learns from the Count. To him, the quiet of Burguete and of San Sebastian are restful rather than boring after the frenetic activities of Paris and Pamplona. Like the Count, Jake learns to recognize the world as a marketplace where one must pay for what he wants, as he reflects in Chapter XIV and again in Chapter XIX:

> I thought I had paid for everything. . . . No idea of retribution or punishment. Just exchange of values. You gave up something and got something else. Or you worked for something. You paid some way for everything that was any good. I paid my way into enough things that I liked, so that I had a good time. Either you paid by learning about them, or by experience, or by taking chances, or by money. Enjoying living was learning to get your money's worth. . . . The world was a good place to buy in. (148)
>
> Everything is on such a clear financial basis in France. It is the simplest country to live in. . . . If you want people to like you you have only to spend a little money. I spent a little money and the waiter liked me. He appreciated my valuable qualities. He would be glad to see me back. I would dine there again some time and he would be glad to see me, and would want me at his table. It would be a sincere liking because it would have a sound basis. (243)

There is, of course, a hint of irony in the second quotation because between the two chapters Jake has been exposed to a more fully developed code hero and a code which transcends the Count's. But finally, Jake's last remark in the novel—"Isn't it pretty to think so?"—suggests that he has at last attained the detachment that will allow him to observe Brett without being manipulated and thus, like the Count, to maintain his self-respect.

The Count, then, is an important character, not only in *The Sun Also Rises* but in Hemingway's work as a whole. Appearing as he does in the earliest section of a book written in 1925, he anticipates the code heroes of "Fifty Grand" (1927), "In Another Country" (1927), "The Gambler, the Nun, and the Radio" (1933), and "The Short Happy Life of Francis Macomber" (1936), as well as Pedro Romero. The only code hero story that appeared in print before *The Sun Also Rises* was "The Undefeated," and it appeared, significantly, during the summer of 1925, just when Hemingway was struggling with the beginnings of his first novel.[5] While the Count is not the perfect code hero, and suffers by comparison with the more finely-finished concept embodied in Romero in the latter part of the novel, he does illustrate the courage, the grace under pressure, and the peculiar code of honor associated with code heroes. Among the purposeless lost souls of postwar Paris, the Count stands out: he knows who he is, and he has learned to take the limited pleasures that the world can give him without bemoaning the fact that he cannot have more. His philosophy of life, while by no means the complete answer to the ills of the twentieth century, is enough to allow him to face the wasteland of modern life.

Notes

1.   Frederic Joseph Svoboda, *Hemingway & "The Sun Also Rises"* (Lawrence: University Press of Kansas, 1983), pp. 24–27.
2.   As first described by Philip Young, the code hero exemplifies the importance of a code which informs his life. *Ernest Hemingway: A Reconsideration* (New York: Harcourt, Brace & World, 1966), pp. 63–74. See also Earl Rovit, *Ernest Hemingway* (New York: Twayne, 1963), pp. 53–77 and Arthur Waldhorn, *A Reader's Guide to Ernest Hemingway* (New York: Farrar, Straus and Giroux, 1972), pp. 21–29. Hemingway's code heroes are often unlikable, flawed characters who have serious moral defects or who have petty faults that make them appear unsympathetic on first readings. However, when they are engaged in their own particular fields of endeavor—like Manuel Garcia of "The Undefeated" or Jack Brennan of "Fifty Grand"—they are clearly superior to those around them. They know what rules they intend to live by, and they live by them with remarkable consistency. Garcia, for example, is illiterate and perhaps even stupid; he lacks sufficient skill to go along with his determination to return to the bullring. But because he refuses to admit his defeat, he could say with Santiago, "Man is not made for defeat. He can be destroyed but not defeated." Jack Brennan, of "Fifty Grand," not only commits a crime that would get him barred from further fights—he bets against himself in a championship fight—but is also undercut by his stinginess. He tips poorly and communicates with his wife by letters rather than by telephone because a letter costs only two cents.
3.   Ernest Hemingway, *The Sun Also Rises* (New York: Charles Scribner's Sons, 1970), p. 28. All future references are to this edition and are inserted parenthetically.
It is significant that everybody calls the painter "Zizi." The term is used to refer to the penis in France when talking to small children. Applied to the Count's little friend, it might suggest mild contempt or even that Zizi was a homosexual as his real life model was presumed to be. See James Charters, "Duke Zizi" in *Hemingway and "The Sun" Set*, Bertram D. Sarason, ed. (Washington, D.C.: NCR / Microcard, 1972), pp. 271–274. Robert McAlmon, "On the Characters in *The Sun Also Rises*," also in Sarason, pp. 225–227, identifies Count Mippipopolous as possibly a Spanish painter, but says little about him.
4.   Svoboda, p. 27.
5.   "Stierkampf," *Querschnitt*, 5 (1925), 521–535 and 624–633.

Signs, Motifs, and Themes in
The Sun Also Rises

MICHAEL S. REYNOLDS*

At the beginning of chapter five, as Jake takes us down the boulevard with him on his way to work, he notices three familiar street people: the man with the jumping frogs, the man with the boxer toys, and the man pushing the roller that leaves a damp word—CINZANO—on the sidewalk (35). While inviting readers to read these signs with him, Jake does not analyze them for us. One might say there is no need to analyze them, for not everything that happens on the surface of a novel bears significance: the street signs may be nothing more than accurate surface details. Yes, they are that, but streets are full of details, indeed so full that were Jake to tell us everything he saw on his way to work, the novel would get no further than that single morning. Therefore, these signs chosen by the author / narrator should at least be checked for significance, for of all the detail that Jake takes in on that particular morning, he has selected these signs to suggest what it was like on the boulevard.

Both the man with the jumping frogs (presumably toys) and the man with the toy boxers are selling their merchandise to tourists. Jake steps aside "to avoid walking into the thread with which his girl assistant manipulated the boxers. She was standing looking away, the thread in her folded hands" (35). Ralph Ellison thought this scene significant enough to use a variation on it in *Invisible Man*. Perhaps there is more here than Jake cares to comment on. First, one can say that selling and buying are a part of the novel: a simple exchange of values, as Bill Gorton says. The two pitch-men, we note, do not delay Jake any more than the three-card monte games on the streets of New York catch the attention of the streetwise. Jake is not on native ground, but he is not a tourist. That's the point. He avoids the unseen control threads, for he has watched the game plenty of times before. But the controls are there; someone is always pulling the strings. Like toy frogs, we jump to stimuli; like toy boxers, we respond violently when our strings

*Reprinted with permission of Twayne Publishers, an imprint of Macmillan Publishing Company, from *The Sun Also Rises: A Novel of the Twenties* by Michael S. Reynolds, 74–94. Copyright © 1988 by G. K. Hall & Co.

are pulled. Throughout the novel Jake reacts to stimuli over which he has little control. In Pamplona his strings are pulled and he responds violently with Cohn, a trained boxer, who puts Jake out on the floor. Then at San Sebastian, Brett pulls his string with a telegram and he jumps to her aid. But here in Paris, Jake, the experienced man on the street, is not taken in or delayed by toys. Instead he follows the CINZANO sign the rest of the way to work. When one thinks of the effects of alcohol on *The Sun*'s characters, Cinzano, the staple Italian vermouth, may be an ironic and prophetic sign for Jake to follow.

For a sign to convey meaning, it must be read within a larger language that the reader understands. If one does not read Greek, the signs of Athens will mean nothing. If the reader of *The Sun Also Rises* does not understand that Paris prostitutes were required by law to be checked regularly for venereal disease, then he will miss the significance of Georgette's yellow card, the sign that she is disease free. The sign reaches our attention long after we watched Jake and Georgette in the taxi. There, when Jake told her he was sick, she replied, "Everybody's sick. I'm sick, too" (16). Not knowing at that point she had her yellow card, the reader was justified in thinking that Georgette was admitting to a venereal disease. Once we know about her yellow card, we have to reevaluate her "sickness." It is not sickness of the flesh but of the spirit, and in that sense, everybody in the novel is, indeed, sick. If we do not have the language framework for reading the sign of the yellow card, we never read her remark right.

The fault is not really ours or Hemingway's. Language continually changes: it is never the same river twice. Authors, writing for their contemporary audience, not eternity, rely on their readers' sharing a common language framework. Thus Chaucer used contemporary signs that his readers understood to characterize his pilgrims on their way to Canterbury. Today we no longer, unaided, recognize the meaning of many of Chaucer's signs. A wart on the nose, red hair, a gap-toothed smile—none of these signs means today what it did to Chaucer's readers. The same is becoming true for Hemingway's signs.

Today we have to explain more of them than was necessary when the novel was first published. In another hundred years, several pages of footnotes will be required to read the book Hemingway wrote. Examples from Jake's fishing trip to Burguete should suffice. Bill Gorton's apparently amusing conversation about "irony and pity" is a contemporary sign that no longer points to any clearly understood meaning. In 1925 "irony and pity" were current buzz words among the literary establishment. Their source was probably Anatole France, and they were a critical shorthand in New York where Max Perkins, Hemingway's editor, appreciated the satire. The average 1926 reader in Kansas City probably missed that sign altogether. Some things in books, Hemingway later insisted, were put in only for the amusement of other writers. Surely Jake's remark about "Henry's bicycle" (115) falls into this category. In the type draft sent to Scribner's, Bill's advice to Jake read: "That's what you ought to work up into a mystery. Like Henry James' bicycle." Bill was referring to the obscure rumor that Henry James had suffered an accident which had rendered him impotent. Charles Scribner's and Sons refused to print the statement, for they were James's publishers. Although the great man was dead (1916), his New York publisher still felt honor bound to defend him. Hemingway dropped the "James'," leaving the anecdote even more obscure than it began.

Other signs during the Burguete excursion are equally obscure today because they referred to topical events long forgotten. For example, when asked to say something ironic when asking the Burguete waitress for jam, Jake says, "I could ask her what kind of jam they think they've gotten into in the Riff" (114). No reader today can be expected to know about the 1925 guerrilla war being fought in the northern reaches of French and Spanish Morocco. Berbers, under the leadership of Abd-el-Krim, were fighting for their freedom against both French and Spanish colonial forces. By the late summer of 1925, the Spanish forces under the leadership of General Rivera were mired down in an unpleasant war with no end in sight. Jake's waitress is as unamused as contemporary readers for whom mention of a Riffian war is a meaningless sign.

It is worth noting that signs need not be words. Each day of our lives we read and sometimes misread hundreds of nonverbal signs. When Jake is returning to his rented rooms (29), he passes the statue of Marshall Ney where he stops to read the inscription on a wreath of faded flowers. Ney's statue is a sign that Jake understands; Ney was a heroic military leader who did his duty in a losing cause. Ney commanded the rearguard action during Napoleon's disastrous retreat from Moscow and rejoined Napoleon in his ill-fated attempt to regain power after his Elba exile. When Napoleon went under at Waterloo, Ney was executed for treason. Ney represents an earlier set of values no longer current in the postwar world that troubles Jake. Considering the debacle that Jake is about to be involved in, the Field Marshall's statue is an ironic sign for the reader who knows a little French history. This sign also says that Jake Barnes knows enough to pause knowledgeably at the statue. Thus we have double signs: first the statue itself; then Jake standing in front of the statue. Each sign conveys meaning without explanation, just as everyday people convey meaning to us through appearances.

We speak of reading the character of a person, which is analysis of verbal and nonverbal evidence. Georgette, herself, is a sign who requires reading. Most of the foreigners at the *dancing*, particularly the Braddocks, misread her. They take Jake's irony seriously and treat the whore as if she were a respectable lady. Brett and the homosexual men read Georgette perfectly, and so does the landlord's daughter. At Pamplona, Brett and Pedro Romero have no difficulty reading each other's body language. When

Brett wants to listen to Jake's confession, he tells her it will be in a language she does not understand. Literally, of course, it will be spoken in a foreign language, but Jake is really saying that Brett would not understand the concepts of guilt and forgiveness that Catholic confession entails. Afterward at the gypsy camp, Brett has her palm read in a language she does understand. That is, she understands pagan ritual but not Christian ritual. She is, by her own admission, "damn bad for a religious atmosphere" (208). There are plenty of signs to verify Brett's self-analysis. While the religious procession of San Fermin passes in the street, Brett is down cellar with a rope of garlic around her neck with drunken men dancing about her in pagan hilarity.

A more difficult sort of sign is the one that seems to read in a straightforward manner, or one that sounds familiar enough that we assume we understand it. In foreign countries, armed with a smattering of the language, tourists continually get themselves into difficulty by assuming that some foreign word has the same meaning as the American word which it looks like. The same sort of difficulty arises when we watch Jake Barnes balancing his checkbook (30). Because it is something most readers have done and because the figures seem familiar enough, we read past the sign without giving much thought to it. First, we should note that this scene follows hard on the heels of Brett's promise to meet Jake at the Crillon. "I've never let you down, have I?" she asked (29). Well, yes, actually she has in the past let him down, and as we know, she will continue to do so. In his room Jake balances his bankbook, now concentrating on money, the one value that he can count on.

We have no problem understanding that part of the sign, for the larger context that provides its meaning has not changed since 1926. However, those figures from Jake's American bank account bear closer inspection. He tells us that since the first of the month he has written four checks. Carefully he subtracts the four unidentified checks: the opening balance of $2432.60 becomes $1832.60. Without totaling the checks, Jake has given us the mathematical signs to conclude that since the first of the month he has withdrawn $600 from his American bank account. Given the writer's task of choosing details to inform the reader, we might ask why Hemingway and Jake included this detail. What does the sign tell us? First, it tells us that Jake has more money than he spends. He's not in debt. He's not dependent on anyone else to support him. Given the financial condition of Mike Campbell, Brett Ashley, and Robert Cohn, Jake's independence is important in characterizing him. The bank balance, in spite of the $600 expended, also tells us that Jake saves money—an American virtue in the Franklin tradition.

Another meaning is equally clear: Jake is not wealthy in the way that Count Mippipopolous is, but neither is Jake poor. But what we cannot say is how much that money is worth in 1926 terms. Of course, Hemingway's readers in 1926 had no such problem with the sign. Today the reader tends to register the figures in the framework of his own bankbook and today's money, which is to misread the sign. Some comparisons will clarify my point. This table is for American prices then and now.

GOODS	1926 PRICE	1987 PRICE
Flour (5 pounds)	$0.30	$0.79
Pork Chops (per pound)	$0.40	$1.99
Bacon (per pound)	$0.50	$1.99
Butter (per pound)	$0.53	$2.03
Potatoes (10 pounds)	$0.49	$2.29
Coffee (per pound)	$0.50	$2.99

Since 1926, the consumer price index and the wholesale price index have tripled. The average personal income has grown from $705 in 1926 to $3943 in 1970. In terms of today's dollar, Jake's six-hundred-dollar expenses would be closer to three thousand dollars.

But comparing American prices from two different eras is not the point. Jake was in Paris, not New York. Today in Paris, prices have risen to match New York prices. But in 1925, when the novel was written, American tourists flocked to Paris to take advantage of the incredibly low prices, for the exchange rate was twenty-five French francs to the dollar. At that exchange rate, a nickel bought a half liter of beer, and a furnished flat rented for forty dollars a month. In Hemingway's own feature story—"Living on $1000 a Year in Paris" (1922)—he claims that a decent breakfast costs about six dollars *a month*, decent suppers about fifty cents each. "There are," he wrote, "several hundred small hotels in all parts of Paris where an American . . . can live comfortably, eat at attractive restaurants and find amusement for a total expenditure of two and one half to three dollars a day."[1] In another assessment, written the same year as *The Sun Also Rises*, the author says that on $2500 a year in Paris one can live in a comfortable hotel, take tea at the smart places two or three times a week, spend winter in Florence or on the Riviera, and summer on the Brittany beaches or in Switzerland.[2]

Re-reading Jake's bank statement using the 1926 frame of reference shows us how badly we misread the sign the first time through. Our narrator has spent enough money "since the first of the month" to support a more frugal man for six months. What conclusions can we now draw? One can safely say that Jake is spending more money than a single man in Paris needs to spend, but there may be mitigating circumstances. Jake is a journalist; he may have professional expenses that he's not telling us about. But we have no evidence to indicate that he has expenses at the $600 level. Looking at the habits Jake tells us about, we notice that he takes taxis without ever thinking about the bus or the metro. He buys drinks at the cafés and bars. On his night on the town, he treats Georgette to supper at Madame Lavigne's, which she says is "no great thing of a restaurant" (16). Sarcastically, Jake suggests that she can keep the cab and go on to Foyot's for dinner. Even at Foyot's, an expensive restaurant of the highest class, a modest dinner for two people would have been only two hundred francs, or eight dollars at the exchange rate. Jake is not an extravagant spender. During the rest of the night, he pays for three taxi rides, buys several drinks for himself and others, and leaves two dollars (50 francs) for Georgette. All around, it has not been an expensive evening for Jake who, as we have seen, prides himself on getting good value for his money.

When he returns to his rented rooms, we see only a living room, bedroom, and bath—nothing palatial certainly. What, then, is the point of his bank balance? An obvious conclusion is that Jake is not telling us everything about his life. I do not mean to suggest that Jake Barnes is leading a secret life, only that he is arranging his story, telling us what he thinks is relevant, stage managing the details. I do not think he is trying to mislead us: he is not an untrustworthy narrator. Neither is he a narrator who takes special pains to explain everything to his reader. If he picks up more bar bills than are his fair share, he does not feel compelled to talk about them.

Perhaps I am making more of this bank statement than it warrants, yet there it is on the page for us to deal with. It seems somewhat extraneous; we do not need to know the exact figures. Given Hemingway's usual careful selection of detail, we are being tacitly asked to deal with this data in a sensible manner. We never will know what Jake spent his $600 on. There are no old bills to dig up: Jake Barnes has no life beyond these pages, which contain all the data we will ever have. The manuscript sheds no better light on the matter: what you see on the printed page about the bank balance is what Hemingway wrote in the blue exercise book on the first draft. I suggest, therefore, rather than directing us inward toward smaller supporting details to account for the spent $600, this sign directs us outward toward larger issues. Hemingway has placed a marker early in the text telling us to pay close attention to money transactions, for, in some way, they will be important to our reading of the novel. This conclusion reinforces what I suggested in the last chapter: money is the only value that has meaning in this cross section of the postwar world.

Money, of course, is not a moral value, being neither good nor evil; affluence or bankruptcy do not disclose one's spiritual condition. Paying one's bills on time is a social value, not a moral one. Nowhere in the New Testament does Christ advise those seeking spiritual salvation to place their faith in their bank balance. Jack the Ripper probably paid his bills promptly the first of every month. Would-be followers of Christ are advised in the New Testament to give their money to the needy and follow their Leader. And we all remember what Christ did to the moneylenders in the Temple. In this context, the point becomes clear. If money has become the only operative value for this postwar generation, then it is spiritually sicker than it knows. That is the wider truth toward which the sign of Jake's bank balance points. When the only criteria for moral behavior becomes "getting good value for one's money," then we are truly bankrupt, spiritually and morally.

In June of 1925, a month before he began writing *The Sun Also Rises*, Hemingway read and praised *The Great Gatsby*, written by his friend F. Scott Fitzgerald. As several commentators have noted, there is more than a passing similarity between the two books. Indeed, when twenties historians quote from fiction, they almost always draw from both books, for each indicts a sick society that has lost its moral bearings. Fitzgerald's narrator, Nick Carraway, contributes to the formation of Jake Barnes. The two are both seemingly minor-character narrators who think that they are less important than the story they are telling. Both men are bewitched by a woman with whom they cannot have sexual relations: Nick by Daisy Buchanan, his cousin and a married woman; Jake by Brett Ashley. Both men act as procurers: at Gatsby's request, Nick arranges for him a clandestine meeting with Daisy; Jake, as we've seen, arranges for Brett her meeting with Pedro Romero. Both narrators are left alone at the end of their stories to clean up after the careless main participants.

Such parallels are not coincidental. Hemingway, who was competitive about everything, particularly writing, approached his novel like a challenge match with Fitzgerald. After breaking his contract with his publisher, Boni and Liveright, Hemingway switched to Fitzgerald's publisher, Charles Scribner's and Sons, where he worked with Fitzgerald's editor, Max Perkins. This change of publisher was carried out at Fitzgerald's urging, for he genuinely admired the young Hemingway, who seemed to be leading the active, uncompromising life that Fitzgerald saw slipping away from himself. Hemingway was flattered by the established writer's interest, and their correspondence for a couple of years is one of the funniest of American's literary relationships. Between the two of them, they anatomized the moral condition of America in the mid-twenties. Fitzgerald at home and Hemingway in Paris were taking the same pulse, hearing the same sick wheezing in the national respiration. Both writers focused on the same symptom: moral confusion in which money became the principal measurement. Daisy Buchanan's voice sounds like money to Gatsby, and the sound of money tinkles satirically through Jake's narrative.

When the slightly drunk Bill Gorton tries to get Jake to buy a stuffed dog, he tells Jake, "Simple exchange of values. You give them money. They give you a stuffed dog" (72). Throughout the novel Jake is faced with moments of simple exchanges of values: he gives Georgette a meal for her conversation; he pays for drinks, for food, for tickets; at Pamplona he exchanges his membership in Montoya's club to satisfy Brett Ashley's desire for Romero. All about him, money is a steady issue. At Burguete, Bill Gorton says jokingly, "One group claims women support you. Another group claims you're impotent" (115). Jake, as we know, is self-supporting, but Robert Cohn, Mike Campbell, and Brett Ashley are dependent one way or another on family support. As Count Mippipopolous knows, money buys affection, support, agreement, and service in an age when no other principles have survived the war. One of the nicer counterstatements to this cynical view takes place when Jake tries to tip the barmaid in a small Spanish town: "I gave the woman fifty centimes to make a tip, and she gave me back the copper piece, thinking I had misunderstood the price" (106). That, too, is a sign: a miscommunication; a conflict of two value systems; a reminder to Jake that not everyone is for sale.

At the end of the fiesta, when the group has rented the car to Bayonne (229–32), their parting is soured by the bill, which, as Jake told himself earlier, always came. Mike cannot pay his bar bill or his share of the car. Jake pays for the rental car. As Jake tips his way out of France and back to San Sebastian, his ironic tone of voice almost loses control: "Everything is on such a clear financial basis in France. . . . No one makes things complicated by becoming your friend for any obscure reason. If you want people to like you you have only to spend a little money" (233). When Brett calls him to Madrid, Jake finds that Romero has paid the hotel bill, in effect paying for his brief affair with Brett.

Adrift in a world with its moral compass broken, Jake makes do as best he can. He did nothing to create the "clear financial basis" for human relationships that surrounds him. In Pamplona, in one of his rare self-examinations, Jake told us: "You paid some way for everything that was any good. I paid my way into enough things that I liked, so that I had a good time. . . . Enjoying living was learning to get your money's worth. . . . The world was a good place to buy in. It seemed like a fine philosophy. In five years, I thought, it will seem just as silly as all the other fine philosophies I've had" (148). Five years after the publication of *The Sun Also Rises* was 1931, and America, along with the rest of Western civilization, was deep in the Great Depression. What Hemingway, through his narrator Jake Barnes, has carefully described are the careless attitudes of the generation that carelessly spent its way into the whirlpool. In retrospect, Jake's bank balance is a clear sign pointing toward one of the novel's central issues that even the most casual reader finally understands.

At the beginning of chapter 3 a more elusive sign appears that needs our attention. Enroute to their dinner at Madame Lavigne's, Jake and Georgette pass the New York *Herald*'s window of clocks (15). Georgette asks what they are for. Jake tells her, "They show the hour all over America." She replies, "Don't kid me." At first reading, this exchange seems to characterize Georgette as a less-than-sophisticated citizen who does not believe in foreign time zones. She is perfectly existential, living entirely in the present tense and, for that matter, in the present time zone. If the *Herald*'s clocks were the novel's only sign calling our attention to the problem of time, we might be able to ignore them. However, time references so proliferate that eventually one must question their presence.

These time references vary: some refer to time of day; some to day of week; some to the year. Many take curious turns that are sometimes perplexing. Some moments in the novel last longer than others. At Pamplona, Bill and Mike argue about how long the run before the bulls in the street lasted. Mike says it was fifteen minutes. Bill replies: "Oh, go to hell . . . You've been in the war. It was two hours and a half for me" (200). Duration depends upon the observer. At San Sebastian, Jake has to reset his watch, having gained an hour crossing the frontier (234), an arbitrary time line. Early in the novel Frances Clyne complains that no one keeps appointments punctually anymore. So when Brett promises to meet Jake at the Crillon Hotel at five the next day (29), neither Jake nor the reader is greatly surprised when Brett fails to keep the rendezvous. Throughout the novel, Brett is late. She is late getting to Pamplona and late returning, for she operates on her own standard time. No one finds fault with her failing, nor does she take particular notice of it. However, one way to read this sign would be the same way we should have read the *Herald*'s clocks: time is relative; it depends on where you are. Brett's time is also relative to herself: she arrives as she pleases, declaring her own time zone.

Brett's self-centered time is easily accommodated, but what are we to make of the calendar derived from the specific dates that Jake provides in the course of the novel? Jake tells us that on Monday, 20 June, he and Bill attended the Ledoux-Kid Francis boxing match (70, 81). In fact, Hemingway witnessed the fight himself, but not on 20 June. The real fight took place on Tuesday, 9 June 1925. Today no one remembers the fight or when it took place, but in 1926 some of the Paris readers might have remembered. Why would Hemingway have Jake cite the wrong date of a known fight? Furthermore, 20 June did not fall on a Monday in 1924 or in 1925, the only two years in which the action of the novel could have taken place. Later we are told that the San Fermin festival began on Sunday, 6 July, which would fit the 1924 calendar, but would not fit with the death of Bryan. Perhaps Hemingway simply made mistakes, forgot the correct date. It is not the sort of mistake he tended to make, but it is possible. But why even give us the exact date? It does not contribute to our following the narrative flow. There was no need to call our attention to the date, but, with Hemingway's approval, Jake gives us other specific dates in chapter 9. We learn that Jake plans to leave for Spain on 25 June (81), and that he does not see Brett again until 24 June. Why are we being given this information that seems to add nothing to the novel? Certainly the conflict is not dependent on readers knowing the correct date.

A similar piece of seeming irrelevant information is placed in the spot-light at the very end of the novel. While Jake and Brett are drinking martinis in Madrid (244), Brett remarks that Romero was only nineteen years old. A few lines later she tells Jake that Romero was born in 1905. "Think of that," she says. Jake replies somewhat laconically, "Anything you want me to think about it?" Brett tells him not to be an ass, and they order another round of drinks. But Jake's question needs attention: what should the reader think of this information, this sign. What does it say? That Romero was younger than Brett? We knew that already. That 1905 was nineteen years ago? Add it up: that makes the action take place in either 1924 or 1925, depending on when his birthday came in the year. Knowing *The Sun Also Rises* was published in 1926, the reader can now say that the action took place in one of the two previous years. But no matter how hard we try, we will not be able to make the novel's action fit into the calendar from either year. That is the catch and maybe the point of those dates at the end. If we follow the clues and construct the calendar, the dates do not work. Something has gone wrong with time in this novel, whose title assures us that the sun rises, that time is relevant to our reading.

If you still think this mountain looks more like a mole hill, consider the drunken conversation between Jake and Bill on their fishing trip. When Bill jokes about William Jennings Bryan, Jake says that he read about Bryan's death in the paper the day before (121). Bill then gives a funny oration about Bryan, aping the famous orator's inflated rhetoric and referring obliquely to the Scopes Monkey Trial in which Bryan was a principal defender of the fundamentalist law that prohibited the teaching of evolution in the Tennessee school system (122). This mention of Bryan's death seems to establish the novel's year as 1925, but it raises an even greater time problem. Bryan died on 26 July 1925, and as Jake points out in the opening lines of chapter 15, the fiesta of San Fermin began on Sunday 6 July (152). Since the fishing trip is before San Fermin, Jake has the great orator dying almost a month before his actual death. How could either Hemingway or Jake have made such a mistake? The manuscript shows that Hemingway revised this passage heavily; the first draft refers more directly to the "monkey business," but not until his revisions did Hemingway add the information on Bryan's death.

Another time reference during the Burguete interlude confuses the perceptive reader even further. Close to the end of the fishing trip, Jake tells us they had stayed five days at Burguete (125). The first draft of the manu-script shows the number as three, then four, and finally five as if Hemingway were trying to correct the skewed calendar. None of the numbers works. On the next page a letter arrives from Mike Campbell; dated Sunday, it says he and Brett will arrive in Pamplona on Tuesday: " 'What day of the week is it?' I asked Harris. 'Wednesday, I think. Yes, quite. Wednesday. Wonder-ful how one loses track of the days up here in the mountains.' 'Yes. We've been here nearly a week' " (127). Nearly a week is either the five days Jake mentioned, or perhaps six days. But if the day is Wednesday, it should also be 29 June based on when Jake and Bill left Paris. But, no surprise, there was no Wednesday, 29 June, in either 1924 or 1925: the problem of days has multiplied.

No matter where you begin to construct a linear narrative for *The Sun Also Rises*, time falls out of joint: days disappear or multiply; hours stretch and shrink. At the San Fermin festival, time becomes irrelevant: Jake does not know what time he gets to bed (147); Cohn falls asleep and loses two hours (159); Bill and others are up all night and sleep to noon (161). For that week in Pamplona the only measurement of time is when the bullfights begin and end; the times of other activities exist relative to the central spectacle in the bull ring. It is not just in the mountains that one loses track of time in this novel, but what is the point? Why is Hemingway playing these time games with us?

The easiest answer is that he simply made sloppy mistakes. In learning about narrative construction on the job, he was not able to get all the joints to fit evenly. The biographical reader would say that Hemingway conflated two summers at Pamplona into one novel. The good fishing trip of 1924 came after the festival, not before it. In transposing the trip, he simply made serious calendar mistakes. Another biographical reader might say that Hemingway was so worried about libel suits that he deliberately constructed a time scheme that he knew would not fit either 1924 or 1925, the two years that contributed to the novel. But what do we make of the death of Bryan? He certainly knew when Bryan died, and he certainly moved the date. And why even give us the specific dates or the birth year of Romero? Why call our attention to specific time at all?

That question takes us right back to Jake and Georgette in the taxi passing the *Herald* clocks—the measurement of standard time all over the United States. "Don't kid me," Georgette said. What Hemingway did not say on the surface of the novel was that Albert Einstein would have agreed with Georgette: in the realm of his mind experiments there was no standard time. Time and space were relative in a universe whose only constant was the speed of light. In Einstein's now classic mental experiment, two men— one on a passing train and the other on the platform—each carries a clock and a measuring rod. The train moves at the speed of light; the man on the platform is stationary. As the train passes the platform, each man measures the window on the train. The man on the platform's measurement is shorter than the man on the train's measurement. The man passing at the speed of light measured a stationary window; the stationary man measured a window passing at the speed of light. Both measurements were relatively correct, but neither measurement was correct for both men. The length of the window varied depending upon the position of the measurer in time and space relative to it. Moreover, the two clocks appeared to run at different rates: to the platform observer, the train clock ran more slowly than the stationary clock.

"Don't kid me," you might well reply. Unfortunately the Newtonian world of standard measurements broke down in the early part of this century. In a quantum universe of probabilities, nothing is absolute, nothing certain but the speed of light. All else is relative. In March 1922, while Hemingway was learning his way about Paris, Albert Einstein was in town delivering a series of lectures. Einstein, whose first theoretical paper on relativity was published in 1905, had, by 1925, become a world celebrity whose picture needed no caption. His name and his ideas were bandied about in the popular press as frequently as they appeared in scientific journals. Between 1922 and 1928 the *New York Times* carried 172 stories about Einstein; during the same period almost a hundred articles about Einstein appeared in English and American periodicals. There is no evidence that Hemingway ever read anything that Einstein wrote, but the young author could not have avoided a general understanding of the physicist's ideas that had permeated the air of the twenties.

Let us look closely at the train station scene in Pamplona where Jake, Bill, and Robert Cohn are waiting for Brett and Mike to arrive (95–99). The three men are standing on the platform as the train pulls into the station. Cohn and Bill have a hundred-peseta bet on whether Brett arrives on time. Jake hedged, saying she would arrive but maybe not on time. Of course Brett is not on the train. Her telegram implies she might arrive the next day; Cohn waits for her; Jake and Bill leave for Burguete. Brett does not arrive until almost a week later. To stage this scene on a railway platform in a book where time is out of joint might suggest that Hemingway was having a bit of fun with Einstein's experiment.

Hemingway's point, however, is less theoretical than Einstein's and more straightforward: time simply does not have the same meaning to Brett as it does to Robert Cohn or to Jake Barnes. Jake has learned to accept her behavior. When she woke him up in the Paris night banging on his door, her appearance was neither questioned nor criticized. It was 4:30 A.M. and Brett said she "had no idea what hour it was" (32). While not moving at the speed of light, Brett does move at her own standard pace. Her erratic sense of time complements the erratic sense of values that has left this postwar generation to their own moral devices. There are no longer any fixed standards for behavior any more than there is a standard meter in the post-Einsteinian universe. In a novel depicting the loss of standards, it seems perfectly appropriate for time to be skewed.

There will be readers for whom a literate, allusive Hemingway does not match their inherited expectations of the writer. What these readers sell short is the milieu that nurtured *The Sun*'s rising and Hemingway's competitive nature, which turned the simplest activity into a challenge match.

Shortly after Hemingway arrived in Paris in December 1921, he met Ezra Pound, Gertrude Stein, James Joyce, and Sylvia Beach. While Pound was corresponding with T. S. Eliot on *The Waste Land*'s final draft, Hemingway was a frequent visitor in Pound's apartment. When Sylvia Beach published Joyce's *Ulysses* (1922), Hemingway was one of the first and most enthusiastic readers of that experimental novel. In 1926, shortly after *The Sun*'s publication, Hemingway and Einstein were among the 167 who signed a petition to keep Joyce's *Ulysses* from being pirated in the United States.

Wherever Hemingway looked in those days, the new masters of his trade were playing time games: Eliot's poem fragmented time; Pound was launched on his epic time-voyage he called *The Cantos*; Joyce lavished his considerable skills on a single day in Dublin's life; and Gertrude Stein composed in her curious "continuous present" tense. By 1925, when Hemingway wrote his novel, his literate friends, acquaintances, and enemies were the leading edge of cultural change: Scott Fitzgerald, John Dos Passos, Ford Madox Ford, Ernest Walsh, Archibald MacLeish, Harry Crosby, Edmund Wilson, Joyce, Pound, and Stein. Nothing ordinary would be sufficient for readers such as these. Hemingway had his eye on the main chance, the wider audience, but for his own pride, he needed to write a novel that might amuse his heady friends. In *The Sun Also Rises*, he left us, his less creative readers, a sufficient number of signs so that we could follow his game and his meaning. The very title calls our attention to one of the few certainties that remained for that postwar generation: the sun rising on another day as disjointed as the preceding one.

A no less prevalent sign is the water, whose presence in scene after scene requires our attention. Count up the bathing references and see that *The Sun* is one of the best-washed novels you have read. In a bathrobe, Jake meets Brett and the Count at his apartment door: a bath interrupted. Perhaps not significant, but a beginning for the theme. Later, when Brett has just returned from her San Sebastian excursion with Robert Cohn, she stops Jake and Bill Gorton on the street (74): " 'I say I'm just back. Haven't bathed even. Michael comes in tonight.' 'Good. Come on and eat with us, and we'll all go to meet him.' 'Must clean myself.' 'Oh rot! Come on.' 'Must bathe. He doesn't get in till nine.' " Coming back from a week of casual fornication with a newly met friend, Brett truly needs a deep cleansing before meeting her fiancé. The night after Mike Campbell arrives, Brett tells Jake again of her need to bathe (83). The hotel where Mike and Brett have registered is, according to Campbell, a brothel, a symbolically appropriate place for Brett, perhaps, but the least likely and most ironic place for a cleansing bath.

One might be reminded of T. S. Eliot's *Waste Land* brothel madame, Mrs. Porter: "O the moon shone bright on Mrs. Porter / And on her daughter / They wash their feet in soda water." In the bawdy song to which Eliot referred, it was a well-used part of their anatomy more closely associated with their trade that Mrs. Porter and her daughter so dutifully washed. Brett Ashley, indeed, needs just such a washing. To connect Hemingway's novel with Eliot's bleak poem of modern times is not as unlikely as it might seem. Remember that Hemingway read *The Waste Land* soon after meeting the poem's editor, Ezra Pound. In his own library, Hemingway would later accumulate all of Eliot's work, and he left allusive statements to the poem in *A Farewell to Arms* (1929) and *Death in the Afternoon* (1932). Like *The Waste Land*, *The Sun Also Rises* focuses on failed sexual relationships as metaphors for the postwar human condition. Both poem and novel use man's sexual inadequacies as a sign of his moral and spiritual failings. In the poem the land's fertility is not renewed by needed water, and the rituals no longer work. Similar rituals, both Christian and pagan, fail to restore sexual order in Hemingway's bleak view of modern life: neither the religious feast of San Fermin nor the pagan fertility ritual of the bullfights restore order. And in both poem and novel, no temptation is without its taker. Hemingway's use of Eliot's *Waste Land* as an informing context for his novel is not surprising. Scott Fitzgerald used the poem successfully in his "valley of ashes" section of *The Great Gatsby*. In 1926, with *The Waste Land* on every literate mind, no one could write a novel in which water and bathing figured as prominent signs and *not* call up Eliot's poem.

Throughout the book, water is a shorthand sign with multiple meanings. Sometimes, as in Brett's bathing, the need for water is the need to be washed of the moral grime that this novel's flesh is all too heir to. At Pamplona, just after we are told that, like Circe, Brett turns men into swine (144), she says, "I must bathe before dinner." After she has been down cellar with the garlic wreath and the dancing men, she needs a bath (159). After the drunken Pamplona evening during which Jake Barnes pimps for Brett and is knocked out by Cohn, he needs "a deep, hot bath" (193), but when he finds the stone tub, the water will not run. Confession and prayer in the Pamplona church did not make Jake feel much better about his moral condition, and there is no absolution for his acting as a procurer in the Pamplona bar. Montoya will never forgive him for assisting in the corruption of Pedro Romero. Thus it is a fitting sign that Jake finds the deep, stone tub, but the water, when he has most need of it, will not run. At San Sebastian, alone and a little depressed by the Pamplona experience, Jake checks into a hotel and takes a shower (234). After lunch he swims out to the harbor raft, where he finds a young couple talking and laughing. Jake does not tell us to remember that San Sebastian is where Brett took Cohn for their brief fling, but we should make the ironic connection. Jake dives deep in green, dark water, but no amount of water can wash away the week in Pamplona. The sign reminds us of the purification by baptismal water, the holy water that washes the soul clean of original sin. Jake's need is real and deep, but ritual cleansing does not work in modern times.

Notes

1. Ernest Hemingway, "American Bohemians in Paris," *Dateline: Toronto*, ed. William White (New York: Scribners, 1985), p. 114.

2. R. F. Wilson, *Paris on Parade* (Indianapolis: Bobbs Merrill, 1925), pp. 305–06.

ORIGINAL ESSAYS

◆

Second Thoughts:
Hemingway's Postscript to *The Sun Also Rises*

ROBERT E. FLEMING*

Many scholars—including Michael Reynolds, Matthew Bruccoli, Frederic Svoboda, and William Balassi—have examined the material that Ernest Hemingway deleted from the manuscript of *The Sun Also Rises*, particularly the nearly three galleys that he cut from the opening of the novel.[1] Working with this material, they have shed a good deal of light on the evolution of the novel from a short story focusing on Cayetano Ordoñez (Niño de la Palma), to a book designed to depict Lady Brett Ashley, and, finally, to a sophisticated novel exploring the inner landscape of its complex narrator, Jake Barnes.

There have been theoretical reservations about the use of material cut from the novel, about the role it should play in interpretation of the published work. "What are we reading when we read *The Sun Also Rises?*" Jim Hinkle asked, at the Fourth International Hemingway Conference in Boston in 1990. Implicitly, Hinkle was objecting to the use of evidence external to the published novel. His objections rest on solid ground; Hemingway revised the early holograph manuscript as well as the typescript before submitting the novel to Scribner's, and he willingly cut the first galleys from the proofs after F. Scott Fitzgerald objected to several aspects of the opening of *The Sun Also Rises*. On the other hand, T. S. Eliot has written "what happens when a new work of art is created is something that happens simultaneously to all the works of art that preceded it" and that "after the supervention of novelty, the *whole* existing order must be, if ever so slightly, altered."[2] Much the same might be said about the manuscript versions that precede a published work of art. Once read, they forever alter the reader's perception of that work. To know the "Fiesta" manuscript is necessarily to read *The Sun Also Rises* in a new light.

The truncated opening and the other materials excised from Hemingway's first novel provide glosses on the book, answer questions on such practical matters as Jake's newspaper syndicate, and offer surprises, such as the news that in an early version of the manuscript Brett Ashley, like her

*This essay was written specifically for this volume and is published here for the first time by permission of the author.

163

real-life prototype Duff Twysden, had a son living in England with his paternal grandparents. Both the holograph manuscript and the excised galleys thus offer helpful insights into the backgrounds of characters in the novel.

But there also exists an excised *coda* to the novel, and perhaps it too can shed light on *The Sun Also Rises*. A nine-page holograph fragment that has been catalogued under the deceptive title "Jimmy the Bartender," it is an abortive sequel or afterword to the novel that recalls Carlos Baker's report in *The Writer as Artist* that "after the book was published, Paris gossip asserted that its title should have been *Six Characters in Search of an Author—With a Gun Apiece*."[3] Baker enlarged upon that remark in his later biography of Hemingway, reporting that Duff Twysden was "furious" when she first read the book, that Kitty Cannell was so angry that "she took to her bed for three days," and that Harold Loeb "felt as if he had developed an ulcer" because of his treatment in the novel.[4] More than thirty years later, Loeb would of course publish his own version of the events that formed the background of *The Sun Also Rises* in his purportedly factual *The Way It Was* (1959).[5] Hemingway's fictional fragment treats the aftermath of publication more lightly.

Dating the fragment is something of a problem. An internal reference to the publication of Jake's book "a year ago in the fall" suggests that "Jimmy the Bartender" was probably written sometime in the autumn of 1927, since *The Sun Also Rises* appeared on 22 October 1926. Michael Reynolds has reported that during the last months of 1927 Hemingway was working on his "Jimmy Breen" manuscript, in which he was "making everything up," rather than relying on experience and observation, and experimenting with other short sketches that seemed to lead him nowhere.[6]

In this sketch, Jake Barnes is drinking in the Dingo Bar with Jimmy the bartender about a year after the publication of his book. "Jimmy" is of course James Charters, a well known bartender of Montparnasse, who later wrote a book of his own about the era, with an introduction by Hemingway himself. In view of the fact that most people had long ago identified the sources for Brett and Mike, Charters is extremely discreet. Although he mentions the names of Duff "Twisden" and Pat Guthrie in his memoirs, when he devotes a chapter to "The Sun Also Sinks," he uses Hemingway's fictional names for the principals and does not otherwise identify them. As he puts it, "to give their real names would be pointless, and in any case I promised 'Mike's' mother that I would not, for it would reflect on a very fine old Scotch family. . . ."[7]

Like Hemingway, Jake is forced to confront the source for his characters at last. Mike Campbell and Brett Ashley walk into the bar, and the conversation turns to literature and literary people, circling around the tense subject of Jake's having used his two current companions as major characters in a book that has achieved a *succès de scandale*. The fragment ends inconclusively with Brett telling Jake that it is a "dreadful bore" to be pointed out "as a character in a book." Jake apologizes weakly but assures her that he too has suffered from his sudden fame.

It is impossible to state unequivocally how Hemingway might have thought of the "Jimmy the Bartender" fragment. He might have intended it for eventual publication. He could have seen it as part of an introduction for a later edition of the novel. He could have been experimenting with a sequel to *The Sun Also Rises*. Or it might have been an attempt to come to terms with what some have seen as an act of betrayal by which Hemingway settled the score with his former friends by libelling them.

Probably the latter alternative is closest to the truth. Although most likely Hemingway did not see his subjective recreation of actual events in *The Sun Also Rises* as a vicious attack on his former friends and acquaintances (as Harold Loeb, for example, regarded it), he might well have begun to suffer doubts as to the responsibilities of a writer who uses in his fiction not only his own experiences but those of his acquaintances as well. Hemingway had already been called to account for creating literary characters whose sources were too easily identifiable by Chard Powers Smith, who had attacked Hemingway in a letter for using him and his wife as characters in "Mr. and Mrs. Elliot," first titled "Mr. and Mrs. Smith."[8] If an author chooses to relinquish his own privacy, it does not necessarily follow that he may also intrude upon the privacy of others.

Hemingway claimed in a letter to Scott Fitzgerald that he had made his peace with Duff Twysden. The general outline of what he told Fitzgerald obviously forms the basis for the "Jimmy the Bartender" sketch, with some significant differences. On 15 September 1927, Hemingway reported to Fitzgerald: "I ran into her one night—she wasn't sore about the Sun—said the only thing was she never had slept with the bloody bull fighter."[9] However, Pat Guthrie was not with Duff on this occasion because, as Hemingway explained to Fitzgerald, "after Duff . . . got her divorce [Pat] wouldn't marry her because she had lost her looks. . . ."[10] Obviously, "Jimmy the Bartender" must be regarded as fiction, perhaps as the way things should have been rather than the way they were.

The sketch begins with Jake and Jimmy the bartender drinking and listening to the phonograph when Brett and Mike walk into the bar. " 'Hello you sots,' Brett said. 'Hello Mr. Barnes.' She was very happy and looking well. 'I've brought Mr. Campbell.' 'The novelist' Mike Campbell said. 'Mr. Barnes the novelist.' 'Mr. Campbell,' I said. 'Will you have a drink Mr. Campbell?' 'I never drink with novelists,' Mike said. It was the first time we had met since the book came out a year ago in the fall. I had seen him several times and had heard things he had said but we had not met."[11] If this fragment can indeed be taken as Jake's examination of his artistic conscience, the passage on Brett Ashley can be posted on the positive side of the ledger. Jake notes that Brett is "happy" and that she is "looking well." She has not been seriously harmed by her appearance as the amoral but fascinating heroine of *The Sun Also Rises*. Brett opens her conversation with the same sort of joking insult that characterized her in the novel, and her conversation continues in a breezy vein.

Mike Campbell is another matter. He manages to call Jake a "novelist" three times in eleven words of dialogue, and the context makes it clear that he does not mean to congratulate Jake on his literary accomplishment. Surprisingly, Mike says that he never drinks with novelists, although the reader knows from *The Sun Also Rises* that Mike will drink anything with anybody. Furthermore, Jake says that it is their first meeting since the book appeared although he has seen Mike "several times." He leaves the reader wondering why they did not meet when he saw Mike earlier. Mike may have cut Jake. Jake might have avoided Mike to save himself the embarrassment of a face-to-face meeting or to avoid feelings of guilt. Jake also states that he has heard "things that [Mike] had said," leaving the reader to wonder about the exact nature of Mike's remarks. Two Freudian slips link Mike to his real-life model. Just as he had done in the original holograph of *Fiesta*, Hemingway twice calls Mike Campbell by the name of "Guthrie."

Another patron of the bar, Captain Scudder, enters the conversation, and he and Jake talk about Braddocks; they detest his constant lies and British affectations. But this talk of lies may cause the reader to reflect that after all, a novelist by the very nature of his profession must "lie." Duff Twysden had complained that, unlike her fictional counterpart, she had never slept with the "bloody bull fighter," but the literary universe is richer because Brett Ashley *did* sleep with Pedro Romero. In a sense, the art of fiction consists in the artistic creation of false stories that nevertheless have the ring of truth. Brett stops their conversation by accusing Jake and Scudder of "talking literary about Braddocks" (p. 4).

In fiction if not in fact, the author and his male character make peace with one another when Mike offers Jake a drink and resumes the joking relationship they shared in *The Sun Also Rises:* " 'Mr. Barnes,' said Mike Campbell. 'Will you have a drink?' 'I'm a novelist.' 'He's a novelist,' said Mike. 'But not a good novelist. James, give Mr. Barnes another whiskey and soda' " (p. 4). Jake tells Mike that he saw him at the Al Brown fight, and they talk about Brown's merits as a fighter. Captain Scudder, however, tries to revive the joke about writers by pronouncing Al Brown a "bloody" writer. Brett cuts him off with a curt " 'Stop it' " (p. 5). In spite of Captain Scudder's awkward interruption, which might have led Mike's conversation back to Jake Barnes as novelist, an uneasy truce has been established. Brett turns the conversation back to Braddocks, supposedly a neutral topic because all present agree that Braddocks is an ass. Yet as they talk of Braddocks, the fact that he is a writer reflects on Jake, who has also become a novelist since the time when he, Brett, and Mike all lived the events he had chronicled in *The Sun Also Rises*.

Brett recalls how Braddocks once tried to tell them what "good people" were and Jake picks up the story: " 'We didn't know what good people were,' I said to Scudder. 'He was explaining it. He said he couldn't explain it to an American' " (p. 5). But lurking beneath the humor of the Braddocks anecdote are unpleasant implications. Ridiculous as Braddocks may be, he is an English gentleman, whose traditional code of conduct specifies that certain things are not done.

Presumably that code would prohibit using one's friends or acquaintances as material in fiction. (It is impossible to know whether Hemingway was aware of the fact that Ford Madox Ford, the model for Braddocks, had used Arthur Marwood as a model for Christopher Tietjens, protagonist of *Parade's End* [1924–1928].) If Braddocks could not explain the concept of "good people" to Jake, the reason might not just have been that Jake was an American, but rather that the rules governing English polite society would be inscrutable to someone with Jake's lack of principles. For example, Jake's remark very early in his narrative establishes his habitual cynicism about human nature. "I mistrust all frank and simple people, especially when their stories hold together. . . ."[12] There is in Jake's character, as there was in Hemingway's, the necessary strand of ruthlessness that makes it possible for him to view his friends and acquaintances as subjects, rather than people.

Mike jokes with Jimmy about hiring him as a secretary, but once again the joke backfires, turning into an unpleasant reminder of the past: " 'Can he read and write? Can you read and write, James?' 'Yes sir,' Jimmy smiled. 'I don't write much of a novel' " (p. 7). Even in the lightest conversation, Jake's culpability as a novelist keeps returning to the subtext of the conversation. This time Scudder joins Brett, who once again comes to the rescue, turning the conversation to the safe topic of hangovers and how to survive them, a subject of interest to all present.

Yet even Brett is drawn back to the subject of Jake's book at the close of the fragment. She complains to Jake: " 'Darling,' said Brett. 'It's getting to be a dreadful bore to have people come into bars and point me out as a character in a book.' 'I'm awfully damned sorry,' I said. 'It's a bore. And it's bloody annoying when you don't feel that way.' 'I know. I have the same thing' " (p. 9). Jake's response to Brett seems to suggest that the penalties of fame do not differ that much from the penalties of infamy. That Jake sees these two public reactions as similar would seem to absolve him, at least in his own mind, from any possible guilt over having used Brett as grist for his own literary mill. The reader, on the other hand, need not necessarily accept Jake's easy equation of the two types of public reaction to "fame." If Hemingway had been having second thoughts about his own production of a *roman à clef* starring a number of his own friends and acquaintances, he might have been groping his way toward a similar absolution.

For most of his adult life, Ernest Hemingway was torn between the necessity of using his personal experience as the raw material for his fiction and the realization that to do so relinquished his privacy. Moreover, he must have realized that it was an even worse invasion of privacy to shine the spotlight on the private lives of his friends and relatives—often altering the facts for fiction—without ever seeking their permission. The "Jimmy the Bartender" fragment shows that Hemingway was well aware of the consequences of exploiting the lives of others and was struggling with the question of the author's culpability. By using Jake, the persona who had served him so well in the very novel in question, to represent the author guilty of infringing on the privacy of friends, Hemingway in effect distances himself from the problem, and the guilt. Turning the consequences of his fiction into another fiction, Hemingway thus introduces an element of "objectivity" as he examines those consequences and exonerates the fictional author and, by extension, himself.

Fragmentary and inconclusive as "Jimmy the Bartender" is, it suggests that Hemingway had decided, at least for a time, that the use of one's acquaintances did not do them any lasting harm. Now he was ready to write *A Farewell to Arms*, in which he would use another old friend—and some highly modified events from his own past—as the basis for his second successful novel.

Notes

1. Michael S. Reynolds, "False Dawn: *The Sun Also Rises* Manuscript," in *A Fair Day in the Affections: Literary Essays in Honor of Robert B. White, Jr.*, ed. Jack D. Durant and M. Thomas Hester (Raleigh: UW Winston Press, 1980), 171–86; Matthew J. Bruccoli, *Scott and Ernest: The Authority of Failure and the Authority of Success* (New York: Random House, 1978); Frederic Joseph Svoboda, *Hemingway and "The Sun Also Rises"* (Lawrence: Univ. Press of Kansas, 1983); William V. Balassi, "How It Probably Was: A Reconstruction of the Day-by-Day Writing of the Manuscript of *The Sun Also Rises*," (Ph. D. dissertation, University of New Mexico, 1985); and William V. Balassi "The Writing of the Manuscript of *The Sun Also Rises* With a Chart of Its Session-by-Session Development," *Hemingway Review* 6, no. 1 (1986): 65–78.

2. T. S. Eliot, "Tradition and the Individual Talent," in *The Norton Anthology of American Literature*, 3d ed., shorter, ed. Nina Baym, et al. (New York: W. W. Norton, 1989), 1828.

3. Carlos Baker, *Hemingway: The Writer as Artist* (Princeton: Princeton Univ. Press, 1972), 78.

4. Carlos Baker, *Ernest Hemingway: A Life Story* (New York: Scribner's 1969), 179.

5. Harold Loeb, *The Way It Was* (New York: Criterion, 1959).

6. Conversation with Michael Reynolds, Albuquerque, New Mexico, 25 October 1991.

7. James Charters (as told to Morrill Cody), *This Must Be the Place: Memoirs of Jimmie the Barman*, with an introduction by Ernest Hemingway (New York: Lee Furman, Inc., 1937), 104.

8. Smith to Hemingway, 1 January 1927, Incoming Letters file, Ernest Hemingway Collection, John F. Kennedy Library, Boston, Mass.

9. Carlos Baker, ed. *Ernest Hemingway: Selected Letters, 1917–1961* (New York: Scribner's, 1981), 262.

10. *Selected Letters*, 262.

11. Item 530, pp. 1–2, Ernest Hemingway Collection, John F. Kennedy Library, Boston, Mass. Future references to this manuscript are included parenthetically in the text. Published with the permission of the Ernest Hemingway Foundation, copyright © 1994, The Ernest Hemingway Foundation.

12. *The Sun Also Rises* (New York: Scribner's, 1926), 4.

Brett Ashley: The Beauty of It All

LINDA PATTERSON MILLER*

Since the publication of Ernest Hemingway's *The Sun Also Rises* in 1926, readers and critics have derogated Brett Ashley as Hemingway's ultimate bitch. Whether labeling her a drunkard, a nymphomaniac, or a modern-day Circe who turns men into swine, these interpretations ignore the complexity of Brett's character and the intricate role she plays in the novel, particularly with regard to her stunning beauty. "Take Brett out" of the novel, says critic Harold Bloom, "and vitality would depart." He adds that only when the critic puts aside "the vision of Hemingway's heroine as a Circe" will he discover "there is more inwardness to Lady Brett." That most critics have not yet seen beyond that "vision" helps to illustrate Brett's dilemma as a beautiful woman whose appearance both identifies and traps her.[1]

Hemingway gives few specific details about Brett's physical appearance. She looks "quite beautiful" in a "black, sleeveless evening dress" during a dinner in Pamplona, and, on another occasion, she wears a wool jersey that accentuates the curves of her body "like the hull of a racing yacht."[2] For the most part, she seems to have adopted the natural look, going bare-legged in Paris and brushing her hair back like a boy's (when she is not hiding it under a hat). Besides Jake's statement that Brett is "damned good-looking" (22), and his repeated assertions that Brett looks lovely, or Brett's own admission that she has the "wrong type" of face for a "religious atmosphere" (208), her stark and unconventional beauty becomes known primarily through reactions to her.

Wherever Brett goes, both men and women notice her. When she walks through the streets of Pamplona with Jake, several women come to a wineshop window to watch Brett pass. Robert Cohn, when he first sees Brett, stares dumbfounded. His look of "deserving expectation" (much as "his compatriot must have looked when he saw the promised land") typifies the response that Brett evokes from others, particularly men (22). As Roger Whitlow notes, "every significant male character in the novel at one time or another comments on Brett's female attractiveness."[3] The fiesta scene, in which chanting men dance around Brett, best illuminates her dilemma as

---

*This essay was written specifically for this volume and is published here for the first time by permission of the author.

a woman known primarily for her beauty. As Jake tells it, they want her "as an image to dance around" (155). They do not want her.[4]

Trapped within a superficial and misleading image determined for her by others, Brett Ashley feels increasingly isolated, which Jake recognizes when he says that Brett "can't go anywhere alone" (102). She fears being alone precisely because she is alone, more so than any other character in the novel.[5] Because Jake understands her entrapment and isolation, she relies upon him in her struggle to break free of the image that both defines and smothers her.

When Robert Cohn, having just met Brett, comments that she is remarkably attractive and that "she seems to be absolutely fine and straight," Jake tries to counter Cohn's idealism and his presumptuous assertions. "She's a drunk," Jake tells Cohn. "You talk sort of bitter," Cohn replies defensively. "Sorry. I didn't mean to. I was just trying to give you the facts." Throughout the conversation with Cohn, Jake reveals his understanding that as men idealize Brett, falling in love with their image of her rather than with the real person (complete with human foibles), they progressively undermine her sense of self. Jake emphasizes to Cohn that while "her name's Lady Ashley," "Brett's her own name" (38–39). To a great extent, the novel revolves around Brett's nascent assertiveness and self-awareness as she struggles to realize, finally, "her own name." As Jake narrates Brett's story, he uses parallel structures and mirroring devices that reveal Brett within a larger emotional framework and emphasize the fact that appearances can both deceive and destroy.

Although Brett does not appear in the novel until the middle of chapter 3, the opening scenes anticipate her through the character of Georgette, the French *poule* who is pretty until she smiles. More a parody of Brett than an autonomous character, Georgette does not reappear after this chapter. Since her circumstances and physical attributes mirror those of Lady Ashley, the prostitute serves to foreshadow and heighten Brett's entrance later at the Bal Musette. Whereas Brett enjoys collecting men (as she admits to Jake), Georgette makes a profession of it. Both women are regarded as pretty (although Georgette's smile undermines that view), and both wear a hat they adjust down over their foreheads before meeting the crowd. Georgette keeps her hat on even while dancing on the crowded dance floor, and the hat becomes an identifying trademark for both women (none of the other women in the novel are mentioned as wearing hats). Both women share a taxi ride with Jake and then engage him in mock romance without sex. To the extent that she is a foil, these events involving Georgette identify and illuminate the thematic motifs important to understanding Brett. As these scenes repeatedly contrast pretense with authenticity, they emphasize that Brett's appearance or image is not the real person and that all such surface appearances cover reality.[6]

When chapter 3 opens, Jake is sitting "at a table on the terrace of the

Napolitain." Robert Cohn has just left him, and the growing darkness, along with the circling crowds, emphasizes Jake's isolation (which parallels that of Brett). As Jake watches "a good-looking girl walk past the table and . . . up the street," he loses "sight of her" until he watches "another" and then finally catches Georgette's eye. After she comes to sit down with him, and they have ordered drinks, Jake teases her for ordering Pernod, which is "not good for little girls." "Little girl yourself," Georgette retorts, emphasizing that while she might *appear* to be young, she is really old in street knowledge. When Jake notes that Pernod is "greenish imitation absinthe" that only "turns milky" when water is added, Georgette grins to disclose that she is not so pretty as she had seemed "with her mouth closed" (14–15).

Later, as they ride together in a cab to dinner, they talk about his being sick, and Georgette notes that Jake, in the face of this sickness, should not drink Pernod, the imitation drink they had ordered earlier. Although Georgette takes literally the idea that everyone in Paris is sick with some form of sexually transmitted disease, and that drinking Pernod exacerbates the disease for men only, her comments in conjunction with the imitative nature of the drink imply that only something authentic will cure a sickness that feeds on deception. As the cab carries Georgette and Jake along a "broad and shiny" but "almost deserted" avenue, they pass "locked" shop doors and store windows that appear invitingly luminescent and promising but are in reality inaccessible (15). When the cab pulls up in front of the restaurant, Georgette does "not like the looks of the place." "This is no great thing of a restaurant," she says. Later she decides that the restaurant is not as bad as it had at first appeared (16).

This emphasis upon appearances that belie reality continues to intensify prior to Brett's entrance. When Jake and Georgette enter Madame Lavigne's restaurant, where they meet up with Robert Cohn, Frances Clyne, and the Braddocks, the play on the word "friend" and the idea of mistaken identity begins. Jake tells Georgette that "a friend" is calling him, and when Mrs. Braddocks tells Jake to bring his "friend" over to meet them, she laughs, as if acknowledging Georgette's "friendly" relationship to Jake. Since "friend" here is equated with a kind of fakery, Georgette's follow-up question to Jake, "who are [his] friends," clearly implies that these "friends," who, according to Jake, are "writers and artists," are also pretenders: "There are a lot of those [phonies] on this side of the river," Georgette states. "Too many," Jake replies (17). As these characters variously use the word "friend," its connotative meanings undercut the denotative meaning, thus foreshadowing Pedro Romero's later assertion to Brett that he kills his "friends" so that "they don't kill" him (186). The insider joking around "friend" emphasizes that friends are not necessarily friendly and that appearance does not necessarily represent the truth.

When Jake introduces Georgette as his fiancée, the singer Georgette Leblanc, the idea of pretense and fakery is further intensified. Georgette is neither Jake's fiancée nor a singer, and her real name differs from this pseudonym. When Mrs. Braddocks tells her husband that Jake has purposefully misrepresented Georgette as a "joke," Braddock takes the "joke" to yet another level when he claims to have known Georgette Hobin "for a very long time." Here, perhaps, the "joke" is on Mrs. Braddocks, whose husband has claimed to know a prostitute. When Mrs. Braddocks speaks French and is "astonished" that it comes out "really French," it seems certain that all of these "friends" are indeed pretenders, people who appear to be something other than what they are. Although Frances Clyne sees Paris as "so extraordinarily clean," Georgette Hobin states a blunter truth. Behind the clean facade, Paris is actually quite "dirty," and she does not like it. "You have nice friends," she concludes sarcastically to Jake (18–19).[7]

Georgette's remark, with its final reference to "friends," embodies all of the irony regarding pretense that has built up throughout these scenes that precede Brett's first appearance in the novel. Emphasizing that almost nothing is what it seems, and that words can say one thing but mean another, the ironic intonations of these scenes continue to reverberate when Brett enters the Bal Musette where Georgette and Jake have gone to dance. Georgette's remark just prior to Brett's entrance introduces Brett by encapsulating her dilemma as a beautiful woman confined within an image. "My God," Georgette says of dancing on the crowded floor, "What a box to sweat in!" (19). When Jake then tells Georgette to take off her hat, Brett enters. This juxtaposition underscores the significance of Brett's disguised identity and her entrapment. To take off her hat would mean self-revelation and vulnerability, which frighten Brett. Whenever she is nervous in the crowd, she pulls her hat down farther over her face, indicating her fear of exposure. Ironically, while the outer image traps Brett, it also shields her from confrontation. Her entrance into the bar with a group of homosexual men, with whom she is physically safe, demonstrates her personal alienation: "When one's with the crowd I'm with," Brett tells Jake, "one can drink in such safety, too" (22).

Brett's alignment with the homosexual men angers Jake, both for Brett's sake and for his own. When he sees them under the light, with their "white hands, wavy hair, white faces, grimacing, gesturing, talking," he feels like hitting them, "anything to shatter that superior, simpering composure" (20). Jake's anger is complicated by impotence, of which the effeminate men remind him, and also by their sham appearance, which the wavery, almost dreamlike description of them emphasizes. Jake associates this posturing with Brett (who is very much "with them") as she allows herself to be molded by the crowd, becoming what the crowd desires. When Jake comes back to the bar later, he cannot hide his contempt for the foppery of it all: "What's the matter with you?" Robert Cohn asks. "You seem all worked up over something?" "Nothing," Jake replies. "This whole show makes me sick is all. Brett came up to the bar" (20–21). Jake's direct association of

Brett with the "show" is not happenstance, for he recognizes how the public "show" both identifies and destroys Brett. Her association with it persists throughout the novel in significant variations, as Brett struggles to break free of the image that both identifies and traps her.

The pretense emphasized in this scene intensifies as Georgette, Brett's "double," is "taken up by" the homosexual men, each one dancing with her in a parody of heterosexual attraction (20). This crowd parallels the crowd that tries to carry away Brett. The initial dialogue in this scene implicitly suggests this irony: "It's a fine crowd you're with, Brett," Jake says. "Aren't they lovely?" Brett responds. "And you, my dear," she adds. "Where did you get it?" (22). Her reference to Georgette's ambiguous identity, as emphasized by her use of "it," reinforces the thrust of the preceding scenes and thus underscores Brett's own indeterminate character. When she is with Jake alone, however, her character becomes sharply etched and irrefutably her own. Indeed, the cab scene that follows their departure from the bar highlights her exposure and vulnerability as it foreshadows her self-realization in the conclusion of the novel.

"Well, we're out away from them," Jake says, prior to their getting into a taxi, which carries them "up the hill" past the "lighted square, then on into the dark, still climbing." Jake and Brett (previously "sitting apart") are "jolted close together," and he notes that her hat is "off," which reinforces the idea that Brett's taking off her hat represents self-exposure. With her head thrown "back," the physical contours of Brett's face glow in the almost surrealistic lighting of the scene: "I saw her face in the lights from the open shops," Jake says. "Then it was dark, then I saw her face clearly." This view of Brett, highlighted by the glare of the workmen's acetylene flares on her face and neck, emphasizes her beauty: Her "face was white," Jake says, "and the long line of her neck showed in the bright light of the flares. The street was dark again and I kissed her" (24–25).

As the keen darkness repeatedly shifts into a sudden and intense light, the surrealistic highlighting and distortion of Brett's physical form allows for a glimpse into her emotional interior, and Brett's eyes match this movement as they shift from flatness to open exposure, like the lens of a camera: "Her eyes had different depths," Jake says, and "sometimes they seemed perfectly flat. Now you could see all the way into them." As Brett looks out, Jake also looks into Brett: "She was looking into my eyes with that way she had of looking that made you wonder whether she really saw out of her own eyes. They would look on and on after every one else's eyes in the world would have stopped looking. She looked as though there were nothing on earth she would not look at like that, and really she was afraid of so many things" (26). Although Jake cannot penetrate Brett physically, he can realize her spiritually, as her eyes become the windows of her soul. When Brett is in the public sphere, however, she tries to remain protected, and her eyes flatten and shield. Jake senses her isolation when he says that

Brett stares "straight ahead" or that her eyes wrinkle (or close up more) at the corners.[8]

As Brett leaves the taxi to go back into the bar with the crowd, her immediate sense of isolation is revealed by the way she puts on her hat with a shakey hand and asks Jake if she looks "too much of a mess." Aware again of the public show, she pulls "her man's felt hat down" farther on her head. It is significant that it is a "man's" hat and that she feels the need throughout to counteract the physical trap by downplaying the feminine. When she joins the same group at the bar, she aligns herself once again with the "chaps": "Hello, you chaps," Brett says, "I'm going to have a drink." As everyone flocks around her, they want her attention, and Zizi is the first to acknowledge her directly. As Zizi calls out "Oh, Brett, Brett," Jake reports that Zizi is a "portrait-painter, who called himself a duke" (28). (This echoes Georgette's asking Jake earlier what he is *called*, as opposed to "What is your name" or "Who are you?") The identification of Zizi as a portrait painter aligns Brett with portraits that convey the external details of individuals, rather than their emotional depth. This is precisely Brett's dilemma, for others cannot see or touch her real self.

Variations of the word "touch" occur in different contexts. When Georgette reaches out to touch Jake physically, he puts her hand away. Later, in the cab scene with Brett, she is the one to tell Jake not to touch her: "When you touch me," she tells him later, "I simply turn all to jelly" (26). Throughout the novel, characters are repeatedly thrust into close contact despite the fact that, in a spiritual sense, they do not touch at all. In the cab, Brett and Jake make contact at first only because the cab jolts them close together, and the dance hall is so confined that actual movement is prohibited: "It was so crowded," Jake says, "we could barely move. . . . We were caught in the jam, dancing in one place" (62). Such contrived intimacy underscores the suggestion that true human touching can be found only by reaching inward to discover one's own resources.

Although genuine intimacy might seem impossible for these characters, the idea of "actual touching," as opposed to physical contact, is defined within the context of bullfighting. Through her involvement in Pamplona with Pedro Romero, Brett comes to realize what Jake already knows about the significance of the bullfighter, who is real. Jake introduces the concept of "actual touching" when he sees Montoya and shakes hands with him on the hotel stairs. Montoya smiles "in his embarrassed way" and touches Jake again by putting his hand on his shoulder: "He always smiled as though bull-fighting were a very special secret between the two of us," Jakes says, "a rather shocking but really very deep secret that we knew about. He always smiled as though there were something lewd about the secret to outsiders, but that it was something that we understood" (130–31). As this passage continues, it introduces the idea of "*aficion*," which Jake says means "passion": "An aficionado is one who is passionate about the bull-fights." The commercial bullfighters, those who write "flattering inscriptions" on their photos that "did not mean anything" and who "simulated" but did not have *aficion*, did not stay in Montoya's hotel. Jake knows that with Montoya he will have "the pleasure of discovering" what they "each felt": "When they saw that I had aficion, and there was no password, no set questions that could bring it out, rather it was a sort of oral spiritual examination with the questions always a little on the defensive and never apparent, there was this same embarrassed putting the hand on the shoulder, or a 'Buen hombre.' But nearly always there was the actual touching. It seemed as though they wanted to touch you to make it certain" (131–32).

This "actual touching" carries over into the characterization of Pedro Romero, who is "real." Montoya wants Jake to meet him, and he takes Jake to Romero's room just prior to his first fight of the fiesta. As soon as the door to Romero's room opens, he is spotlighted under a ceiling light in a "gloomy room" that fronts the "narrow street" and holds "two beds separated by a monastic partition." The words "narrow," "separated," "monastic," and "partition" emphasize Romero's isolation and confinement. As his handlers wind the sash around his waist, he stands "very straight and unsmiling" in his tight-fitting garb, and he seems distanced from the others: "They were just finishing winding his sash," and "his black hair shone under the electric light. He wore a white linen shirt and the sword-handler finished his sash and stood up and stepped back. Pedro Romero nodded, seeming very far away and dignified" (163).

In its intensity and evocative power, especially as it focuses on Romero standing center stage under the glare of the electric lightbulb, this scene parallels the earlier cab scene in which Brett's beauty and vulnerability were highlighted by the harsh lighting of the workmen's flares. In many respects, Brett and Romero parallel each other so closely that he becomes her male counterpart. Jake's descriptions of them repeatedly echo each other, as when Jake leaves Romero's room and then looks back to see him standing "alone except for his sword-handler, and the three hangers-on" (163). Romero's remarkable isolation, the "hangers-on" who surround him, and his rigid posture all mimic Brett and her relationship to others.

What most characterizes Brett and Romero is their exceptional beauty. After the door to Romero's room has been thrown open, and Jake sees him standing there, he thinks to himself that here was "the best-looking boy" he had "ever seen." His later response to Montoya's assertion that Romero is "a fine boy, don't you think so?" is to state openly, "He's a good-looking kid" (163). His statement echoes his earlier qualification of Brett as "damned good-looking," and he repeats this once again: "He's a damned good-looking boy," Jake tells her. "When we were up in his room I never saw a better-looking kid" (167). Brett herself notices Romero's good looks: "Oh, isn't he lovely. And those green trousers" (165). The repeated emphasis on Romero's physical beauty, to the exclusion of other qualities, suggests his alignment with Brett, who likewise is most noted for her beauty.

Like the parallels with Georgette, the similarities between Brett and Romero are too pointed to ignore: They wear clothes that hug the curves of their bodies, and they wear hats that accentuate (while also partially hiding) the fine contours of their faces. When Brett first meets Romero, he tips his hat "down over his eyes" in a way that mimics Brett's own pulling her hat down over her forehead. She immediately identifies herself with him by saying that she "would like a hat like" his. Romero assures her that she will get one, implying that she will not only have a hat like his but will be like him as well (186).

If Brett is recognized for the way that she collects and devastates men, adding to her trophies, Romero is identified by the way he collects and kills bulls, enhancing his reputation with each new victory. To the extent that Romero is a foil for Brett, it is significant to note how his dilemma as a bullfighter who is both "real" and yet imagined relates to Brett's own quest to become "real." Jake uses the same phrasing to describe Romero as he has used for Brett, particularly in aligning both of them directly with "the show." On the second day of Romero's fighting, as Brett watches intently, Jake states how "Romero was the whole show. . . . It was all Romero." Six times Jake repeats the phrase "Brett saw" to underscore how her watching, with those cameralike eyes of hers, aligns her directly with Romero (167).

As Brett's responses and Romero's moves become intricately related, a symbiotic relationship builds that revolves around motifs central to Brett. Unlike Brett, Romero does not do anything awkward because he is not afraid and is "real." He is in control because his actions are not contrived; Brett "saw what it was all about" and saw "how close Romero always worked to the bull" whereas "the other bull-fighters used to make it look as though they were working closely" (167). Unlike Belmonte, Romero is not a phony imitation of himself, and he does not use trickery: "Romero never made any contortions, always it was straight and pure and natural in line. The others twisted themselves like corkscrews . . . to give a faked look of danger" (167–68).

The description of Romero's bullfighting underscores the contrast between appearances and reality that is central to Brett's role in the novel. Brett's alienation drives her toward fake actions, and her "fake emotional feeling" leaves her both "safe" and unconnected, as she seems to recognize when she remarks to Jake that she is "so safe" with the homosexual crowd. Montoya recognizes in relation to Romero, who is the real thing, that the crowd can corrupt the real and make of it what they want.[9]

Romero's third day of fighting graphically illustrates this idea. Although Romero looks good fighting the color-blind bull, the crowd does not understand the little sidesteps he uses to compensate for the bull's deficiencies, and they think he is afraid: "They preferred Belmonte's imitation of himself or Marcial's imitation of Belmonte" (218). They "take a boy like [Romero]," Montoya tells Jake, and "they don't know what he's worth. They don't know what he means" (172). To the degree that the "boy" gives in to the crowd's desires, allowing the crowd to mold him, he no longer possesses himself. Instead he has Belmonte's bitterness and despair, his inability to please the crowd, and his contrived actions that leave an unpleasant aftertaste. Belmonte illustrates the way the crowd creates the phony image of the real; when he "retired the legend grew up about how his bull-fighting had been, and when he came out of retirement the public was disappointed because no real man could work as close to the bulls as Belmonte was supposed to have done, not, of course, even Belmonte" (214).

Belmonte becomes the foil of Romero in the way he foreshadows Pedro's destruction by the crowd; Romero, in turn, parallels Brett to foreshadow her potential destruction. During Romero's last fight, "the crowd made him go on," for they "did not want it ever to be finished." Increasingly, as Romero fights, becoming "one with the bull," the crowd gains control, running "from all parts of the arena" to make "a little circle around" the dead bull and "to dance around the bull," much as the fiesta crowd circled and danced around Brett. As Romero tries to escape by "running to get ahead of the crowd," he comes toward Jake and Brett but "the crowd were all about him," and finally they carry him away as Romero looks back helplessly and "apologetically" at Jake and Brett. Just as Brett is taken up by the boys in the bar, the dancers in the processional (who want Brett as an "image to dance around"), and the drunks, so Romero is carried off by "the crowd [which is] the boys, the dancers, and the drunks" (219–21).

Brett reveals her own helplessness when she tells Jake "I've got to do something. I've got to do something I really want to do." As she and Jake talk about Romero, they walk "away from the crowd and the lights of the square" and past wineshops from which come "light" and "sudden bursts of music." Significantly, when Jake asks Brett if she wants to go in (to the usual crowds, noise, and drink), Brett declines. She has already said that she does not want to be the center of attention but to break free of the crowd that traps her in an image of herself (182–84).

The juxtaposition of crowds and isolation, public show and private revelation, culminates as the fiesta takes on its "close, crowded hum." The repetition of the word "crowd" begins to build a sense of inevitability and a reminder of the crowd's mindless power (161, 170). The sense of frenzy associated with Brett's desperation also builds. As "the dancing kept up, the drinking kept up, the noise went on," Jake says, "everything became quite unreal finally and it seemed as though nothing could have any consequences." In the end, "you had the feeling, even when it was quiet, that you had to shout any remark to make it heard" (154–55).

After Brett has met Romero, their tables at the cafe "almost touching"

(173), she gives Romero her hand, and they leave to spend the evening together. By morning, Robert Cohn has knocked out Jake and worked over Romero, and Jake has awakened early to watch the running of the bulls through the street and into the ring. At noon, as Jake goes to the "crowded cafe," "the town was crowded" as well. "Every street was full," and everything and everyone is "absorbed into the crowd." Then Brett comes "through the crowd in the square," seeming almost to part it, "walking, her head up, as though the fiesta were being staged in her honor" (205–6). Brett chooses not to go where she can "see the crowd walking," for she does not "want staring at just now" when she wishes to talk with Jake. Standing fully exposed "in the sunlight" and looking out at the "yellow wall of the chapel" of San Fermin, Brett asks Jake, "Is that San Fermin's?" "Yes," he replies. "Where the show started on Sunday." This reference suggests that Brett's "show" had started and intensified, and that it might end at the close of the fiesta. Brett goes into the chapel where the show began in order to "pray" (unsuccessfully) for Romero and, by association, for herself (207–8).

This scene occurs prior to Brett's watching Romero fight on the last afternoon of the fiesta, after she has spent the night with him, and Jake notes that she seems "radiant" (207). Earlier, when Brett had asked Jake to help her meet Romero, she told Jake that she felt good about what she was doing: "I don't say it's right," she says. "It is right though for me. God knows" (184). What is "right" here for her is that she is discovering herself. Once she has finally met and gone with Romero, Brett tells Jake, "I'm not worried about him at all. I just feel happy about him." Jake says, "It was the first time I had seen her in the old happy, careless way since before she went off with Cohn." After Brett and Jake part at the hotel, he emphasizes her self-assurance and her determination: "She went straight down the hall and into Romero's room," Jake says. "She did not knock. She simply opened the door, went in, and closed it behind her" (208–9).

Not wanting to become a ludicrous self-parody as she ages, one of those "bitches that ruins children" (243), Brett Ashley nonetheless, pursues Romero, who becomes the catalyst for her personal breakthrough. Brett's central attraction to Romero is not based mostly on a sexual craving but rather on the fact that she has seen in him the mirror of herself. With eyes that have "different depths" and an incredible potential to see beyond what others apprehend, Brett has already watched Romero, and she has learned what it means to be real. Her relationship with him ultimately helps her to see that she can be known for herself and not just for her image. By the time Brett meets Jake in Madrid at the end of the novel, she has already begun to realize, and verbalize, her personal breakthrough.

As Brett reports to Jake, Romero had unwittingly encouraged her to break free of that image of herself when he asked her to grow her hair long. His friends had "ragged him" about Brett "at the cafe," seemingly because of her unconventional appearance, which somewhat embarrassed Romero. But in telling Brett to grow out her hair, Romero was perhaps less concerned with what others thought than with encouraging Brett to become "more womanly" in the traditional Spanish sense and to get rid of that masculine "cover" that the boyish hairstyle epitomizes: "Me, with long hair. I'd look so like hell," Brett tells Jake. The fact that Romero seemed initially a bit "ashamed" of her "was rather a knock" for Brett, but then she came to realize that Romero actually loved her and not any particular image of her. "He wanted to marry me, finally," she tells Jake. "Maybe he thought that would make him Lord Ashley," Jake replies. "No. It wasn't that. He really wanted to marry me" (242).

Jake's statement regarding Brett's title as Lady Ashley alludes to the idea repeated throughout the novel that titles (Duke Zizi, Count Mippipopolous, Lady Ashley, Baron Mumm) and false names disguise identity and behavior. When Brett and Jake discuss titles with the Count, Brett finds it "wonderful" that they "all have titles" and wonders why Jake does not also have a title. Although the Count assures Jake that a title "never does a man any good" and that "most of the time it costs you money," Brett rejoins that a title can be "damned useful" if used "properly." She has had "hell's own amount of credit" on hers. Directly following these statements, however, Brett reveals that she may not be as high-class as her title implies, for she carelessly flicks her cigarette ashes on Jake's carpet. Only when she sees that Jake has noticed does she acknowledge her indiscretion and ask for an ashtray: "I say, Jake," she says, "I don't want to ruin your rugs." Brett's rather low-class behavior, especially as it occurs in the midst of their discussion of high-class titles, reinforces the idea that appearances deceive (57).

If titles can readily represent a convenient cover, they can also represent a personal entrapment, the self trapped within a contrived image of itself. The Count openly encourages Brett to get out from behind the image that traps her, telling her that she does not need her title for she has her own class: "You got class all over you," he says. Brett tries to deflect his praise by mocking it, but he persists. "I'm not joking you," he says. "You got the most class of anybody I ever seen. You got it. That's all" (58).

Although Brett is clearly embarrassed, the Count will not be sidetracked as he encourages Brett to be herself. He seems to recognize, as does Jake, that Brett's skittish behavior and her attempts "to joke" disguise her insecurity and isolation. Brett says that "this is a hell of a dull talk" and that they should have some champagne. Certainly drinking is the most popular escapist tactic for the characters in this novel, but the Count recognizes the seriousness of the issue and keeps Brett from having her drink until he can make sure she has heard him out: " 'You're always drinking, my dear. Why don't you just talk?' 'I've talked too ruddy much. I've talked myself all out to Jake.' 'I should like to hear you really talk, my dear. When you talk to me you never finish your sentences at all.' 'Leave 'em for you to finish. Let any one finish them as they like.' 'It is a very interesting system. . . . Still I would like to hear you talk some time' " (58).

Besides encouraging Brett to talk openly, rather than allowing others to determine her words and thoughts, the Count also urges Brett to act on her feelings and marry Jake. Again Brett feels threatened by a serious discussion and tries to "get out of this" by replying flippantly to the Count that she and Jake do not marry because they have their "careers" (61). Since she fears a confrontation with her feelings, she tries to get them all to go back into a bar where it is crowded and noisy. The count recognizes that she gravitates toward noise and crowds as a means of escape from herself. Once inside Zelli's, "it was crowded, smoky, and noisy. The music hit you as you went in," Jake states, and as he and Brett dance, they are "caught in the jam" (62). Only later do they get "out from the crowd" where they can be alone (64). Standing in front of her hotel door, however, Brett "pushed [Jake] away" and "turned quickly and went into the hotel" (65).

This scene with the Count, who encourages Brett to break free of her "cover" in the midst of her mounting hysteria, reinforces Brett's movement toward self-realization. Essentially it is a movement back and forth between quiet and noise, crowds and isolation, and it reflects Brett's vacillating emotions and fear of feeling stranded and isolated. As Brett tries to break free of her image to become "real," her insecurity intensifies. She simultaneously feeds and denies the image, which only exacerbates her nervous edge.[10]

When Brett tells Jake that she has lost her "self-respect," she is trying to find the courage to "do something" to break free. As her desperation mounts, her behavior becomes more frenetic. Her skittishness, her incomplete sentences, her carelessness, her restlessness, all reflect her increasing sense of her unrealized self. Since Brett's physical beauty gives her a heightened awareness of uncertainty and flux, she yearns to get to the inner truth of herself. She bathes obsessively (as if to wash away the outer layers), she assumes rough speech and a boyish air, she covers her cropped hair and her forehead with a cap, and she mocks her appearance: "Beautiful. With this nose?" (79).

Brett finally comes to recognize, as she tells Jake, that Romero loved her and not the idea of her: "He thinks it was me," Brett repeats emphatically. "Not the show in general." "Well, it was you," Jake responds. "Yes. It was me" (245). Whereas Brett previously felt that she was doing the "right" thing in going with Romero, she now believes that she is correct in sending him away. She would not be good for him, she seems to feel, because she would distract him from bullfighting. Brett tells Jake that she feels "rather damned good" having made this decision (245), and her new self-assurance is reflected in her sobriety. She recognizes that she does not need to drink and run from her feelings. Jake comments that while he has drunk three bottles of rioja alta, Brett has not "drunk much of it." When Jake orders his fourth and fifth bottles of the wine, Brett restrains him: "Don't get drunk, Jake. . . . You don't have to." Her admonition to Jake echoes the Count's earlier statement to her that she did not have to drink in order to be herself (246).[11]

Although Brett is visibly shaken when Jake arrives at the hotel in Madrid, and she feels small when he holds her in his arms, she has discovered a new sense of self. She has come to realize what Jake tried to tell Cohn in the beginning of the novel, that "you won't get away from yourself by moving from one place to another" (11). When Jake first sees Brett in Madrid, her hat is off, she is brushing out her hair, and she has bared her wounds, stripping off her protective garb to expose her naked and vulnerable self. As Brett rests comfortably against Jake in the taxi in Madrid, she seems at peace for the first time in the novel. Her final statement to Jake ("Oh, Jake, we could have had such a damned good time together") reflects her sad but realistic recognition of time lost.

Brett is the one who has the potential for the clearest vision, and the emphasis upon her eyes, her "watching" and "seeing," endorses her final recognition that she has herself. As Brett walks out of the Madrid hotel with Jake, she says to him forthrightly, and perhaps with some bemusement, "I haven't seen Madrid. I should see Madrid" (246). Her statement implies that previously she did not see well (more because of her shielded vision than because of any disability), and that now she will see expansively and intensely. In the themes of appearance and reality, and of personal growth and self-realization, *The Sun Also Rises* is very much her novel, and she stands at the center of it, beautiful, vulnerable, and finally herself.

Notes

1. Harold Bloom, ed., *Major Literary Characters: Brett Ashley* (New York: Chelsea House, 1991), 1–2. This collection of reprinted articles focuses on Brett and attempts to redress some of the critical neglect and malignment of Hemingway's heroines. When critics have not dismissed Hemingway's female characters as less interesting or less complex than their male counterparts, they have tended to categorize them as either goddesses, like Catherine Barkley, or bitches, like Brett Ashley. Edmund Wilson, in his *The Wound and the Bow* (Cambridge: Houghton Mifflin, 1941), describes Brett as "an exclusively destructive force" (238), and he is usually credited with initiating what Roger Whitlow, in *Cassandra's Daughters: The Women in Hemingway* (Westport: Greenwood Press, 1984), calls the "Brett-the-bitch" school of criticism (51). Whitlow provides an excellent overview of the critical reaction to Hemingway's women, including Brett (10–15). He focuses more directly on Brett as a character and the critical reaction to her in "Bitches and Other Simplistic Assumptions" (49–58). Whitlow believes that critics "almost to a person . . . rely on Brett's own pronouncements for their interpretation, particularly the assertion that Brett makes to Jake after she leaves Romero: "You know it makes one feel rather good deciding not to be a bitch" (51). The 1980s marked a significant shift in Hemingway criticism, as scholars began to reassess Hemingway's fictional treatment of women, particularly in the short stories. Linda Wagner-Martin's groundbreaking article "Women in Hemingway's Early Fiction," *College Literature* 7, no. 3 (1980): 239–47, argues that Hemingway's female characters demonstrate a greater

complexity and strength of character than their weaker male counterparts, thus overshadowing them. Charles J. Nolan, Jr., continues this revisionist trend in his "Hemingway's Women's Movement," *Hemingway Review* 3, no. 2 (1984): 14–22, pointing out the degree to which "Hemingway the writer is much more sympathetic to women and their plight than readers have generally recognized" (22). Nevertheless, such revisionist readings have not prevailed. Brett continues to be judged more than understood by critics, something that Delbert E. Wylder (in "The Two Faces of Brett: The Role of the New Woman in *The Sun Also Rises*," *Kentucky Philological Association Bulletin* [1980]: 27–33) attributes to the residual Victorian attitudes of many male critics (28).

2. *The Sun Also Rises* (New York: Scribners, 1926), 146, 22. Further quotations will be cited within parentheses in the text.

3. Whitlow, 50.

4. Sam S. Baskett (in "An Image to Dance Around: Brett and Her Lovers," *Centennial Review* 22, No. 1 [1978]: 45–69) sees Brett as an "uncertain image of great value" to her several lovers (45). Although Baskett implies that Brett is trapped within this image, he does not analyze the implications for Brett so much as focus on the male characters in relation to her. Baskett suggests that Jake is the only of her lovers who recognizes both her mysterious, almost spiritual, power and her "ordinary, human dimension," and Baskett allows for a more "complicated characterization" of Brett because of her "symbolic beauty" than have most critics to date (46–48).

5. In part because many critics persist in regarding Brett as belonging to an "insider" group, they fail to recognize her aloneness and isolation. H. R. Stoneback ("From the rue Saint-Jacques to the Pass of Roland to the 'Unfinished Church on the Edge of the Cliff,' " *Hemingway Review* 6, no. 1 [1986]: 2–29) points out that for all of Brett's "facile assumption of an insider's 'code' knowledge or style," she is actually "quite alone and quite without the values that sustain such characters as Jake, the Count, Montoya, Romero" (22).

6. E. Roger Stephenson (in "Hemingway's Women: Cats Don't Live in the Mountains," in *Hemingway in Italy and Other Essays*, ed. Robert W. Lewis [New York: Praeger, 1990], 35–46) also points out parallels between Georgette and Brett in arguing that they "change places," with Brett coming to recognize her "kinship with Georgette" as a whore. Stephenson aligns Brett with the major females in Hemingway's other novels who "are not literal whores" but are "*presented* as metaphorically whore-like" (36). Stephenson's argument is consistent with the bulk of Hemingway criticism, which analyzes these heroines only to the degree that "Hemingway *uses* them to characterize his men," who regard these women "as whores or at least whore-like" (35).

7. Louise R. Achuff (in " 'Nice' and 'Pleasant' in *The Sun*," *Hemingway Review* 10, no. 2 [1991]: 42–46) suggests that words like "nice" and "pleasant," as repeated throughout the novel, demonstrate Hemingway's "ability to let simple words express their full range of meaning and association." In particular, "as these people find amusements to help them avoid pain, so their vocabularies find words that evade the truth of what they are and do" (45). Achuff argues that such words, when applied to Brett, suggest "a shallowness and a frivolity as vacuous as Brett's life" (46).

8. Wirt Williams (*The Tragic Art of Ernest Hemingway* [Baton Rouge: Louisiana State University Press, 1981]) suggests that the "incandescence" of this scene reveals the metaphorical truth that Brett and Jake have now entered hell (54). Stoneback agrees with Williams while also regarding the passage as a "microcosm of the larger action, the journey, hell, and hope of the book" as structured around Jake's quest for "the same qualities of courage, loyalty and freedom from agonizing self-consciousness that . . . Roland epitomized" (8, 17). I would argue that Brett, despite what Stoneback regards as her "lack of discrimination" and carelessness, also undergoes a similar quest for freedom from "agonizing self-consciousness" toward self-discovery. As Stoneback articulates well, the novel is "concerned with vision" and Jake's search for clarity with regard to Brett. Ironically, this scene emphasizes

that Brett has the most penetrating and far-ranging vision, and it is pivotal in understanding Brett's movement away from the crowds and into herself.

9. Kim Moreland (in "Hemingway's Medievalist Impulse: Its Effect on the Presentation of Women and War in *The Sun Also Rises*," *Hemingway Review* 6, no. 1 [1986]: 30–41) suggests that Brett's association with the ideal, or the imagined ideal, relates to Hemingway's "nostalgia for the courtly love tradition," which the modern world distorts (40). Distortions "primarily result from and thus act implicitly to criticize Brett's morals, actions, and personality, and therefore the morals, actions, and personality of the new modern woman . . . who makes true knighthood an impossible goal for modern man" (31). As such, the old purity of line that Romero embodies becomes distorted and perverted in Brett. Moreland is not the only critic to see Brett as a corrupting influence because she is "fickle," "promiscuous," and "incapable of fidelity." Milton A. Cohen (in "Circe and Her Swine," *Arizona Quarterly* 41, no. 4 [1985]: 293–305) sees her as relegated to "a Manichaean pole of evil, whose only counterweight of Hemingwayesque good is Pedro Romero" (293). She is a "sexually aggressive" Circe who "dominates" and devours her lovers; and though she "does exude a religious aura," it is "pagan and totemic" in contrast to Romero's monasticism, his religious ascetism and purity as embodied in his bullfighting (295, 299).

10. Wendy Martin, in "Brett Ashley as New Woman in *The Sun Also Rises*," in *New Essays on The Sun Also Rises*, ed. Linda Wagner-Martin (Cambridge: Cambridge University Press, 1987), 65–82, suggests that Brett's vacillation and edginess reflect her position as a woman poised between two eras. The Victorian era repressed and idealized women, who in the modern era seek autonomy while recognizing the risk involved. Brett's dilemma is that she is "both the idealized other whom men seek as a prize for their prowess and the autonomous woman who tries to make her own decisions" (71).

11. Martin argues that Brett's new assertiveness reflects her final emergence as the modern woman, no longer torn between conflicting identities. Whereas "Jake must learn to accept the discomfort and uncertainty that come with his loss of authority" in the modern era, "Brett must learn to make choices for herself and to take responsibility for those choices" (75).

Good Old Harris in *The Sun Also Rises*

JANE E. WILSON*

Jake and Bill's fishing trip to Burguete is often recognized as a crucial episode in Ernest Hemingway's *The Sun Also Rises*. Temporally and spatially, it occurs in the center of the novel, between the scenes in Paris and the festival in Pamplona. Structurally, the episode is a significant moment of tranquility between the frantic action of the two cities. Many scholars, Linda Wagner-Martin among them, assert that the fishing trip is an idyllic interlude in the midst of the unsettling events that characterize the rest of the novel; it is a chance for Jake to experience the regenerative aspects of nature in the company of his best friend. In a contradictory interpretation by Warren Wedin, the trip to Burguete is an unsuccessful return to nature, and the events of the trip foreshadow Jake's final disillusionment. In these two lines of argument, the role of Wilson-Harris (the Englishman on a fishing holiday who is befriended and renamed "Harris" by Jake and Bill) is essential for a complete examination of this episode.

The association of nature and fishing with health and refreshment can be traced directly to Hemingway's Nick Adams stories. Nevertheless, Warren Wedin points out some interesting differences in the depiction of the fishing trip in *The Sun Also Rises* and the fishing scenes in the short stories. "For Hemingway, learning how to live in the world is often closely associated with knowing how to fish in it. . . . [Fishing] is viewed as a means of physical, psychological, and spiritual survival."[1] Wedin contends that Jake's preoccupation with Brett and Cohn, his flat description of the river, and his fishing methods all point to an overall "emotional deadness" that "completes the pattern of loss through self-betrayal."[2] In this reading, the fishing expedition becomes exemplary of the losses that Jake will experience in the course of the novel.

The interpretive debate centers on whether the fishing trip is indicative of healthful rejuvenation or degenerative loss for Jake. The narration of the conclusion of the fishing episode, especially when the introduction of Harris is considered, adds to the case for the former. In contrast to most of the novel, which is narrated in detailed episodic segments (even to the point of

*This essay was written specifically for this volume and is published here for the first time by permission of the author.

elongating the time spent at the fiesta), Jake compresses the activity of the fishing trip: "We stayed five days at Burguete and had good fishing. The nights were cold and the days were hot . . . so that it felt good to wade in a cold stream, and the sun dried you when you came out and sat on the bank."[3] This passage is "a decided exception" for a narrator "possessed of an obsessive aversion to the iterative."[4] Although Wedin points to a lack of evidence of "good fishing," Jake's simplification of the trip and his delineation of its healthful, natural aspects indicates that he, at least, remembers the trip as a good one. Furthermore, the introduction of Harris at this point in the narrative emphasizes the positive aspects of the fishing expedition.

Harris is on his own trip to Burguete. From the very beginning, the trio of Jake, Bill, and Harris appears as separate and different from the other groups in the novel: "In the evenings we played three-handed bridge with an Englishman named Harris. . . . He was very pleasant and went with us twice to the Irati River. There was no word from Robert Cohn nor from Brett and Mike" (125). This group is independent (they do not even need a fourth for a bridge game), and their interactions are never touched by the disruptive forces of Jake's other friends. Harris is associated with Jake and Bill and dissociated from Cohn, Brett, and Mike. Just as Burguete offers a tranquil rest from the settings of Paris and Pamplona, Harris offers a healthful interlude from Jake's relationships with the other characters.

The manuscript of the novel offers evidence of the development of the episode and the characters in it. Hemingway changed the duration of the fishing trip from three to four to five days in his manuscript revisions.[5] He also condensed a conversation between Jake and Bill about their travel plans for the larger group. These revisions increase the role of the fishing trip and reduce the intrusion of outside forces. In the manuscript, Harris is referred to only as an "Englishman" until the morning he gives Jake the letter from Mike: "The Englishman, his name was Harris, was [looking] reading the paper again."[6] In the final version of the novel, however, Harris is named when he is first mentioned. The emphasis on the trip and the immediate identification of Harris indicate that the character and the episode were being given greater importance in the final version.

The most obvious points of association between Harris, Jake, and Bill are their shared love of fishing and their continual acknowledgment that they enjoy each other's company. Harris, like Jake, has "not had much fun since the war" (129), and he displays a need to return to natural sport. He refuses Jake's offer to join them in Pamplona because he has "not much more time to fish" (127). When Jake and Bill leave Burguete, Harris gives them "his card, with his address in London and his club and his business address" (130). In the manuscript, Harris simply gives the Americans "his address in London."[7] Like Jake and Bill (and unlike the others), Harris is not a disillusioned expatriate but a well-established professional, which seems to lend some order and responsibility to his life beyond the trip.

In actual representation, Harris most closely resembles the character of Bill. Both prefer fly-fishing to Jake's method of using worms for bait. Harris even reflects Bill's speech patterns. His observation to Jake that it is "wonderful how one loses track of the days up here in the mountains" (127) echoes Bill's semi-serious, semi-ironic descriptions of the United States, New York, Vienna, and Budapest as "wonderful" (69–70). Harris's reply of " 'What a pity' " (127) to the announcement of Jake and Bill's departure is a repetition of Bill's "irony and pity" refrain (113–14). Jake calls attention to Harris's imitation of Bill's speech ("He had taken up utilizing from Bill" [128]), but he also gives an example of Bill's repeating Harris's assertion that it will "give . . . pleasure" (129) to buy a round of drinks. This points to the flow of their conversation: 'Isn't that a pub across the way?' Harris asked. 'Or do my eyes deceive me?' 'It has the look of a pub,' Bill said. 'It looks to me like a pub,' I said. 'I say,' said Harris, let's utilize it' " (128). The conversations among Harris, Bill, and Jake have the same humorous comfort that distinguishes Jake's conversations with Bill alone. Some of the rhythm of these conversations is built around subtle changes Hemingway made to the dialogue in the manuscript. When the trio leaves the monastery at Roncesvalles, Bill's claim that " 'It's not the same as fishing' "[8] in the draft is changed to " 'It isn't . . . ' " (128) in the novel. This leads to Harris's observation " 'Isn't that a pub. . . . ' " Bill's claim that " 'It has the look of a pub' " originally read " 'It has every appearance of a pub' ";[9] the amended version leads into Jake's " 'It looks to me like a pub' " (128). Finally, as the trio is drinking in the pub in question, Harris expresses his pleasure in their company and Bill responds. In the original draft he tells Harris they have had a " 'damned good time,' "[10] but in the novel the phrase is a "grand time" (129). The revision is closer to Harris's own British style of conversation. In each case the repetition and imitation add to the rhythm of the dialogue and point to the harmony of the group.

An immediate kinship exists among these three men. Gerald T. Gordon claims that "to a degree, he [Harris] is an enigmatic representative of Jake and Bill if only in that he typifies the loneliness of the quest, the loneliness of attempting to survive with grace and dignity."[11] Harris does remain alone, but that choice is not as bleak as Gordon makes it appear. Just as Jake later finds some order and peace when he retreats to San Sebastian at the end of the novel, Harris recognizes that he would be better off fishing alone on the Irati than joining the crowd at Pamplona. Gordon also asserts that a certain distance exists between Harris and his two new friends. He claims that Jake and Bill are at first "put off"[12] by Harris but later warm to him because he passes a series of tests for "code" values. The Englishman, according to Gordon, never quite understands the American pair or reaches their level of verbal sophistication. On the contrary, as is shown in the give-and-take of conversation, Harris is accepted from the beginning by both Jake and Bill.

Harris's similarities to his fishing partners align his character with wholesome, natural values; this association is strengthened in contrast to Mike Campbell, Brett Ashley, and Robert Cohn. As Jake and Bill leave Burguete, they express regret that Harris will not be joining them in Pamplona but immediately acknowledge that "you couldn't tell how English would mix with each other, anyway" (130). The implication is, of course, that Harris is different from and would not mix with the group from Paris. When Jake and Bill tell their companions in Pamplona about Harris, a direct link is drawn between him and Mike by Bill's facetious question, " 'Ever know him, Mike? He was in the war, too' " (134). A comparison is drawn later in the novel, after the fiesta, when Jake, Bill, and Mike roll dice to see who will pay for drinks in the bar at Biarritz. Mike loses and confesses that he has no money; he cannot pay for the drinks or for his share of the car that the trio has rented (229). This contrasts with the scene in Burguete in which Harris will not allow Jake or Bill to pay for their drinks because he has enjoyed their company so much. Harris's present of fishing flies is another payment for his good time. The gift is an ironic one because Jake fishes with worms. Although Jake's method of fishing causes him to be labeled a "lazy bum" (121) by Bill and creates a "rather unsportsmanly image,"[13] Harris shows great faith in his American friend. The gift of hand-tied flies is a precious one; by giving it, Harris openly demonstrates that he respects the values of the American pair and cherishes the time they have spent together. Like Jake and Bill, and unlike Mike, Harris displays an understanding of value and the need for payment.

One night in Pamplona, Jake lies awake and his thoughts travel from his friends' behavior while they were drunk, to morality, to speech patterns: "What rot, I could hear Brett say it. . . . The English spoken language— the upper classes, anyway—must have fewer words than the Eskimo. . . . I liked them, though. I liked the way they talked. Take Harris. Still Harris was not the upper classes" (149). Jake then abruptly turns on the light and begins to read. This becomes a complicated connection between Brett and Harris. Jake seems to associate Brett with undeveloped communication, then tries to create approval for this lack by associating it with Harris, but this association falls through because Harris and Brett are essentially different (according to Jake, because of social class). Finally, Jake gives up and picks up his book, Turgenieff's A Sportsman's Sketches; he says, "I would remember it somewhere, and afterward it would seem as though it had really happened to me. I would always have it. That was another good thing you paid for and then had" (149). This quotation reflects a desire to retreat into a healthy outdoor life and a reasonable system of payment, demonstrated earlier by Harris. Jake is beginning to realize the destructive nature of his relationship with Brett and to contrast it, in some way, with the healthy, natural, and ordered influences in his life.

Harris also displays a striking contrast to Robert Cohn, most obvious in Bill's reactions to each of them. Harris is welcomed into the fishing group and is repetitively assured that he is liked. His shortened name even becomes an indication of his acceptance: " 'Good old Wilson-Harris,' Bill said. 'We call you Harris because we're so fond of you' " (129). On the other hand, while Bill acknowledges that he likes Cohn, he also tells Jake that Robert " 'makes me sick, and he can go to hell, and I'm damn glad he's staying here so we won't have him fishing with us' " (102). Communication is the most striking point of contrast between Harris and Cohn. Cohn's use of Spanish results in a "lousy" (128) telegram: "Vengo Jueves Cohn" (127). Jake and Bill's reaction to the telegram is immediately followed by Harris's admirable use of Spanish to convince the innkeeper not to accept any payment but his; this is further evidence that he recognizes the need to pay for what he enjoys. Finally, Cohn's refusal to go to Burguete contrasts sharply with Harris's refusal to go to Pamplona. Jake sees Cohn's fouled-up rendezvous with Brett and Mike as ridiculous and his excuses as insincere. He sarcastically mentions that Cohn is "sentimental" (101) about not going fishing. Harris's refusal, on the other hand, is narrated as honestly regretful but understandable. He wishes Jake and Bill could stay, but he will not leave because he must do more fishing.

Harris's character remains directly aligned with Jake and Bill and opposed to Mike, Brett, and Cohn. The introduction of Harris at the close of the fishing expedition confirms that the trip is a regenerative one; he becomes representative of health to Jake. Harris espouses the same values Jake holds important, and he directly mirrors Bill, the least destructive and most healthy character in the novel. His appearance in the trip to Burguete links the trip to positive values and to health and normality, and it separates the trip from the chaotic influence of the other characters.

On their last day in Burguete, Jake and Bill accompany Harris to the monastery of Roncesvalles. Their ability to enjoy the visit together is a sanctifying episode in their association. Jake is silent while Bill and Harris acknowledge that the monastery is "remarkable" but "not the same as fishing" (128). The allusion to the betrayal of the hero in the epic *Chanson de Roland* and Jake's silence suggest that traditional and theological values are important to him.[14] There is also the suggestion that he might anticipate the episodes about to unfold in Pamplona, but he quickly begins to banter with the other two about the pub. If Jake does feel foreboding, it can be quickly dismissed in this company.

This peaceful interlude cannot last forever, though. Jake leaves Burguete for the fiesta in Pamplona and enters a vastly different social situation. His relationships with Harris and Bill are based on mutual respect and liking in contrast to those in Pamplona, where each of the human relationships is tinged with irreverence and bitterness. By the end of the fiesta, Jake has forfeited nearly everything he values. He has lost control with Cohn, and he has betrayed his *aficion* for bullfighting and his passion for Brett by introducing her to Romero. He has lost himself; the world "was just very

190 ♦ JANE E. WILSON

clear and bright, and inclined to blur at the edges. . . . I looked strange to myself in the glass" (224). To begin to recover, he must be alone, and he returns to a natural setting to begin the regenerative process.

In Jake's narration, the fishing expedition is the one worthwhile experience he is able to keep. He consistently remembers it as a good time, and his relationships with his fishing companions, Harris and Bill, remain cordial and open. The relationship with Harris is one of the keys to the meaning of the fishing episode and its beneficial aspects. By introducing Harris at the end of the trip, Hemingway allows Jake, as narrator, to close the expedition with a positive force and to remember the episode as an affirmation of humane, natural values in contrast to the degeneration that follows.

Notes

1. Warren Wedin, "Trout Fishing and Self-Betrayal In *The Sun Also Rises*," *Arizona Quarterly* 37, no. 1 (1981): 66.

2. Wedin, 73.

3. *The Sun Also Rises* (New York: Scribner's, 1926), 125.

4. John Atherton, "The Itinerary and the Postcard: Minimal Strategies in *The Sun Also Rises*," *Journal of English Literary History* 53, no. 1 (1986): 215.

5. For the convenience of the reader, I am quoting Hemingway's manuscript of *The Sun Also Rises* from *Ernest Hemingway, The Sun Also Rises: A Facsimile Edition*, ed. Matthew J. Bruccoli (Detroit: Omnigraphics, 1990), 344. Hereafter cited as *Facsimile Edition*.

6. *Facsimile Edition*, 346.

7. *Facsimile Edition*, 355.

8. *Facsimile Edition*, 351.

9. *Facsimile Edition*, 352.

10. *Facsimile Edition*, 353.

11. Gerald T. Gordon, "Hemingway's Wilson-Harris: The Search for Value in *The Sun Also Rises*," in *Fitzgerald / Hemingway Annual 1972*, eds. Matthew J. Bruccoli and C. E. Frazer Clark, Jr. (Dayton: NCR, 1973), 238.

12. Gordon, 238.

13. Wedin, 65.

14. Linda Wagner-Martin, "Hemingway's Search for Heroes, Once Again," *Arizona Quarterly* 44, no. 2 (1988): 61–62.

Index

♦